Weddings /365

Harvey Solomon

GET
THE
365
EDGE®

www.weddings-365.com

Copyright © 2012 by Harvey Solomon

Author: Harvey Solomon / hjs@weddings-365.com
Design: Dawn Sebti / dawnsebti.foliogem.com
Copy Editor: Diane Patrick / dianepatrick.net

365 Edge
P.O. Box 5434
Takoma Park, MD 20913

Printed in U.S.A.

Dedication

To my parents,
on their wedding day
January 4, 1942

Leonard Solomon and Gertrude Epstein met in the White Mountains of New Hampshire and married six months later in New York City. That night they attended a Broadway show, and for the next 60 years lived happily ever after.

Introduction

While researching several books about pop culture, I kept coming across accounts of notable weddings. So many, in fact, that I decided they deserved a book all their own. Not another glossy photo book that offers only a smattering, but an inclusive collection covering every day of the year.

I mean, really, who wouldn't like to know who else got married on the day (or, ahem, days) you were married, or are going to get married? Or the day your parents, siblings or best friends got married?

So I pored over hundreds of original news accounts and books in libraries, familiar terrain for this former history major. But I learned that, alas, many books have their facts wrong. One lavish coffee table book, for example, had an incorrect date for the wedding of the celebrity couple featured on *its cover*! And on-line? Don't get me started. Let's just say that the accuracy of wedding-related information on the Web often leaves much to be desired, and leave it at that.

Putting together **Weddings/365** was a bit like doing a jigsaw puzzle with 366 pieces (yes, Leap Year's here too). Many days offered multiple wedding possibilities; some had almost no weddings of note, so I had to dig deeper.

I've striven to tell a little story every day that captures the feel and flavor of that couple's special day. Did I succeed? I'll let you be the judge. And I couldn't resist including, wherever possible, a description of the fashions, especially those of the bride. Maybe it's because I'm the son of a haberdasher...

Finally, I'd be remiss to not acknowledge Diane Patrick, fashion plate and copy editor extraordinaire, and discerning designer Dawn Sebti. Thank you, talented ladies, for your invaluable contributions.

January

Shania Twain & Frédéric Thiébaud

January 1, 2011

1

"Fred is a romance god, and I lap it up. I'm spoiled rotten, and I admit it." SHANIA TWAIN

January 1 (2011)
Shania Twain & Frédéric Thiébaud

Sure, she sang the song, but applying it in real life proved a lot harder. "(If You're Not in It for Love) I'm Outta Here!" brought Canadian country singer Shania Twain her second chart-topping single. A decade later her best girlfriend stole away her husband/manager (and the song's co-writer). Today at sunset on a Puerto Rican beach, Twain, 45, makes a memorable comeback by marrying Swiss businessman Frédéric Thiébaud, 40, the ex-husband of that home-wrecking former friend. Prime material, perhaps, for another cheatin' heart country tune? Twain wears a long white gown with a black sash and full veil. Her nine-year-old son Eja gives her away at a small ceremony attended by 40 friends and family members who later **serenade the newlyweds with the Beatles' classic "All You Need is Love."** Engaged last October, the couple kept it a secret until two weeks ago when Twain showed off a $100,000, three-carat emerald-cut diamond engagement ring.

January 2 (2010)
Kyla Weber & Vince Vaughn

No sign of any wedding crashers. Capping a lo-ong New Year's Eve celebration that began with a bash at his Chicago penthouse apartment, Vince Vaughn, 39, marries Kyla Weber, 31, at the picturesque Armour House at Lake Forest Academy near Lake Michigan. A small gathering of 65 friends and family, bussed in from the nearby landmark Knickerbocker Hotel, witnesses the union of the hyper macho actor (*Swingers, Couples Retreat*) and his real estate agent bride, his girlfriend of several years since his breakup with Jennifer Aniston.

January 3 (2004)

Britney Spears & Jason Allen Alexander

Oops... I got married! Winding up a wild New Year's blowout in Las Vegas, two high school pals are partying hearty at a hip bar at the Palms Casino Hotel when word goes out for a limousine. Pronto. And so at 5:30 a.m., pop goddess Britney Spears and Jason Allen Alexander, both 22, get hitched at the quickies-are-our-specialty Little White Wedding Chapel on the Strip. A hotel bellman walks the bride, wearing jeans and a baseball cap, down the aisle. The bombshell news makes worldwide headlines, with non-stop follow-up coverage detailing their impulsive, alcohol-infused misadventure. "We were just looking at each other," said Alexander later, "and said, "**Let's do something wild, crazy.**Let's go get married, just for the hell of it.'" Two days later a local judge accepts her lawyers' filing for an annulment.

"*Plaintiff Spears lacked understanding of her actions to the extent that she was incapable of agreeing to the marriage.*"

FROM THE ANNULMENT PETITION

MARIO LOPEZ and ALI LANDRY

And They Said It Wouldn't Last...

A baker's dozen of the shortest celebrity marriages:

106 days	*Lisa Marie Presley & Nicolas Cage* (2002)
72 days	*Kim Kardashian & Kris Humphries* (2011)
38 days	*Drew Barrymore & Jeremy Thomas* (1994)
32 days	*Ernest Borgnine & Ethel Merman* (1964)
21 days	*Gig Young & Kim Schmidt* (1978, ends by murder/suicide)
14 days	*Eddie Murphy & Tracey Edmonds* (2008)
9 days	*Dennis Rodman & Carmen Electra* (1998)
8 days	*Mario Lopez & Ali Landry* (2004)
8 days	*Dennis Hopper & Michelle Phillips* (1970)
48 hours	*Britney Spears & Jason Allen Alexander* (2004)
24 hours	*Robin Givens & Svetozar Marinkovic* (1997)
24 hours	*Zsa Zsa Gabor & Felipe de Alba* (1982)
6 hours	*Rudolph Valentino & Jean Acker* (1919)

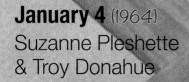

January 4 (1964)
Suzanne Pleshette
& Troy Donahue

A match made in Hollywood heaven: the heartthrob blond teen idol, who gets hundreds of fan letters each week, and the dark-haired, fast-rising actress. Troy Donahue (born Merle Johnson, Jr.), 27, and Suzanne Pleshette, 25, who met while filming the romantic comedy *Rome Adventure*, marry this evening at the Beverly Hills Hotel in what one columnist calls **"one of the quickest, quietest Hollywood weddings within memory."** She wears a white lace gown and headpiece with a long sheer veil, accompanied down the aisle by her father, a vice president at ABC. In three minutes the service is over, and the hundred guests proceed to a reception room where a string trio plays *Moon River* for the couple's first dance. The show biz-heavy crowd includes Richard Chamberlain, Robert Conrad, Rock Hudson, Jerry Lewis, Carl Reiner, Connie Stevens, Inger Stevens and Gig Young.

Her first of three, his second of four, lasts eight months

"I hope you retain humor, frankness, and above all, patience."

JUDGE EDWARD BRAND

January 5 (2000)

Celine Dion & Rene Angelil

Married in a lavish church ceremony in Montreal in 1994, the musically magnificent couple decides to remarry in **an opulent but rather less pious locale**: Las Vegas. Rene Angelil, 58, recently recovered from throat cancer, and Celine Dion, 31, transform the chapel at Caesars Palace into an Arabian mosque to honor his Lebanese and Syrian roots. She wears a metallic gold gown by Givenchy, and afterwards guests repair to a cavernous ballroom that continues the Arabian theme. Berber tents erected inside represent scenes from *A Thousand and One Nights*, complete with exotic birds, camels plus jugglers, dancers and singers. Food, naturally, consists of Moroccan and Middle Eastern fare that guests enjoy while seated on plush cushions. Next month Dion begins an intensive round of in vitro fertilization treatments that next year produces their long-desired result: her first child, son René-Charles. "This was their dream," says record producer and longtime friend David Foster. "It's bigger than any hit record, bigger than anything for them."

January 6 (1940)

Diana Lewis & William Powell

Fans rejoice and gossip columnists snipe as debonair William Powell takes a bride more than a quarter century his junior. Famous for his role as Nick Charles (opposite Myrna Loy as his wife Nora) in the popular *Thin Man* detective series, Powell, 48, weds starlet Diana Lewis, 21, at a dude ranch in Warm Springs, Nevada. **They met in rather unusual fashion.** Last month MGM photographers arrived at his Beverly Hills home to shoot publicity stills of Lewis around Powell's pool and patio. But he wasn't away as they'd been told, and he amicably strolled out of his house to chat them up. Taken by the petite brunette beauty, he invited her to dinner that night and their relationship soon blossomed. The romance ended a dark time for Powell, recovering from cancer and the unexpected death of his paramour Jean Harlow, the "Blonde Bombshell," from kidney failure three years before at age 26.

His third, lasts 44 years until his death

January 7 (2006)
Pink & Carey Hart

From the X Games to motocross to a sunset wedding on a Costa Rican beach. Quite the ride for Pink, 26, and Carey Hart, 30. After they met at the X Games in Las Vegas, she held up back-to-back signs from the pit during a motocross race in Mammoth, California: **"Will you marry me?"** and "I'm serious!" To the strains of "She's Always a Woman" by Billy Joel (Mar. 23), she strolls down the aisle barefoot, with pink highlights and a black ribbon in her hair, in a two-piece ivory Monique Lhuillier gown with a black sash around her waist. He sports a black Gucci jacket with a custom-made lining of silkscreened photos of his bride. The ceremony, before 130 guests, includes personal vows, excerpts from *The Prophet*, and them pouring of two kinds of sand into a vase and exchanging wedding bands with the inscription "'Til Death." After returning to L.A., they jet off on a snowboarding honeymoon.

> "She came into my flat and into my life forever. It was as simple as that. I had heard of love at first sight but never really believed in it, yet here it was."
>
> **MICHAEL CAINE**

January 8 (1973)
Shakira Baksh & Michael Caine

Unlikely though it seems, **late night television delivered true love** to British actor Michael Caine. Watching the telly one night in his London flat, he was instantly smitten by a dark-skinned young woman in a Maxwell House coffee commercial. Within a day he'd secured her name, rang her up for a date, and... their lifelong relationship commenced. After several happy years, she became pregnant. So on a trip to Los Angeles to promote his latest film, *Sleuth*, Caine, 40, and Indian (and former Miss Guyana) Shakira Baksh, 25, fly to Las Vegas. After a short ceremony, for which they fork over extra for Polaroids and orchids, their fairy-tale romance is official. Back in L.A., the hotel gives them an Indian-themed bridal suite in which the bed hangs from the ceiling on four chains. With four bells suspended underneath, anyone hovering outside the door should know when the marriage is being consummated. In July they welcome daughter Natasha.

January 9 (2005)

Lia Gerardini & Vince Neil

Does a surreal life lead to **a surreal wedding?** "It's Hammer time!" cries '80s has-been turned pastor M.C. Hammer as he approaches the altar at the Four Seasons Hotel in Las Vegas. There he unites *The Surreal Life* castmate and Motley Crue vocalist Vince Neil, 33, and Lia Gerardini. She wears a body-hugging, champagne-colored full-length gown with a crisscross halter top. Vince ops for a traditional, dark pinstriped suit with a rose boutonniere that mirrors the bride's bouquet. A nice touch, yes, but between her way too revealing top and messily piled up blonde hair (which reminds one reporter of a bad Pamela Anderson impersonator) and his recent all-too-obvious facelift, it is indeed a garish, surreal sight. Guests include Motley Crue cohorts Nikki Sixx and Tommy Lee, plus Dennis Rodman. Leopard-skin furnishings help convert a ballroom into a nightclub for the rockin' reception.

His fourth, her second

January 10 (1958)
Loray White & Sammy Davis, Jr.

Uncoupled: **segregated America has been buzzing** over the interracial affair between blonde actress Kim Novak, fresh off her starring role in Alfred Hitchcock's *Vertigo*, and Sammy Davis, Jr. Grooming Novak as Columbia's answer to Marilyn Monroe, enraged studio mogul Harry Cohn threatens to "put out Sammy's other eye." The black entertainer, 32, gets the message and today marries obscure black chorus girl Loray White, 23, at the posh Sands Hotel in Las Vegas. Harry Belafonte serves as best man. Sammy gives his bride a $3,000 mink stole, a diamond ring, and bankrolls a $10,000 shopping spree. Next month Cohn dies of a heart attack, and nine months later the couple divorces. Two years later, when interracial marriages remain illegal in 31 states, the actor-singer-dancer again shocks America by marrying statuesque blonde Swedish actress May Britt. Frank Sinatra serves as best man at that service held at Sammy's house high in the Hollywood Hills.

> **His first of three, lasts nine months**

January 11 (2003)
Idina Menzel & Taye Diggs

A few years ago he romanced Angela Bassett here in *How Stella Got Her Groove Back*. Today hunky Taye Diggs, 32, **returns to cap a real-life romance** as he ties the knot with Idina Menzel, 31, at the elegant Round Hill resort in Jamaica. She wears a strapless white Badgley Mischka gown with a touch of ornate crystal beadwork, he wears an off-white suit by John Varvatos and no tie (it's the islands, mon). A handful of family and friends witness the Caribbean nuptials of the couple that met while co-starring in *Rent* on Broadway. Soon they're making regular acting appearances opposite each other in *Wicked* and an Off-Broadway production, *The Wild Party*. For more than a half century Round Hill has enjoyed a vacation reputation as a playground for the elite including Noel Coward, Clark Gable, Audrey Hepburn (Sept. 25), Grace Kelly (April 19), Jackie O and John Kennedy, with more recent celebs including Demi Moore and Bruce Willis, Michael Douglas and Joan Collins.

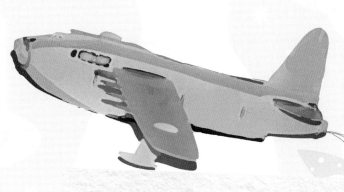

January 12 (1957)

Jean Peters & Howard Hughes

The calls arrive at 4 a.m. from their famously reclusive boss: get to Hughes Aircraft in L.A. within the hour. Soon the aide and lawyer, plus their boss and his girlfriend are aloft in a brand-new TWA plane en route to hardscrabble Tonopah, Nevada. At an unassuming motel, a justice of the peace marries G.A. Johnson and Marian Evans. Actually those are assumed names for reclusive mogul Howard Hughes, 51, and "B" movie starlet Jean Peters, 30. He slips a ruby ring onto her finger, and within an hour they're flying back home. After having dalliances with many women (and perhaps men) over the years, the paranoid and enigmatic Hughes has chosen to wed his 12-year, on-and-off girlfriend for reasons, as usual, unknown. Rumors swirl, but it's not until two months later that **the press breaks news of the wedding**—though it gets the date and location wrong.

His second of three, her second of three, lasts 14 years

"My life with Howard Hughes was and shall remain a matter on which I will have no comment."

JEAN PETERS (IN 1972)

January 13 (1958)
Jayne Mansfield & Mickey Hargitay

With a history of staged publicity stunts that exposed her ample cleavage, actress Jayne Mansfield (*The Girl Can't Help It, Will Success Spoil Rock Hunter?*) shows off her voluptuous figure today in a a wedding dress that newspapers report "was **so form-fitting that it appeared painted on**." More than 1,500 fans surround the all-glass Wayfarer's Chapel aside the Pacific as Mansfield, 24, marries bodybuilder (and former Mr. Universe) Mickey Hargitay, 32. The ceremony begins a half-hour late to accommodate the bride's photo session. Photographers nearly outnumber the guests, ensuring images splashed on front pages worldwide tomorrow for the blonde bombshell frequently touted as a contender to the crown of Marilyn Monroe (below).

"He was always, before and after the divorce, her best friend."

ALLAN SNYDER, MARILYN'S MAKE-UP ARTIST

January 14 (1954)
Marilyn Monroe & Joe DiMaggio

What's a poor girl to do? Serving her first (but not last) studio suspension, Marilyn Monroe takes the steps that millions of fans have been anticipating—down the aisle. **The storybook romance comes true today for the movie star and the baseball star** as Joe DiMaggio, 39, whisks her in his dark blue Cadillac to San Francisco City Hall. Tipped off by 20th Century Fox only an hour before a hundred reporters and photographers converge. Marilyn, 25, wears a dark brown broadcloth suit with a white ermine collar, and the couple graciously poses for pictures and answers questions before and after the short ceremony. But a rocky road lies ahead since the former glory of the straight-laced, ex-N.Y. Yankees star pales before the luminous glow of his wife's fast-rising career. By the way, that suspension? For her refusal to play the lead in *The Girl in Pink Tights*, a picture that's soon shelved as Marilyn moves on to *The Seven Year Itch*.

Her second of three, his second, lasts nine months

"Milko is more than my husband. He is my physician, my favorite reporter, my tennis coach, my business manager. Above all, he is the guardian of my happiness."

GINA LOLLOBRIGIDA

Don't you hate it when that happens? Gina Lollobrigida (right) and Elizabeth Taylor wear identical dresses by Christian Dior at the Moscow Film Festival in July 1961.

January 15 (1949)
Gina Lollobrigida & Milko Skofic

Daughter of a furniture maker, this beautiful young lady grew up taking part in, and winning, beauty pageants. She had her heart set on an acting career – but detoured long enough to marry a doctor she'd met at a New Year's Eve party two years ago. "He understands me," she wrote in her diary. "He likes me. **He is the husband type.** I hope we will get engaged real soon. I am sick and tired of single life." Today Gina Lollobrigida, 21, and Milko Skofic ski to a small church in mountain town of Terminillo, Italy, and marry before a couple of close friends. Within several years he gives up his medical practice to become her manager, for his gorgeous wife has progressed from extra to supporting player to leading lady. Setting the film world on fire with her face and figure, "La Lollo" ascends to international stardom in 1955 after starring in *The Most Beautiful Woman in the World*, a.k.a. *Beautiful But Dangerous*. Soon she conquers America too, starring in a string of Hollywood movies opposite top leading men like Yul Brynner, Tony Curtis, Rock Hudson and Anthony Quinn.

Her first, his first, lasts 22 years

January 16 (1943)
Ginger Rogers & Jack Briggs

Hearts fluttered as Fred Astaire and Ginger Rogers **danced across the silver screen** in a string of '30s movie musicals like *Top Hat*, *Follow the Fleet* and *Swing Time*. But she knows how to keep her personal life private. Today she quietly marries private first class Jack Briggs at the First United Methodist Church in Pasadena. Rogers, 31, wears a tailored brown suit with matching accessories, and clutches a spray of tiny white orchids. They'd met during her tours to support the war effort when he escorted her around a Marine Corps base in San Diego. Soon the starlet (who began her career by winning a Charleston dance contest at age 14) and her beau, an ex-Hollywood bit player, were off playing tennis and enjoying ice-cream sodas at the soda fountain. Their stealthy romance flew under the radar, but tomorrow her nuptials make front-page news in papers coast to coast. After a quick honeymoon she's back filming an adaptation of a Moss Hart play, *Lady in the Dark*.

"When two people love each other, they don't look at each other—they look in the same direction."

GINGER ROGERS

Her third of five, lasts six years

January 17 (1973)
Denise Nicholas & Bill Withers

Only **her hairdresser knows for sure**. Denise Nicholas, a familiar presence on ABC's earnest high school drama, *Room 222*, broke the news first to her Hollywood hairdresser that she was secretly marrying singer/songwriter Bill Withers. After today's quiet service in a Van Nuys church, Nicholas, 28, and Withers, 34, jet off for a Parisian honeymoon. Hits like "Ain't No Sunshine," "Lean on Me" and "Use Me" have catapulted the late-blooming, longtime bachelor to overnight success. But cracks in their seemingly fairy-tale romance have already surfaced. "For her sake, I hope the marriage turns out to be more serene than their courtship," writes gossip columnist Marilyn Beck. "Denise suffered a few severe bruises last month as a result of a fuss with Withers. Love conquers all, they say."

> His first of two, her first of three, lasts one year

January 18 (1987)
Eugenia Crafton 𝄞 Steve Winwood

Call it **a shotgun wedding**: not only is the bride pregnant, but the couple met at a concert of Junior Walker, whose signature tune was the '60s R&B smash "Shotgun." Two years after their chance meeting at NYC's Lone Star Cafe, wedding bells chime for a college student from a tiny Tennessee town and a storied English rocker. Eugenia Crafton, 26, and Steve Winwood, 39, marry at the Fifth Avenue Presbyterian Church, where her preacher from back home helps with the service. Families from both sides wing in from Nashville and London, respectively, and over the weekend they attend a most appropriate Broadway show, *Me and My Girl*. The happy couple honeymoons on the Caribbean island of St. Barts, interrupted only by a quick return trip to NYC for the Grammys where the comeback kid's "Higher Love" wins two awards including Record of the Year. Four months later she gives birth to daughter Mary Claire, the first of their four children to date.

> His second, her first

"I thought he must have been interested because on everybody else's autograph he wrote 'Regards from Steve Winwood,' and on mine he wrote 'Love from Steve Winwood.' I thought…mmm!" **EUGENIA CRAFTON**

January 19 (1957)
Vivienne Verwey & Gary Player

Under an archway of **golf clubs held aloft by groomsmen**, a promising young South African golfer takes a bride in Johannesburg. Gary Player, 21, marries Vivienne Verwey, 20, daughter of a club pro who is mentoring the young phenom. Their first child soon arrives, and the family takes to the road as Player hits the international golf circuit. Two years later the Black Knight, so nicknamed for his penchant for dressing in black, wins the prestigious British Open. Eventually the whole family, numbering six children, travels along, often necessitating three taxis to hold the entourage and their luggage. But after Vivienne dubs herself "the world's #1 golf widow," he agrees to tour only six months a year. Over the next half century he travels more than 14 million miles and racks up more than 160 tournament wins.

"They were the Douglas Fairbanks/Mary Pickford of our time. Cool, nomadic, talented and nicely shocking."

**PETER EVANS, PHOTOGRAPHER
ON POLANSKI AND TATE**

January 20 (1968)
Sharon Tate & Roman Polanski

If you're going to London, **be sure to wear some flowers in your hair**. Actually the song suggests San Francisco, but lovebirds Roman Polanski, 34, and Sharon Tate, 24, settle on London, rather than their hometown of L.A., for their wedding. The hot young actress, fresh off upbeat reviews for Valley of the Dolls, indeed wears flowers in her hair and a cream-colored taffeta mini dress, the mercurial director wears an olive green Edwardian jacket with a frilled ascot. Their 11 a.m. sharp marriage at the Chelsea registry office on Kings Road draws an avalanche of photographers and fans, but only a select few guests including Keith Richards, Vidal Sassoon and David Bailey. The reception at the Playboy Club runs 'til 5 a.m. and attracts a Who's Who of swinging Londoners and more including Warren Beatty, Candice Bergen (Sept. 27), James Fox and Laurence Harvey. A mix-up finds the newlyweds cutting a three-tiered cake inscribed "Happy Retirement Hilda."

His second of three, her first, lasts 18 months until her murder by the Manson family

'George, with velvet brown eyes and dark chestnut hair, was the best-looking man I'd ever seen. At the break for lunch I found myself sitting next to him, whether by accident or design I have never been sure. We were both shy and spoke hardly a word to each other, but being close to him was electrifying.' PATTIE BOYD

January 21 (1966)

Pattie Boyd & George Harrison

As the titanic wave of Beatlemania washed across the universe, the Beatles began shooting their first movie, *A Hard Day's Night*, in 1964. On the first day George Harrison became **smitten with a beautiful but rather shy young model**, cast in a non-speaking role as a schoolgirl. He asked her out but she refused. By her second day of shooting, ten days later, she'd dumped her boyfriend and they went out on that first date – chaperoned by Beatles manager Brian Epstein. A week later she took George home (alone) to meet the family, and that was that. Today Harrison, 22, and Pattie Boyd, 21, marry in a quick service at a registry office in Surrey. The tall, waiflike bride wears a short red silk dress by Mary Quant, with cream-coloured stockings and pointy red shoes. Since it's winter she also wears a red fox fur coat, and George a black Mongolian lamb coat, both courtesy of Quant. Paul McCartney serves as best man, and tomorrow Epstein arranges a press conference before the newlyweds depart for a honeymoon in Barbados.

His first of two, her first of two, lasts 11 years

January 22 (2005)
Melania Knauss & Donald Trump

With a name **synonymous with extravagance**, Donald Trump, 58, spares no expense for his Palm Beach wedding of the decade at Bethesda-by-the-Sea Episcopal Church, which overflows with gardenias, roses and orchids. His Slovenian model bride Melania Knauss, 34, wears a strapless $100,000 Christian Dior gown with 1,500 hand-stitched pearls and crystal rhinestones, a 13-foot train and 16-foot veil. The glitzy guest list includes Bill and Hillary Clinton (Oct. 11), Katie Couric, Simon Cowell (who gives it a nine) and Shaquille O'Neal. The reception at Trump's Mar-a-Lago Estate is even more opulent, with its 17,000-square foot ballroom made to resemble Versailles. Appetizers include caviar, lobster and truffles, and the main course features steamed shrimp salad and beef tenderloin. Knauss slips into a lightweight tulle Vera Wang (June 22) gown so she can dance to live songs including Billy Joel doing "Just the Way You Are," Paul Anka crooning "My Way" and Tony Bennett's "Always." Dessert? A five-foot, 200-pound, seven-tier Grand Marnier chiffon cake decorated with 3,000 icing roses.

His third, her first

January 23 (1976)
Joanna Shimkus & Sidney Poitier

Interracial marriage is no longer the shock it was back when his pal Sammy Davis, Jr. married May Britt in 1960. In fact, when pioneering black actor Sidney Poitier (*In the Heat of the Night, Guess Who's Coming to Dinner*) and Joanna Shimkus tie the knot in his Beverly Hills mansion, guests include two other mixed couples: Quincy Jones and Peggy Lipton, and Harry (best man) and Julie (matron of honor) Belafonte. Poitier, 49, and Shimkus, 32, met in 1969 after his producer spotted her photo in *Vogue*. A little-known Canadian model/actress splitting time between Paris and London, she landed a role (despite refusing to audition) in Poitier's next film, *The Lost Man*. The movie was a flop, but **sparks flew** and soon the two were a living together in his home in the Bahamas. Later they relocated to Beverly Hills, and two of today's most special guests are their daughters Anika, three, and Sydney, two.

January 24 (2001)

Halle Berry & Eric Benét

The select guests had received **the proverbial message in a bottle**: a bottle in the mail with directions to a wedding. Today on a secluded Southern Californian beach, actress Halle Berry, 34, and singer Eric Benét, 33, marry. She wears a Ristarose gown, he wears a white silk suit. A quiet honeymoon in the scenic Maldives follows. The world doesn't learn of the nuptials until early next month when Berry, onstage at a Black Entertainment Television party in Burbank, casually announces, "Here is my husband, Eric Benét." Previously unlucky in love, Berry had suffered through the breakup of her high-profile marriage to baseball star David Justice. By year's end she's starring in *Monster Ball*, a role that wins her an Oscar: the first ever for a black actress in the category Best Actress. But her unlucky-in-love streak continues, and her marriage to the serially unfaithful Benét fans tabloid headlines before imploding.

Her second, his first of two, lasts four years

January 25 (1964)
Camille Hanks & Bill Cosby

Momma always warned her to stay away from those seedy showbiz types. So at first the college coed rejected his advances, but **this ambitious young man wouldn't quit**. And her parents gradually warmed, especially after learning his fast-rising stand-up career earned him as much as $1,500 a week! Today Camille Hanks, 20, marries Bill Cosby, 26, in a church in Olney, Maryland. Off they head on a whirlwind quasi-honeymoon: San Francisco, where he's appearing at the Hungry i, Los Angeles (the Crescendo) and Lake Tahoe (Harrah's). The Cos's affable, low-key demeanor meshes perfectly with a rising wave of kinder, gentler comedy led by folks like the Smothers Brothers. Next year he spies his first (of five) children, and a breakthrough TV role in the tongue-in-cheek espionage adventure, *I Spy*.

"The second week I knew him he asked me to marry him. Three months later I said yes." CAMILLE HANKS

January 26 (1997)
Catherine Martin & Baz Luhrmann

Their audaciously flashy, punk version of **one of the greatest romance stories of all time**, *Romeo + Juliet*, is burning up the box office worldwide. So director Baz Luhrmann, 34, and production designer Catherine Martin, 32, decide to officially cement their longtime union. It's a three-fer for Martin: her wedding on her birthday and Australia Day, the country's national holiday. Tomorrow the couple celebrates with a lavish reception at the Sydney Opera House, where they build a church on the stage. "You wouldn't believe it," says Luhrmann, who burst to international prominence five years ago with *Strictly Ballroom*, an art house sleeper that became a runaway international hit, "but with all of our experience with stage management, the bride was incredibly late." The couple met ten years ago when Luhrmann needed a designer for an experimental opera, and they've been together personally and professionally ever since.

January 27 (1949)

Linda Christian & Tyrone Power

All of Rome's horses and all of Rome's policemen —plus a cordon of Jeeps—cannot keep the adoring crowds penned in. Thousands of **screaming bobbysoxers riot** around the 10th century Santa Francesca Romana church, a stone's throw from the Colosseum, anticipating a Hollywood-style extravaganza: the wedding of movie star Tyrone Power, 35, and starlet Linda Christian, 25. The "breathless and beautiful" bride, arriving 20 minutes late, must fight her way through the surging crowd in which several women faint. She wears a high-necked white satin gown with a long train decorated with lace and pearls, and a small matching white bonnet. Barely any of the 200 guests who aren't seated in the church's first few rows can hear a word of the service amidst the din outside. Immediately afterward the couple departs for a special audience at Vatican City with Pope Pius XII, who presents her with a rosary and him with a silver pontifical medal.

His second of three, her first of two, lasts seven years

January 28 (1982)

Rhea Perlman & Danny DeVito

It's lunchtime, want to grab a bite? I don't know, **why don't we get married** instead? On their lunch break from filming the hit sitcom *Taxi*, Danny DeVito, 37, and longtime girlfriend Rhea Perlman, 33, marry in the garden of their Hollywood Hills home. A bit of rain, rather unusual for Southern California, complicates the small civil ceremony but the comedic couple interjects a shot of levity by strolling down the aisle to a recording of Alfalfa from *Our Gang* singing "I'm in the Mood for Love." One of DeVito's nephews serves as best man, her sister Heidi as maid of honor. Afterwards it's back to work, though Perlman soon departs her recurring role on *Taxi* for a co-starring gig on *Cheers* beginning this fall.

January 29 (1958)

Joanne Woodward & Paul Newman

Life may be no picnic, but that's actually where **one of film's most celebrated couples** first met. In a 1953 stage production of William Inge's *Picnic*, Paul Newman made his Broadway debut in a supporting role while Joanne Woodward worked as an understudy. He was married with a growing family, but the attraction was undeniable between the movie-star handsome Newman and his understated new love. Their careers heated up, especially his, with films like *The Long Hot Summer* and *Cat on a Hot Tin Roof*, while she'd recently broken out with an Oscar-winning turn in *The Three Faces of Eve*. Today, two weeks after co-starring as husband and wife in a live *Playhouse 90* television drama, Newman, 33, and Woodward, 27, marry at the El Rancho Hotel on the Las Vegas Strip. The small party of guests includes newlywed singers Steve Lawrence and Eydie Gorme. Then they jet off for a honeymoon in London, with stardom beckoning for him—though it'll take another 30 years 'til he matches her *Eve* Oscar with a win on his seventh nomination, for *The Color of Money*.

> "Sexiness wears thin after a while and beauty fades, but to be married to a man who makes you laugh every day? Ah, now that's a real treat."
>
> **JOANNE WOODWARD**

His second, her first and only, lasts 50 years until his death

'Gala... the good fairy of my equilibrium, who banished the salamanders of my doubts and strengthened the lions of certainties.' SALVADOR DALI

January 30 (1934)

Elena Ivanovna Diakonova & Salvador Dali

A surrealist legend finds **his mate, his muse, his manager**—and the legend only grows. Used to occupying an often outlandish spotlight, Salvador Dali, 29, and Gala, 39, marry in an uncharacteristically quiet civil ceremony in Paris. They're just back from a triumphant U.S. tour, where his one-man show at an upper crusty Manhattan gallery attracted considerable if puzzled attention. At a farewell ball she wore a costume Dali designed that featured a doll, perched on her head, that was crawling with ants and having its head squeezed by a phosphorescent lobster. The costume inadvertently stirred a tempest when a journalist likened it to the kidnapped Lindbergh baby, a case then sweeping the nation. Gala becomes the model for the singular Dali's artwork, and their unusual (platonic, nonexclusive, with issues) relationship lasts nearly half a century.

His first, her second, lasts 48 years until her death

January 31 (1960)

Anne Francis & Robert Abeloff

Two weeks ago a veteran gossip columnist reported: "**It must be love**. Anne Francis's admirer, Beverly Hills dentist Dr. Robert Abeloff, flew to New York to see her." Francis, a blonde actress with a prominent beauty mark who's best known for her role as a teenaged tempest in the sci-fi classic *Forbidden Planet*, later calls her suitor "a gentle soul who seemed to have wonderful understanding." Today Francis, 29, and Abeloff, 34, marry in Las Vegas and then honeymoon in Hawaii. But soon it appears to be more of a misunderstanding, and the birth of a daughter in 1962 doesn't ease their marital woes. After on-and-off separations she files for divorce, but a judge refuses to grant alimony since "it appears that this lady makes more money than her husband." In the mid-'60s Francis achieves small screen success as sexy sleuth *Honey West*, a short-lived but beloved detective drama.

Her second, his second, lasts four years

February

Maureen Cox
& Ringo Starr
February 11, 1965

February 1 (1986)
Diana Ross & Arne Naess, Jr.

There **ain't no mountain high enough** to keep diva Diana Ross from strolling down the aisle. In a 10th century church in a Swiss town nestled in the Jura mountains, she rather fittingly marries adventurer Arne Naess, Jr., 48, who last year led the first Norwegian team to the top of Mount Everest. Serenaded by the Norwegian Boys of Silver choir, and Stevie Wonder singing "I Just Called to Say I Love You," Ross, 41, wears a long satin dress with a veil of antique Belgian lace. The newlyweds met last summer in the Bahamas, where their six kids (three from each) bonded. Naess soon began occupying front-row seats at Ross's concerts in Paris, Los Angeles, London and Stockholm, where she took to dedicating "Reach Out and Touch (Somebody's Hand)" to her new love. From mountains to islands, the couple jets off—after a lavish reception at a five-star hotel in nearby Lausanne—to honeymoon on his private Tahitian islet.

Her second, his second, lasts 13 years

February 2 (1985)
Nicole Brown & O.J. Simpson

Though his storied pro football career has ended, O.J. Simpson remains a popular presence with a sportscasting gig on *Monday Night Football* and a hugely successful ad campaign running through airports for Hertz. Still, his marriage today merits almost no media coverage except **a one-line *Parade* magazine mention** nearly two months after the event: "O.J. Simpson, 37, married Nicole Brown, 25, a curvaceous interior decorator, on Feb. 2." The couple, who met back in '77 when she was waitressing at a Beverly Hills nightclub, celebrates with a huge affair at his Brentwood mansion that attracts 400 guests. During dinner a homemade video of their previous seven years together screens on multiple monitors and induces lots of crying. Happy tears, quite the opposite of years to come which include frequent spousal abuse, a divorce, and her brutal murder by parties unknown for which O.J. is notoriously acquitted.

His second, her first, lasts seven years

"There was so much love. Everybody was so happy for Nicole and me."

O.J. SIMPSON ON HIS WEDDING DAY

February 3 (2006)
Glenn Close & David Shaw

Over the years she's been **romantically involved mostly with fellow entertainers**. Today veteran actress Glenn Close, 58, and boyfriend David Shaw, 54, a biotech entrepreneur, tie the knot in a private fireside ceremony at his beachside home on historic Prout's Neck in Scarborough, Maine. Though she's come close on many occasions, Close has never won an Oscar despite six nominations to date. The respected actress has won many other awards including two Golden Globes, three Emmys and three Tonys. Her new husband founded Idexx Laboratories, and has served on the faculty of Harvard's John F. Kennedy School of Government. Last year the couple bought an upper level penthouse in the swank Beresford (neighbors? John McEnroe, Diana Ross, Jerry Seinfeld) overlooking Central Park, a $6 million unit reportedly once owned by Rock Hudson that includes two balconies and a private elevator.

Her third, his second

February 4 (1974)
Roseanne Barr & Bill Pentland

Telling her parents she was going to visit a friend in Colorado, the mouthy 18-year-old left her Utah town—and never looked back. Arriving by bus, she and her friends went off to a motel where she met the night clerk: **"The cutest guy in the world**—his hair was really long and he had on a jean jacket, torn up, torn up jeans, leather moccasins and a cigarette dangling out of his mouth." Love dawns, and today Roseanne Barr, 21, marries Bill Pentland. They raise a family and she starts dabbling in stand-up comedy at various Colorado clubs. Then she gets the urge for going, again, and heads to Los Angeles where more stand-up gigs lead to a career-making appearance on *The Tonight Show Starring Johnny Carson*. Her blue-collar sitcom *Roseanne* brings fame and fortune, though her tyrannical behavior on the set and out-of-control spending makes her a tabloid favorite.

Her first of three, lasts 16 years

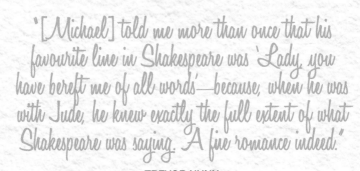

"[Michael] told me more than once that his favourite line in Shakespeare was 'Lady, you have bereft me of all words'—because, when he was with Jude, he knew exactly the full extent of what Shakespeare was saying. A fine romance indeed."

TREVOR NUNN

February 5 (1971)

Judi Dench & Michael Williams

Appearing in a traveling production of *Twelfth Night* in Australia, she was **shocked one night to discover an old chum onstage** as an extra. He'd flown all the way from England to surprise her. He proposed on a sunny day in Adelaide, but she demurred until he proposed again on a rainy night back at home, and she accepted. Judi Dench, 36, and Michael Williams, 35, marry in Hampstead's Catholic church, walking to the service from her house around the corner. Her eldest brother Peter gives her away. Ian Richardson and Alec McCowen serve as ushers, and afterwards they celebrate with a reception at the London Zoo. Director Trevor Nunn gives them a special advance wedding present: co-starring roles as young lovers in the Royal Shakespeare Company's production of the comedy *London Assurance*, followed by brother and sister roles in a tragedy, *The Duchess of Malfi*. On and off stage, it's a long happy union.

Her first, his first, lasts 30 years until his death

February 6 (2010)
Amy Robach & Andrew Shue

Say, **is that a birthday cake or a wedding cake?** *Weekend Today* anchor Amy Robach enjoys a combination today on her 37th birthday. The wintry weather outside The Lighthouse at Chelsea Piers is frightful, but the mood inside is delightful as she marries ex-*Melrose Place* stud Andrew Shue, 42. She wears an off-the-rack dress from Saks Fifth Avenue and Christian Louboutin heels for the family-friendly event. Shue's mother Anne Harms officiates, the two deliver their own vows, and the wedding party includes his three sons (with ex-wife Jennifer Hageney) and her two daughters (with ex-hubby Tim McIntosh). Notable guests include his sister Elizabeth and husband Davis Guggenheim, a director, plus her colleagues Ann Curry, Kathie Lee Gifford (Oct. 18) and Meredith Vieira. Work played a big part in today's festivities, since the couple met last year during a book party for *Today's Moms*, penned by two of the show's producers.

February 7 (1988)
Robin Givens & Mike Tyson

Given his out-of-control history, it seems like a bad idea to just about everyone on the planet—except the bride. So after attending the N.B.A. All-Star Game together, actress Robin Givens (*Head of the Class*), 22, **walks down the aisle** with "Iron" Mike Tyson, 21, the world's undisputed heavyweight champion. A Roman Catholic priest performs the ceremony, in front of a hundred family members and friends, in the chapel of Holy Angels Church. Then she's back to L.A. to film her sitcom, while he's off to New York to train for his next bout against Tony Tubbs. Givens quickly gets a taste of life with Mike when she informs him that she nailed an audition for the TV miniseries *The Women of Brewster Place*, and instead of offering congratulations he explodes. Before the year's out they appear on *20/20*, where she tells Barbara Walters that their life together has been "torture, pure hell, worse than anything I could possibly imagine."

His first of three, her first of two, lasts one stormy year

February 8 (1977)
Jeanne Moreau & William Friedkin

An odd couple: **the legendary new wave French actress and the brash director** of *The French Connection*. They met when he was scouting locations for his drug chase thriller, which he followed up with an even bigger hit, *The Exorcist*. Jeanne Moreau, 48, and William Friedkin, 41, marry in a brief civil service in Paris with only two witnesses: director Alain Resnais and his wife Florence Malraux. Afterwards the two couples lunch at the storied Le Grand Vefour restaurant in the gardens of the Palais-Royale. Moreau relocates to his Beverly Hills mansion, and next month he produces the Oscar awards telecast at which she presents the prestigious Best Director award (to? John Avildsen for *Rocky*). But plans for professional collaborations fizzle, as does the marriage. "It was the most passionate relationship of my life," Moreau says, "and you know, I have had many." To wit: Pierre Cardin, Louis Malle and François Truffaut, among others. But at least the union doesn't end as badly as in *The Bride Wore Black*, Truffaut's 1968 revenge flick in which widow Moreau avenges her husband who was accidentally killed on their wedding day.

> His first of four, her third, lasts two years

"When he proposed there was some sort of magic thread between us. Perhaps we should have stayed lovers. Being lovers permits you greater freedom."

JEANNE MOREAU

February 9 (1980)
Carole Anne Boone & Ted Bundy

On the brink of conviction, serial killer Ted Bundy confounds the courtroom today by taking advantage of an old law still on the books in Florida. While questioning character witness Carole Boone, a former coworker and groupie, he asks her to marry him—and she accepts. Despite the shock and outrage of state authorities, their stealth plan works and the marriage stands. Tomorrow Bundy is convicted, and in the ensuing years the handsome, charming psychopathic killer meets Boone in the lone room where Death Row inmates have that privilege. Despite a lack of conjugal rights, Boone becomes pregnant and gives birth in 1982 to a daughter, Rosa. Again the authorities are enraged, but the new mother is as defiant as her lethal husband: **"I don't have to explain anything about anyone to anybody."**

> His first, her first, lasts nine years until his execution

Stampede!

Blushing brides need not apply. Bride-zillas welcome. The exact date has been lost to history, but in 1947 the flagship Filene's Basement in downtown Boston offered a special sale on bridal dresses. So began a tumultuous tradition that came to be known as the "**Running of the Brides.** " After only a couple years the shopping ritual had become legendary. "Brides from all over the world," wrote *The Boston Globe* in 1950, "have proudly displayed a Filene's Basement trousseau."

Drawing international media coverage, the event ran for more than half a century until the chain's closing in 2011. It became so popular that customers would fly in from around the country and line up the night before, eager to do battle with their fellow shoppers to find that once-in-a-lifetime wedding dress at bargain prices.

"Down From Upstairs, Further Reduced: Filenes Main Store STOCKTAKING CLEARANCE — Remaining lots were transferred down to the BASEMENT for final clearance under our FAMOUS AUTOMATIC PLAN. "

FILENE'S AD IN *THE BOSTON GLOBE* , FEB. 9, 1947

February 10 (1966)
Rita Anderson & Bob Marley

For a struggling rock steady ska singer/producer and his girlfriend, a nurse and aspiring singer, life is tough in hardscrabble Kingston, Jamaica, mon. But love wins out, and this morning Robert Nesta Marley, four days after turning 21, marries Rita Anderson, 19, in **a simple ceremony at a friend's home**. For the occasion he'd gotten a close-cropped razor cut, and wears his best clothes: a sharp black suit and fancy shoes supplied by his record label employer. She wears a ruffled white party dress with a mother-of-pearl tiara and short lace veil. Their celebratory breakfast consists of curried goat, rice and bananas. Tonight his band, the Wailers, plays its biggest concert yet at Kingston's National Stadium, but tomorrow he flies back to Wilmington, Delaware, where his mom lives and he looks for work. Rita flies over a few months later, and he returns to Jamaica in November, poised to unleash the hypnotic Rastafarian reggae sounds that'll catapult him, against all odds, to worldwide fame and fortune.

February 11 (1965)
Maureen Cox & Ringo Starr

Given all the hoopla over the Beatles' raggedy mop tops, it seems perhaps a tad ironic that **drummer Ringo Starr marries a hairdresser**. In a stealthy, five-minute early morning ceremony at London's Caxton Hall registry office, Ringo Starr (Richard Starkey), 24, marries Maureen Cox, 18, daughter of a Liverpool ship's steward. Manager Brian Epstein serves as best man, with only George and John (plus wife Cynthia) in attendance; Paul's off on a North African holiday with his squeeze, Jane Asher. Off the newlyweds pop for a brief honeymoon on England's south coast, staying at a friend's apartment. With Beatlemania in full flush, the nuptials make worldwide news on a week that the band tops both the U.S. and U.K. charts with the #1 single ("I Feel Fine") and album (*Beatles '65* in the U.S., *Beatles for Sale* in the U.K.). As the papers dutifully report, this leaves only two unmarried Beatles: Paul and George. Is there perhaps more weeping mixed in with their ardent female fans' screams?

His first of two, lasts ten years

February 12 (1948)

Marjorie Willett & Dick Van Dyke

With some 15 million listeners tuning in, budding entertainer Dick Van Dyke, 22, and his high school sweetheart, Margie Willett, marry this afternoon on the popular *Bride and Groom* radio program. Newly arrived in L.A. from his native Illinois, small town boy Van Dyke and a partner have been doing a live variety act at the Chapman Park Hotel on Wilshire Blvd., where the radio show tapes. Each episode tells the story of one couple's courtship and culminates with their wedding, off mike in an adjoining chapel. (The producers have 30 local clergymen on call to perform the services.) Then they return fresh from the altar, where the host always cadges a kiss from the bride before showering them with gifts: luggage, jewelry, appliances or silver. Then they whisk away on an all-expenses paid honeymoon; the Van Dykes enjoy a ten-day skiing vacation at Mount Hood in Oregon. Over the show's five-year run nearly a thousand couples marry, and after *Bride and Groom* jumps to television another 1,500 couples tie the knot before it ends in the mid-'50s.

"The best part was it didn't cost us a nickel. Which was perfect, since we didn't have a nickel to spare."

DICK VAN DYKE

February 13 (1935)

Dori$ Duke & Jame$ Cromwell

The whole wide world takes notice as **the "wealthiest girl in the world"** suddenly marries this morning. Tobacco heiress Doris Duke, 22, whose wealth exceeds $50 million, weds businessman James Cromwell, 38, of the blue-blooded Stotesbury family of Philadelphia. The bride wears a simple blue crepe dress with a matching hat and fur in a civil service that papers describe as "unostentatious and somewhat mysterious." It takes place in the spacious library of the Duke family's Upper East Side mansion, which is adorned with rare lilies and orchids from the bride's 5,000-acre conservatory in New Jersey. A state Supreme Court justice performs the service, another serves as a witness. Afterwards the couple sails off in an Italian ocean liner for a leisurely, four-month honeymoon that'll extend from Egypt and the Mediterranean to the Far East and Hawaii before a return to California. Papers report that the newlyweds will utilize "almost every conceivable means of transportation: airplane, automobile, boat, train, elephant and rickshaw."

> Her first of two, his second of four, lasts eight years

February 14 (1967)

Raquel Welch & Patrick Curtis

Valentine's Day in Paris. What a romantic time and place to tie the knot. Not. "Film Siren Weds in a Minidress" scream the headlines as buxom sexpot Raquel Welch, 26, marries her Svengali-like manager Patrick Curtis, 31, amidst swarming photographers and reporters. The city's mayor delays the civil service 20 minutes to clear the gilt and rococo room of photographers, claiming, **"This is a solemn marriage. It is neither a fair nor a fashion show."** Tell that to the bride, who wears a brown body stocking under a see-through, crocheted mini-skirted dress. Afterwards the couple descends the city hall staircase as dozens of photographers fire away, then drive off in a Rolls-Royce to a champagne reception. Next week Welch's latest flick *One Million Years B.C.* opens in America, and a shot of her curvaceous figure in a fur bikini and go-go boots turns into a bestselling pin-up poster.

"People were dropping out of the trees to take photographs of us. For three days I had tried to get out to a couture house to buy a wedding dress, but I just couldn't because of the mob."

RAQUEL WELCH

> Her second of four, lasts five years

February 15 (2000)
Darva Conger & Rick Rockwell

Money can't buy you love, but it can snag 23 million voyeurs to tonight's premiere of Fox's much ballyhooed special, *Who Wants to Marry a Multi-Millionaire?* In a quasi-beauty pageant format, 50 young ladies compete for the hand of a wealthy bachelor seen only in silhouette. The five finalists don wedding gowns, and real estate developer Rick Rockwell, 42, chooses emergency-room nurse Darva Conger, 34. Wedding bells chime and the new couple jets off for a honeymoon in Barbados. But there's **trouble in paradise** and then some. Reports quickly surface that he's no multimillionaire but a wannabe stand-up comedian whose former girlfriend has filed a restraining order against him. Conger files for an annulment and admits that participating was a big mistake. But she gets to keep more than $100,000 in prizes, and cashes in on the publicity by posing nude for *Playboy*.

February 16 (1969)
Tammy Wynette & George Jones

Country music royalty. There's simply no other way to describe the storybook union of one of country's finest vocalists and his fast-rising queen. George Jones, 37, and Tammy Wynette, 28, end months of speculation (and purposely false rumors they're already hitched) by marrying in Ringgold, Georgia, a favored out-of-the-limelight spot for Nashville stars (Dolly Parton wed here three years ago). Powered by massive crossover hits "Stand By Your Man" and "D-I-V-O-R-C-E," Tammy's career charge challenges that of her well-established hubby. As they enjoy Top Ten solo hits and sellout concerts, fans follow the marriage through each successive single. But while the music professes their love, the reality of his increasing alcoholism and drug abuse takes its toll. She files for divorce, then they reconcile and hit #1 with "We're Gonna Hold On." But it ain't so.

"A woman who married George Jones and complained that he drank would have been like a woman marrying the Reverend Billy Graham and complaining that he preached."

GEORGE JONES

His third of four, her third of five, lasts six years

February 17 (2002)
Joan Collins & Percy Gibson

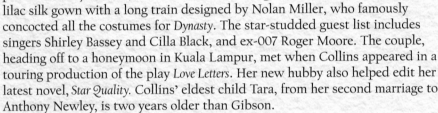

As villainous, scheming Alexis Colby on *Dynasty*, British actress Joan Collins found her signature role—and the acclaim that had eluded her during a long, undistinguished career in "B" movies. Today **she embellishes her lusty off-screen reputation**, walking down the aisle for the fifth time in a classic May/December coupling. At the posh London hotel Claridge's, Collins, 68, marries Peruvian theater producer Percy Gibson, 36. She wears a full-length, lilac silk gown with a long train designed by Nolan Miller, who famously concocted all the costumes for *Dynasty*. The star-studded guest list includes singers Shirley Bassey and Cilla Black, and ex-007 Roger Moore. The couple, heading off to a honeymoon in Kuala Lampur, met when Collins appeared in a touring production of the play *Love Letters*. Her new hubby also helped edit her latest novel, *Star Quality*. Collins' eldest child Tara, from her second marriage to Anthony Newley, is two years older than Gibson.

All my Love, from one of the Gibb brothers

"No one knew me until I met my wife Lulu. Lulu's mother used to ask, 'Which one is Maurice?' For six months she thought Lulu was dating Barry." MAURICE GIBB

February 18 (1969)
Lulu & Maurice Gibb

What better way to cap the swingin' sixties than a **marriage of two harmonizing pop stars**? Crowds gather at St. James Church in Buckinghamshire to catch a glimpse of songbirds/lovebirds Lulu (born Marie Lawrie), 20, and Bee Gee Maurice Gibb, 19. Arriving in her green Rolls-Royce, the bride wears a long white, mink-trimmed coat with a fur hood over a white silk mini-dress. Only close friends and family witness the half-hour service, but it takes a good ten minutes to clear a path outside afterwards amidst a thousand gawkers. Her career's been surging since her double-duty debut two years ago with *To Sir With Love*, appearing in the movie and topping the pop charts with its title track. The Bee Gees have already had several Top Ten hits and will soon catapult to international superstardom.

Her first of two, his first of two, lasts four years

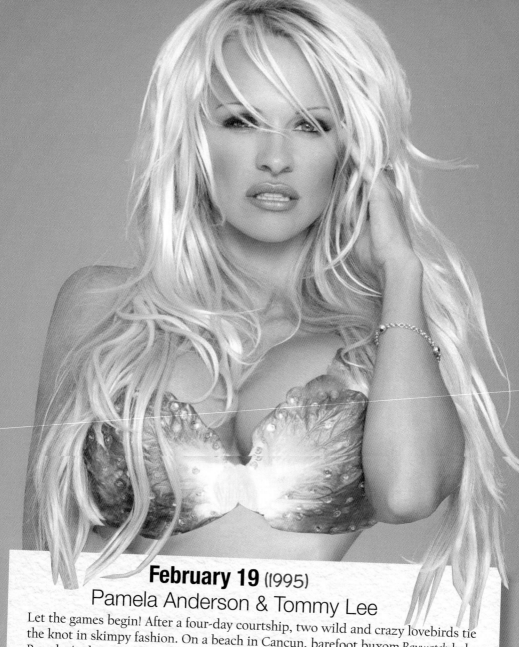

February 19 (1995)
Pamela Anderson & Tommy Lee

Let the games begin! After a four-day courtship, two wild and crazy lovebirds tie the knot in skimpy fashion. On a beach in Cancun, barefoot buxom *Baywatch* babe Pamela Anderson, 28, wears a tiny white bikini while her beloved, Motley Crue drummer Tommy Lee, 31, wears white Bermuda shorts sans shirt or shoes. And so begins **a torrid, made-for-tabloid-heaven marriage** that keeps them in the spotlight. He spends three months in jail for assaulting her while she was holding their infant son Dylan (who has an older brother, Brandon). But reaching ever loftier gutter standards, nothing surpasses the best-selling adult video of 1998, the porn-arific *Pam & Tommy Lee: Stolen Honeymoon*.

Her first of three, his third, lasts three years

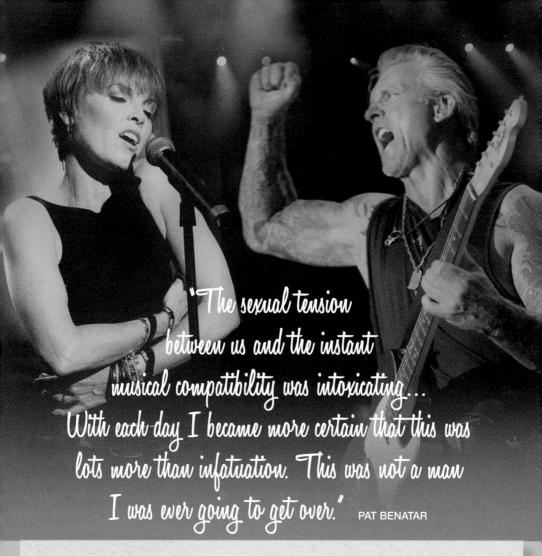

"The sexual tension between us and the instant musical compatibility was intoxicating... With each day I became more certain that this was lots more than infatuation. This was not a man I was ever going to get over." PAT BENATAR

February 20 (1982)

Pat Benatar & Neil "Spyder" Giraldo

Over the last couple of years they've jetted around the globe, staying in countless high-class hotels and partying hearty. But for their wedding they prefer a more secluded spot. So her travel agent suggests the tiny town of Hana on Maui, and as soon as their small plane touches down on a runway carved out of the Hawaiian jungle, they realize it's the right call. The locals have no idea who they are: hard rock chick Pat Benatar, 29, and her guitarist/arranger Neil Giraldo. On this picture perfect sunny day with **birds soaring and waves crashing** against the cliffs, they wed. She wears an off-the-rack white lace dress from Robinsons-May, purchased for $82 before they left L.A. Each sports leis around their necks and garlands of flowers on their heads. After a short honeymoon at the Hotel Hana-Maui, it's back to L.A. and the Grammy awards where Pat wins her second for "Fire and Ice."

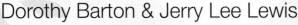

February 21 (1952)
Dorothy Barton & Jerry Lee Lewis

Goodness, gracious, he's a church-goin' boy, but his piano-pounding music smacks of the devil. It got him tossed out of seminary school, but he did meet and fall **in love with a Pentecostal preacher's daughter.** Today Jerry Lee Lewis, 16, marries Dorothy Barton, 18, at a friend's house in his hometown of Ferriday, Louisiana. She moves in with his family while he starts preaching the gospel at a local church and hanging out with his cousin, Jimmy Swaggart. But hellion Jerry Lee just can't cotton to married life, and soon he's out every night, running 'round with friends and playing in whatever honky-tonk bar will have him. Dorothy moves back home, leaving Jerry Lee free to pursue his hard-drinking, hard-playing, hard-living ways. Five years later his version of "Whole Lot of Shakin' Going On" brings success, but his taste for even younger women, i.e., his 13-year-old cousin Myra Gale, leads to a scandal combining cradle-robbing, incest and bigamy.

> **His first of seven, lasts one year**

February 22 (1998)
Tori Amos & Mark Hawley

She's always unconventional, to say the least. So **why not a medieval theme** for her wedding? Why not, indeed, as alternative rocker Tori Amos, 34, and sound engineer Mark Hawley, 33, marry at the 13th century St. Lawrence Church in the tiny village of West Wycombe, Buckinghamshire. Torchbearers dressed like monks lead the assemblage along a gravel path to the gothic church. The bride wears a shimmering silver floor-length, hooded cape over a long, low-cut ice-blue dress, the groom sports a vintage, long-coated black suit with a white boutonniere. Clusters of candles burn in the church windows, and the service features music including Bach and Irish pipes (but no vocals). Many of the 175 guests get into the spirit by wearing capes and velvet suits. Afterwards, an ornate carriage drawn by two jet-black horses carries the couple up a lantern-lit driveway to the reception at a nearby mansion.

'I really feel like my husband is my boyfriend. I am having an affair with my husband, and sometimes plates fly.'

TORI AMOS

February 23 (2002)
LeAnn Rimes & Dean Sheremet

Two weeks ago the Grammy award-winning artist sang "Light the Fire Within" at the gala opening of the 2002 Winter Olympics in Salt Lake City. Today 19-year-old LeAnn Rimes quenches her fire by walking down the aisle with Dean Sheremet, 21, one of her backup dancers, at Perkins Chapel at Southern Methodist University in Dallas. She wears an ivory Vera Wang strapless tulle gown and holds a bouquet of red and white roses, he wears a gray Hugo Boss suit. The foyer displays photos in remembrance of departed relatives, and **she pins to her garter a ring that belonged to her late grandfather**. The family theme continues at the reception where LeAnn shares a dance with her father, whom she'd once sued for theft, to the strains of Nat King Cole's "Unforgettable." Yet the marriage might better be described by her lone #1, "One Way Ticket (Because I Can)," as it disintegrates amidst whispers of her infidelity (with later hubby Eddie Cibrian) and hints of his playing for the other team.

Her first of two, his first of two, lasts eight years

February 24 (1992)
Courtney Love & Kurt Cobain

Brilliant but self-destructive, Kurt Cobain detours from his usual musical and drug-taking routines to **an unlikely destination: marriage**. On a Waikiki beach at sunset Cobain, 25, weds girlfriend Courtney Love, 27, in a brief non-denominational ceremony performed by a minister found through a local wedding bureau. She wears an antique silk dress that once belonged to troubled actress Frances Farmer, the gaunt groom wears blue-plaid pajamas with a woven Guatemalan purse over one shoulder. The best man is longtime pal Dylan Carlson, who flew in both for the role and to bring heroin. Indeed Cobain did some smack just before the ceremony. "Just a little teeny bit so I didn't get sick," he said later. The handful of guests includes no relatives but mostly band crew members.

February 25 (1958)

Paulette Goddard &
Erich Maria Remarque

The haunted writer of the renowned anti-war novel *All Quiet on the Western Front*, and a glamorous screen legend, once married to Charlie Chaplin and since linked romantically to leading men from Clark Gable to John Wayne. **Opposites attract** in a quiet civil ceremony, witnessed only by her two attorneys and their wives, at the Branford, Conn. office of the town's judge. Paulette Goddard, 47, wears a burgundy wool suit with a mink collar, and a brown velvet ribbon hat. Erich Maria Remarque, 59, wears a double-breasted navy suit. Though publicly linked for years, the couple evokes conflicting visions: his writing of the hollow-eyed face of war's futility versus her image of gilt Hollywood excess. A later joint biography, *Opposite Attraction*, captures their unlikely entangled lives.

Her fourth, his third, lasts 12 years until his death

February 26 (2009)
Gisele Bündchen & Tom Brady

Not only does he scout the field, he plays the field. Yes, drop-dead good looks, boatloads of money and three Super Bowl rings have made quarterback Tom Brady **quite the catch**. Late this afternoon Brady, 31, weds Brazilian beauty Gisele Bündchen, 28, in a secret ceremony at a catholic church in Santa Monica. The supermodel wears a Dolce & Gabbana ivory lace strapless dress with a trumpet skirt, and carries a bouquet of ivory roses. He opts for a gray, two-button peak lapel wool suit from Ermenegildo Zegna. His father holds Tom's 18-month-old son Jack (from his relationship with model Bridget Moynahan). Once is apparently not enough, for in April the couple enjoys a short sunset ceremony at her Costa Rican home. For that she wears a designer dress with a 10-foot veil and holds a bouquet of white orchids, while the NFL star wears a gray jacket and white trousers.

February 27 (2010)
Molly Malaney & Jason Mesnick

Planning for a wedding can be plenty stressful. But this bride and groom are **no strangers to the camera**, so the presence of a sizeable film crew doesn't seem all that unusual as *Bachelor* couple Jason Mesnick, 33, and Molly Malaney, 25, marry during a downpour at a plush Palos Verdes resort overlooking the Pacific Ocean. She wears a strapless gown, strolling down the aisle as *American Idol*'s Jason Castro croons "Over the Rainbow." The 15-minute service ends with the release of white doves into the soggy skies. The crowd of 300 includes many fellow TV contestants from ABC's long-running reality dating game shows like Trista and Ryan Sutter (the first couple from the show ever to wed), Jillian Harris, Ed Swiderski, DeAnna Pappas, Jesse Csinsak and Kiptyn Locke. For anyone not invited, not to fear: the network captures all on tape for a two-hour special airing next month.

February 28 (1988)
Joanne Whalley & Val Kilmer

Someone tell Val I filed for divorce.

They met on the set of *Willow*, Ron Howard's sword and sorcery fantasy that's soon to open. Today Val Kilmer, 28, and Joanne Whalley, 23, marry after sending a message to the movie's casting directors with a two-word notation: "**Good casting!**" Soon the British actress appends her husband's last name to hers with a hyphen, and after well-received turns in *Dance With a Stranger* and *The Singing Detective* sees her stock rise internationally with next year's *Scandal*, playing naughty schoolgirl Christine Keeler (Oct. 21). He ascends even higher with a bravura performance as Jim Morrison in *The Doors*, Oliver Stone's biopic. *People* names her one of its 50 most beautiful people in the world, but her career and the marriage falter. After giving birth to their second child, she files for divorce—news that Kilmer reportedly hears on CNN while off filming *The Island of Dr. Moreau*.

His first, her first, lasts eight years

February 29 (1968)
Florence Ballard & Thomas Chapman

It's **a rare happy moment** during an especially rough patch for former Supreme Florence Ballard. In Honolulu, Ballard, 24, marries longtime beau Thomas Chapman, once a chauffeur at Motown. Last year she was forced out of the group, the culmination of an increasingly ugly, acrimonious battle with Motown founder Berry Gordy, who elevated Diana Ross to lead singer and renamed the group Diana Ross and the Supremes. Next month Ballard attempts a comeback by signing a solo contract with ABC Records, and sues Motown for royalties during her time in the successful trio that rang up an astonishing ten #1 hits in less than three years. This fall Ballard gives birth to twin girls Michelle and Nicole, but the marriage sours and her solo career tanks, perhaps due in part to Gordy's draconian contract that prohibits Ballard from mentioning in any promotional materials that she had sung in the Supremes.

Her first, lasts eight years until her death

March

Nancy Davis
& Ronald Reagan
March 4, 1952

March 1 (1968)
June Carter & Johnny Cash

Last month at a concert in London, Ontario, **the man in black proposed onstage** to his country lady. A bit embarrassed to receive a marriage proposal in such a public place, June Carter demurred until the crowd of 5,000, realizing it was for real, egged her on. So she accepted. Today Johnny Cash, 36, and Carter, 38, marry in a small ceremony in a Methodist church in Franklin, Kentucky. Merle Kilgore (her co-writer on "Ring of Fire") serves as best man, and the reception is alcohol free. The wedding caps a busy year for Cash: in January he performed live at Folsom Prison, and the resulting album becomes a huge and enduring crossover hit; and last month the couple won a Grammy, his first, for the duet "Jackson." Delaying their honeymoon until a concert tour of Britain in May, Johnny and June then slip off to Israel, where he's very moved by the sights, sounds and smells of the holy land.

His second, her third, lasts 35 years until her death

"Me to my love and my love to me."
ENGRAVED ON THE RINGS JOHNNY AND JUNE BUY ON THEIR HONEYMOON

March 2 (2007)
Elizabeth Hurley & Arun Nayar

There's no sign of a partridge in a pear tree, but Elizabeth Hurley does have twelve attentive handlers: four make-up artists, three hairdressers, two wedding planners and a personal assistant, photographer and stylist. Today's Britain's most famous model/actress Hurley, 41, marries Indian textile tycoon Arun Nayar, 42, at **a glitzy wedding at a 15th century castle** in tiny Winchcombe in the Cotswolds. *Hello!* magazine pays a reported $3 million for exclusive rights to photograph glitterati guests like Donatella Versace (who designed the wedding dress), Yasmin Le Bon, Jimmy Choo, Elton John, Kate Moss, Elle Macpherson, Patsy Kensit and Valentino. Afterwards, instead of the usual formal toasts and speeches, the bride and groom show a Bollywood-style film that celebrates their lives in singing and dancing. From castles to palaces, the couple wings to India for a traditional Hindu ceremony next week in Jodhpur.

Her first, his second, lasts four years

Lavish Love

When it comes to extravagant weddings, these five celebrity couples take the cake... and spend the cash. A countdown of the Top Five:

$2 million
Elizabeth Taylor & Larry Fortensky (Oct. 1991)
Tom Cruise & Katie Holmes (Nov. 2006)

$2.5 million
Elizabeth Hurley & Arun Nayar (below)
(March 2007)

$3 million
Paul McCartney & Heather Mills
(June 11)

$3.5 million
Liza Minnelli & David Gest
(March 2002)

March 3 (1967)
Liza Minnelli & Peter Allen

Never one to relinquish the spotlight, **the mother of the bride stands center stage** today. After all, it was Judy Garland who'd first met the groom when he was playing in a group at a Hong Kong hotel, and introduced him to her daughter. Several years later the jet-setting "in" couple, Liza Minnelli, 20, and flamboyant (ahem) singer/songwriter Peter Allen, 22, marry at a friend's Park Avenue apartment. She wears an Elizabethan-style gown of white wool and lace designed by her father Vincente. Photographer Paul Jasmin serves as best man at the intimate gathering that includes her long-divorced parents, Yul Brynner, Van Johnson and Allen's mother and sister who'd flown in from their native Australia. Unfortunately for Liza, her new husband is gay, and he reportedly spends this honeymoon night in the arms of a male lover. Two night later, Garland makes the most of her New York visit by appearing as a mystery guest on *What's My Line*.

> Her first of four, lasts two years

March 4 (1952)
Nancy Davis & Ronald Reagan

MGM announced that the minor "B" movie actress, whose last picture bombed, had asked out of her contract. Then it quietly added that **she would marry a higher-profile movie star**. What it never mentioned was that she was pregnant —a story far more scandalous in these staid '50s than even her intended's divorce. Today Nancy Davis, 30, marries Ronald Reagan, 41, on an untraditional Tuesday at the Little Brown Disciples of Christ Church in the San Fernando Valley. No children (he has two with ex-wife Jane Wyman), no relatives, no press. Nancy wears a gray wool suit with a white collar and cuffs, and a small hat, while Ronnie wears a dark blue suit. Actor William Holden and wife Brenda Marshall serve as best man and matron of honor, respectively. After a night at the landmark Mission Inn (where Richard and Pat Nixon married in 1940) in Riverside, the newlyweds are off on a honeymoon to Phoenix, with his mother watching the kids. In October, daughter Patti is born.

> His second, her first, lasts 52 years until his death

March 5 (1989)
Phoebe Cates & Kevin Kline

She didn't get the part, but **she did get the man.** Seven years after they met at an audition for *The Big Chill*, Kevin Kline and Phoebe Cates marry in a small private ceremony in New York. Kline, 41, has been pegged as a most eligible bachelor about town, what with his multiple, well-received stage (*The Pirates of Penzance*) and screen (*Sophie's Choice*) performances. Cates, 25, has enjoyed considerable success though less acclaim for flicks like *Fast Times at Ridgemont High*. Soon she's a stay-at-home mom, and he's winning an Oscar for *A Fish Called Wanda*. The family grows as he carefully chooses his roles, so cautiously that Hollywood execs bestow upon him a nickname: "Kevin Decline."

"We're both sensible, and we don't separate for long periods of time. We take care of the marriage."

KEVIN KLINE

March 6 (2004)
Paula Deen & Michael Anthony Groover

Old time Southern cookin' arrives in **an old time Southern wedding**—and it's on TV to boot! Food Channel chef Paula Deen, 57, ties the knot with Michael Groover, 47, in a ceremony at the tiny Whitfield Chapel in Savannah, with cameras rolling for a special edition of *Paula's Home Cooking* that'll air in June. The full-figured gal wears a dress of crisp white organza with a soft, long-sleeved jacket. The chapel holds only 75 people, but the reception at (where else?) The Lady & Sons offers 650 guests a down-home Southern feast: shrimp and grits served hot in martini glasses, tomato sandwiches, okra sandwiches, crab-stuffed shrimp, white-bread handle sandwiches (drumettes of fried chicken wings with leeks), and wontons stuffed with collard greens and cream cheese. Dessert's a take on the groom's favorite cake that his momma used to make: a pound cake with sour cream, almond and orange extract with butter cream icing.

March 7 (1953)
Virginia Patterson Hensley
& Gerald Cline

She traded in her childhood nickname of Ginny for Patsy, a play off her middle name. Always dreaming of being a singer, she won an $8 a night gig with a band at the Moose Lodge, a well-known local hot spot in Frederick, Md. One of the regulars, a contractor, fancied and wooed **the attractive brunette with the amazing voice.** Today Virginia Hensley, 20, and Gerald Cline, 27, marry at the local United Church of Christ before a handful of witnesses. Her hubby soon buys her a snazzy red Buick Roadmaster coupe, but the passionless marriage fades as he prefers a stay-at-home housewife. Never giving a thought to abandoning her dream, Patsy lands a recording contract next year. Her first song, "A Church, A Courtroom, and Then Goodbye" is a dud. But she perseveres, debuts at the Grand Old Opry and becomes one of country's most celebrated and beloved singers with timeless classics like "I Fall to Pieces," "Crazy" and "Sweet Dreams (of You)" before her tragic death in an airplane crash at age 30.

> **Her first of two, his second, lasts four years**

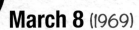

"I'm gonna be something one of these days."

PATSY CLINE

March 8 (1969)
Joan Smith & Ray Kroc

They deserve a break today. Back in 1957 they met in a St. Paul restaurant—a budding burger businessman and a buxom blonde pianist. Sparks flew, but both were married. Years intervened, and his burgeoning McDonald's chain made him a billionaire. Earlier this year they met again at a regional McDonald's convention (her husband was a franchisee). This time the attraction was too strong to ignore and both quickly divorced. Today, Ray Kroc, 56, marries Joan Smith, 40, in front of a massive stone fireplace at his sprawling Southern California ranch. While he continues to expand his empire, the couple enjoys the perks of untold wealth. She becomes an especially prominent philanthropist, he maintains his eagle eye on business and pens an autobiography: *Grinding It Out.*

> **His third, her second, lasts 15 years until his death**

March 9 (1796)

Josephine de Beauharnais
& Napoleon Bonaparte

During an era when **15 is considered a marriageable age**, the bride is an aging 32. But today she lops off four years while her gallant bridegroom adds two, so the marriage certificate falsely shows each to be 28. Yet the groom's so late tonight the mayor departs, leaving a minor official who lacks legal authority to perform the simple civil service. Napoleon Bonaparte arrives three hours late and his witness, an aide-de-camp, is underage so his role is illegal too. All in all, not a particularly auspicious start to a most strange coupling: a promiscuous, featherbrained woman past her prime and not particularly in love, and a besotted, ambitious general. Past ten p.m. in a dingy, second story room of the Parisian mayor's office, the future Emperor of France weds Josephine de Beauharnais. Later on, in bed at her house, as the ardent, sexually inexperienced groom begins enjoying his conjugal rights, her pug dog Fortune bites him in the leg.

"I awake full of you. Your image and last evening's intoxication have left my senses no repose whatever. Sweet and incomparable Josephine, what a strange effect do you produce upon my heart!"

NAPOLEON

March 10 (2000)
Amy Grant & Vince Gill

It's **a classy, country Christian affair**: an outdoor, private ceremony on a Tennessee farm outside Nashville that's devoid of press. Christian crossover pop star Amy Grant, 39, wears a full-length, cream-colored Jane Booke dress with matching cape, and flowers in her hair. She sheds a pair of matching ballet slippers to go barefoot while the shod Gill, 42, wears a formal black Calvin Klein suit. A violin/guitar duo performs during the service, conducted by a local Baptist pastor, and the couple exchanges self-penned vows. Afterwards the Nashville Pipes and Drums bagpipers march over a nearby rise playing "Highland Cathedral" and "How Great Thou Art." More than 400 guests attend the reception at Grant's Nashville home, where the couple takes to the floor for their first dance to the strains of Celine Dion's "Because You Loved Me."

"She's really easy to love. I got lucky, real lucky."

VINCE GILL

March 11 (1968)
Maureen O'Hara & Charles Blair

With her fiery red hair, she earned the nickname "The Queen of Technicolor" as color came to dominate the movies beginning in the '50s. Displaying **an appealing mix of femininity and independence**, she starred five times opposite her good friend John Wayne. Today Maureen O'Hara, 47, marries a man sometimes described as a real-life John Wayne: retired Air Force Brigadier General Charles Blair, 58, a pioneering pilot who flew the first solo flight over the North Pole. It's a small civil ceremony for the couple, friends for more than 20 years, held in a judge's chambers in the Virgin Islands. On St. Croix he builds them a home atop a hill overlooking the crystal-blue Caribbean. Several years into the happy marriage, O'Hara scores on two fronts: she becomes a grandmother, and stars opposite the Duke in their final film together, *Big Jake*.

Maureen O'Hara
in *How Green Was My Valley*

Her third, his third, lasts ten years until his death

March 12 (1992)

Annette Bening & Warren Beatty

The leopard changes its spots, the sun rises in the west, and Warren Beatty gets married. In a town of legendary Lotharios, no man amassed a more curvaceous catalog of conquests: the C's alone include Maria Callas, Leslie Caron, Cher, Julie Christie, Connie Chung and Joan Collins, undoubtedly a partial list. **"Women are his profession, movies are his hobby,"** noted a colleague. In a super secret wedding Beatty, 54, marries Annette Bening, 33, his *Bugsy* co-star. Two months ago she gave birth to their daughter Kathlyn, who's reportedly the ceremony's sole witness. Later this month, on his 55th birthday, the happy couple attends the Oscars, an event Beatty first attended alongside girlfriend/co-star (*Splendor in the Grass*) Natalie Wood in 1962, when Bening was but three years old. Given his prodigious sexual history, many doubt the union's staying power—but to date they have four children and are still together.

"Miss Bening found the one way of pinning him down because he would have been a bachelor forever... The present of sex is something that goes away, but the present of a warm and loving baby, especially a little girl, is forever."

DR. JOYCE BROTHERS

March 13 (1994)
Sarah Kapfer & Cuba Gooding, Jr.

Ah, **who says high school romances don't last?** Seven years after they first met in school, Cuba Gooding, Jr., 25, and elementary school teacher Sarah Kapfer marry in a small sunset ceremony in Pacific Palisades. But the honeymoon's a one-day affair, according to his publicist: "Then he falls into the arms of Halle Berry," referring to his upcoming film, *Losing Isaiah*. But not to fear: the marriage is on solid ground, as Gooding immediately plunks down $600,000 to buy his first house, a four-bedroom ranch-style L.A. home with mountain, canyon and city views. Within a couple years his stock climbs even higher with *Jerry Maguire* and his memorable line, "Show me the money." Three children later, the marriage is still going strong.

March 14 (1983)
Melissa Mathison & Harrison Ford

In a well-timed operation, one of the world's biggest box-office attractions and his intended choose the cover of Oscar mania to conceal their wedding plans. As headlines trumpet the two-horse race between E.T. and *Gandhi*, Harrison Ford, 40, pilots his Porsche into a parking space at the Santa Monica Courthouse. Soon he and screenwriter Melissa Mathison (E.T.), 32, exchange **wedding bands and single white roses** in a 15-minute ceremony. Then it's back to their home in the Hollywood Hills for a small celebration with their parents. It takes the press several weeks to detect the news, which breaks as *Gandhi* (eight Oscars, including Best Picture) steamrolls the then highest-grossing film ever, E.T., and Mathison loses the screenplay award to John Briley (yes, *Gandhi* again). Ford and Mathison met in '76 on the set of *Apocalypse Now*, for which she was an assistant to director Francis Ford Coppola. Within months swashbuckling Ford is back on screen in *Return of the Jedi*, while his screenwriting missus is penning a segment of *Twilight Zone: The Movie*.

> His second of three, lasts 18 years

March 15 (2003)

Kimberly Williams & Brad Paisley

He saw her movie debut, *Father of the Bride*, with a girlfriend. By the time the sequel came out four years later, she'd left him for his best friend so he saw it alone. The by now fast-rising, cute country crooner was smitten all over again, so he asked his silver screen queen to appear in a music video. The two clicked—**the country boy and the city girl** who knew so little about country music she thought they sang opera at the Grand Ole Opry. Tonight guests invited to a wedding rehearsal at a chapel in Malibu (the invitation reads "denim required") are amazed when Kimberly Williams, 31, peels off her denim coat to reveal a wedding dress, and the nuptials proceed with Brad Paisley, 30. At a big reception tomorrow he sings "Toilet Seat Down," a humorous song about married life – and a bit of an inside joke, since he proposed to her at the Venice Beach pier in Santa Monica, right in front of the public toilets.

March 16 (1940)

Dorothy Spence & Robert Mitchum

He's no good, says her family. A bum. He'll never amount to anything. But she won't be dissuaded. Her insurance company coworkers pass the hat and raise $100, and a friend drives the couple to Dover, Del. where Dorothy Spence, 20, buys a dress while her high school sweetheart Robert Mitchum, 22, buys a ring. Off they go to a Methodist minister's house, which is so cold **they marry in the kitchen with a strong smell of cabbage**. Tomorrow it's off on a Greyhound bus to L.A, where they live in a converted chicken coop behind a West Hollywood house holding the rest of the bohemian Mitchum clan. As her family warned, Bob had had a rough'n'tumble background: coal miner, boxer, and chain gang worker while serving time for vagrancy. But when she gives birth next year to a son, he finds a regular job at an aircraft factory. That doesn't work out, but an agent he'd met arranges an audition, and so begins the unlikely career of one of Hollywood's most rugged, popular leading men.

His first, her first, lasts 57 years until his death

March 17 (1961)
Joan Plowright & Laurence Olivier

Last night they appeared on Broadway—him in *Becket*, her in *A Taste of Honey*. Then Hume Cronyn's cabbie drove them to tiny Wilton, Connecticut, where they spent the night at the house of director Joshua Logan. This morning, on St. Patrick's Day, with their respective divorces recently having become final, Laurence Olivier, 53, and Joan Plowright, 29, marry in **a short ceremony held in an office above a drug store**. Delighted that they'd hoodwinked the press, Olivier soon basks in patriotic pride since, given the time difference, the first paper to report the union is the *Times* in London. Then it's back to the city for their respective evening performances. Afterwards Richard Burton, on Broadway in *Camelot*, hosts a bash to which Lauren Bacall brings a three-tiered wedding cake.

His third, her second, lasts 28 years until his death

March 18 (1993)
Nicole Mitchell & Eddie Murphy

The bride wanted a small, private ceremony. The groom didn't. Guess who won? Five hundred guests from James Brown to Bruce Willis gather at the Grand Ballroom of New York's Plaza Hotel for the mega-opulent marriage of Eddie Murphy, 31, and Nicole Mitchell, 25, who'd met at an NAACP Image Awards banquet in 1988. She wears a low-cut, off-the-shoulder silk and satin dress with French Alençon lace and rosettes, with a 12-foot cathedral train and veil **edged in Belgian embroidery with iridescent Austrian crystals and pearls**. The bride enters to "Don't Give Up on Love" from Murphy's *Love's Alright* album, and they (including four-year-old daughter Bria) exit to Whitney Houston's "I'm Every Woman." The lavish spread even includes a dish named after the bride, Chicken Nicole, with Cognac sauce. "One of the most elegant, glamorous, and classiest weddings," says Donald Trump, who'll use the same room next December for his blowout bash to Marla Maples.

His first, her first, lasts 12 years

March 19 (2009)
Regina Lasko & David Letterman

No they're **not getting married in a chateau but in Choteau**, a tiny Montana town not far from their ranch. But they almost don't arrive since their truck gets stuck on a muddy road, so TV talk master David Letterman must hike back to the house to get another car. Off they head to the Teton County Courthouse where Letterman, 61, and longtime girlfriend Regina Lasko, 48, tie the knot in front of a justice of the peace, with only their five-year-old son Harry and a couple friends in attendance. The world doesn't learn of the nuptials 'til he tapes his next show five days later, revealing that he thought married men admired his longtime bachelorhood, "like I was the last of the real gunslingers." Letterman neglects to mention that his bachelorhood hasn't been without considerable drama, what with the unwanted attentions of an infamous, persistent stalker, several affairs with staffers, and multiple lawsuits.

March 20 (1969)
Yoko Ono & John Lennon

Growing up in the seaport of Liverpool, John Lennon knew that **ship captains traditionally perform marriages at sea**. But his plans to wed Yoko Ono on a ferry across the English Channel fell apart due to problems with her passport. So this morning they take a private jet to Gibraltar, the only European country that doesn't require a two-week minimum residency for nuptials. The famous couple is immediately on full display: Ono, 36, in a layered knit white miniskirt with knee-high socks, sneakers and a floppy hat, and Lennon, 28, in a grey corduroy jacket, white polo sweater, white trousers and sneakers. An elderly registrar at the British Consulate performs the quick service with a lone witness: Beatles' jack-of-all trades Peter Brown. Then it's off to Amsterdam, where John & Yoko commence their most unconventional honeymoon: a very public performance art-ish "bed-in" at the Amsterdam Hilton.

His second, her third, lasts 11 years until his death

March 21 (1993)
Jennifer Holliday & Reverend Andre Woods

The star of *Dreamgirls* isn't giving up on her dream. Eight months after a short-lived marriage, Tony Award winner Jennifer Holliday, 32, walks down the aisle at Detroit's Revival Tabernacle Church of Christ with its pastor, Rev. Andre Woods, 38. She wears a long-sleeved, knee-length white lace dress with a sheer neckline and long train, with a white spread taffeta headpiece. The couple met last June at another church in Detroit, and romance soon blossomed. **"We looked up and we were in love,"** says the happy bride, who croons Stevie Wonder's "Ribbon in the Sky" to her new husband. Holliday sports a new svelte look, having lost more than 120 pounds off her former 300-pound frame from her heady Broadway days. Her showstopper, "And I'm Telling You I'm Not Going," catapulted her to fame and won universal critical and audience acclaim. *The New York Times* called it "one of the most powerful theatrical coups to be found in a Broadway musical since Ethel Merman sang 'Everything's Coming Up Roses' at the end of Act I of 'Gypsy.'"

> Her second, his first, lasts one year

March 22 (1984)
Sarah Brightman & Andrew Lloyd Webber

Tonight we're slated to meet the Queen, so what should we do today? Get married? So off they go to the magistrate's office in a small village in Hampshire: one of the world's most acclaimed composers (*Jesus Christ Superstar, Evita, Cats*) and his budding stage star/singer. Andrew Lloyd Webber, turning 36 today, and Sarah Brightman, 23, marry before a handful of guests. Then it's back to London for the gala preview of *Starlight Express* at the Apollo Victoria Theatre. Afterwards **the new couple is presented to Queen Elizabeth**, radiant in a crystal-embroidered coral pink chiffon evening dress. Webber met his bride when she appeared in the original presentation of *Cats*, later admitting that he fell in love with her voice before falling in love with her. The Svengali behind her theatrical success, he creates the role of Christine in his musical extravaganza *The Phantom of the Opera* especially for her.

> His second of three, her second, lasts six years

March 23 (1985)
Christie Brinkley & Billy Joel

On a 150-foot yacht cruising New York harbor, **the piano man and the supermodel** tie the knot. It's a brief ceremony, including James Brown's "I Feel Good," for Billy Joel, 35, and Christie Brinkley, 31. The stunning *Sports Illustrated* swimsuit issue model wears a Norma Kamali satin gown adorned in lace and gold, and carries a bouquet of 50 white roses. They'd met several years ago on a Caribbean holiday when he was holding court at a posh hotel's piano bar. Two other famous ladies were there too: Elle Macpherson, who he dated first, and Whitney Houston. Rebounding from a divorce and a motorcycle accident, Joel quickly reflected his newfound love in his music. "Tell Her About It" professed his love; the follow-up "Uptown Girl" was a pre-nuptial paean to Brinkley who made a rather non-rhythmic appearance in its video.

"He was totally unlike anyone else I had ever met. There was something defensive and untamed about him, like a wild animal."

ANNE FLEMING

March 24 (1952)

Anne Charteris & Ian Fleming

Forty-four years of bachelorhood end today at the gently decaying town hall of Port Maria, Jamaica. Bon vivant and ex-military intelligence officer Ian Fleming, has finally met his match in haughty, sharp society lady Anne Charteris, 38. She wears a pale green silk dress, a Dior knockoff fashioned by a local seamstress; he sports a belted linen shirt and blue trousers. The registrar has such bad breath that, during the short ceremony, he whispers to her, "Try to keep upwind of him." Afterwards the small party, including his pal Noel Coward and secretary, repair to **Fleming's island retreat, Goldeneye** (named after a codeword for a World War II intelligence operation), for a spectacularly awful meal: self-caught turtle (Coward: like "chewing an old tyre"), black crab in its shell ("like eating cigarette ash out of an ashtray") and a cake with lime-green icing, the remainder of which Fleming promptly buries in his garden. Tomorrow morning the couple flies to London, with the rough manuscript in his suitcase of a novel entitled *Casino Royale*: the birth of his James Bond phenomenon.

March 25 (2003)
Liv Tyler & Royston Langdon

For the last few years, her ethereal self has graced the *Lord of the Rings* trilogy. Today Liv Tyler, **the erstwhile elf princess Arwen, comes down to earth** in a most lovely spot, Barbados. There in a scenic Caribbean beach house Tyler, 25, marries musician Royston Langdon, 30, in an intimate candlelit affair attended by a handful of his relatives. Next month in New York they hold a more elaborate ceremony for her family, which is a decidedly unconventional lot. Tyler grew up with mother Bebe Buell and her partner Todd Rundgren, whom she thought was her father until around age ten when she learned her actual papa was Aerosmith's Steven Tyler (May 28). To keep it all in the family, next month Langdon's band Spacehog opens on tour for... Aerosmith? Nope. Rundgren.

March 26 (1968)
Joan Baez & David Harris

It's not every Episcopal church that has **peace symbols plastered all about** and a tree, center stage, covered with paper flowers. Then again, it's not every couple that's been arrested and out speaking on lecture tours, either. Not to mention the nervous bride's upset stomach, for which she's been gulping Kaopectate. Nevertheless, the ceremony goes on. Anti-war activist and folk singer Joan Baez, 27, barefoot, wears a Grecian-style, sleeveless floor-length dress. Draft resister David Harris, 22, with muttonchop whiskers and a walrus moustache, wears a decidedly establishment three-piece suit. A pacifist preacher performs the combo Episcopal/Quaker service, which ends in a prolonged French kiss interrupted by her father's harrumph, while his crew-cut military father stands stiffly and uncomfortably. His son marrying a peacenik?! Judy Collins songs enliven the subsequent champagne toast.

Her first, lasts three years

"The concept of keeping one's name, not to mention identity, was not yet born in me. But the idea of becoming a wife, and, hopefully, a mother, was thrilling. David and I were going to have bushels of babies and save the world at the same time." JOAN BAEZ

"What I had felt for George was a great, deep love. What Eric and I had was an intoxicating, overpowering passion. It was so intense, so urgent, so heady, I felt almost out of control." PATTIE BOYD

March 27 (1979)

Pattie Boyd & Eric Clapton

Two thirds of the world's most celebrated rock triangle come together today: George Harrison's ex-wife Pattie Boyd (Jan. 21), 35, for whom he penned "Something," and Eric Clapton, 33, who wrote "Layla" to describe his anguished amore with his good friend's wife. To confound the press they book several Tucson churches but settle upon an Apostolic Assembly with a Mexican priest who performs the service in Spanish. She wears a cream, silk satin dress with a lace jacket. At a hotel reception the cake cutting turns into cake throwing. "Everyone was drunk and the whole thing turned into chaos," recalled Pattie. **"Not the traditional wedding but perfect rock'n'roll**." Tomorrow night Clapton opens a tour by dedicating "Wonderful Tonight" to his new bride, but the marriage is no rock'n'roll fairytale since infidelities, coupled with his drinking and spiraling heroin addiction, result in an unhappy ending.

His first of two, her second, lasts nine years

March 28 (1920)

Mary Pickford & Douglas Fairbanks, Sr.

The international epitome of romantic love, the modern fulfillment of every love story since Adam and Eve has a happy ending today as **the prince and princess of silent filmdom** marry. America's Sweetheart, Mary Pickford, 27, weds swashbuckling Douglas Fairbanks, Sr., 36, in a short ceremony at the Glendale, California residence of the pastor of the Temple Baptist Church. She wears a simple white tulle dress, and according to tradition, one stocking wrong side out. Tomorrow she wears a piece of adhesive tape over her wedding ring, a plain platinum band, hoping no one will notice. The secret holds for three days until everything explodes and reporters besiege their United Artists studio and private homes. Fevered front-page coverage focuses on her recent divorce in Nevada, and despite their prominence the couple fears condemnation since they're both divorced Catholics. But moral indignation never jells and as the Roaring '20s get underway, their popularity among an accepting public soars.

> Her second of three, his second, lasts 15 years

March 29 (1939)

Carole Lombard & Clark Gable

With the press hovering, MGM didn't want the impending nuptials of two megastars to turn into a media circus. So it ordered a publicist to find an out-of-the-way spot. At dawn the couple piles into his blue DeSoto coupe for an 800-mile round trip to tiny Kingman, Arizona. Stopping for gas, **they hid under a blanket in the rumble seat** so no one would see their unmistakably recognizable faces. Late this afternoon in a Methodist Episcopal church, Clark Gable, 38, and Carole Lombard, 30, marry. She wears a tapered gray flannel suit and a polka-dot blouse designed by MGM costumer Irene Gibbons, he sports a blue serge suit, crisp white shirt and printed tie. They arrive back at Lombard's house in L.A. at 3 a.m. to discover that one of her brothers had hung a shotgun on her bedroom wall. Tomorrow morning MGM stages a press conference in her living room, and front-page stories trumpet the news. Then he's back on set filming a little something called *Gone With the Wind*.

His third of five, her second, lasts three years until her death in a plane crash

March 30 (1946)
Doris Day & George Weidler

America's favorite girl next door embodied post World War II dreams as "Sentimental Journey" became an anthem for returning soldiers. Yet the personal life of pretty, wholesome Doris Day, singer with Les Brown and His Band of Renown, didn't match the sweet song. Today Day, 21, **repeats an earlier mistake by marrying another musician**, swarthy mustachioed George Weidler, 20, a saxophonist in Brown's band, in Mount Vernon, N.Y. Her recording career soars and the movies beckon, but Weidler decides that he doesn't want to become known as Mr. Doris Day. Gossip columnist Hedda Hopper dubs her "a girl who fell in love without pausing for breath." Her success in radio, recordings, film and television remains unrivaled. In 1960, she's America's #1 box-office star, a nose ahead of her romantic screen co-star, Rock Hudson (Nov. 9).

Her second of four, lasts a year

March 31 (1991)
Janet Jackson & Rene Elizondo

When is the wedding of one of the biggest pop divas on earth not an occasion for mega-media coverage? When it's a, ssshhh, secret. In the midst of her sizzling *Rhythm Nation World Tour*, Janet Jackson inked a $50 million deal with Virgin Records several weeks ago. Today Jackson, 24, and dancer/songwriter Rene Elizondo, Jr., 28, marry in her northern San Diego estate before a handful of family and friends. As her longtime musical collaborator, Elizondo co-writes many of her songs and produces her videos. But for the next decade they maintain **the guise of being, uh, good friends**. Next September, it is Rene's hands cupping Jackson's bared breasts on a controversial cover of *Rolling Stone*. Only when he files for divorce in May 2000 does the news that they're married become public.

Her second, his first, lasts 12 years

"I hope my fans will understand that I tried to keep my marriage private in an effort to have a normal family life." **JANET JACKSON**

April

Tia Mowry &
Cory Hardrict
April 20, 2008

April 1 (1979)
Patty Hearst & Bernard Shaw

The most famous bank robber in America marries her bodyguard cop?!
It's no April Fool's joke as Patty Hearst, 25, weds mustachioed Bernard Shaw, 33, in a flower-bedecked chapel at the Treasure Island naval base in San Francisco Bay—especially chosen since armed sentries guard all gates. She wears a bare-shouldered silk gown of white organza, satin and French lace, and carries a lily-of-the-valley bouquet. Around her neck hangs a white gold and diamond pendant on a strand of pearls, an heirloom from her grandmother. Her ex-bodyguard bridegroom wears black tails, satin-striped trousers and a striped cravat. The maid of honor is her childhood pal Patricia Tobin, whose father is president of the San Francisco bank that Hearst and her Symbionese Liberation Army cohorts robbed five years ago to a blaze of media attention. More than 300 guests attend the lavish, three-hour reception two months to the day after she was released from federal prison after her sentence was commuted by President Carter.

"I've never seen Patty so happy. Don't you think it's about time?" **FEDERAL MARSHAL JANEY JIMENEZ**

April 2 (1949)

Zsa Zsa Gabor & George Sanders

Some enchanted evening, you may see a screen star across a crowded room... At a cocktail party at the swank St. Regis hotel in New York, **an ambitious, avaricious divorcee** in a clingy black jersey silk dress, dripping in diamonds, spotted her prey: a handsome, debonair leading man. He didn't stand a chance. Today the reputed former Miss Hungary of some year in the late '30s, Zsa Zsa (born Sari) Gabor, 32, gets her man: dashing Englishman George Sanders, 42. They jet from L..A. to Las Vegas, heading straight to the Little Church of the West where his brother, actor Tom Conway, serves as best man at the quickie ceremony. Blonde, vivacious, twice-divorced Zsa Zsa—whose $2,000 monthly alimony from ex Conrad Hilton, the hotel magnate, is cut in half with this remarriage—tells reporters, "This definitely is the last time."

"He was infuriating and charming, intelligent and educated, a cad and a gentleman, a man who knew how to treat women and how to torture them... I loved George from the moment I first saw him up on the screen in The Moon and Sixpence—and made up my mind to marry him." **ZSA ZSA GABOR**

Here Comes the Bride—Again!

"I'm an excellent housekeeper. Every time I get a divorce, I keep the house."

ZSA ZSA GABOR

Burhan Belge (1937)
Conrad Hilton (1942)
George Sanders (1949)
Herbert Hutner (1962)
Joshua Cosden, Jr. (1966)
Jack Patrick Ryan (1975)
Michael O'Hara (1976)
Felipe de Alba (1983)
Frederic Prinz von Anhalt (1986)

Zsa Zsa Gabor's nine strolls down the aisle

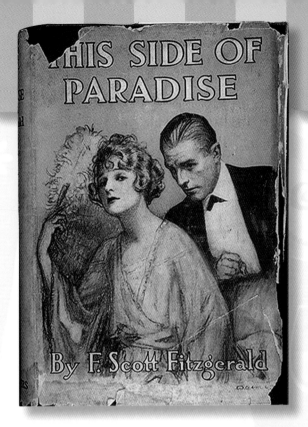

"Of the things they possessed in common, the greatest of all was their almost uncanny pull at each other's hearts."

FROM *THE BEAUTIFUL AND DAMNED*

April 3 (1920)

Zelda Sayre & F. Scott Fitzgerald

They're young and they're beautiful. At the doorstep of achieving stunning professional and financial success, F. Scott Fitzgerald, 23, marries Zelda Sayre, 19, this morning in the rectory of St. Patrick's Cathedral in Manhattan. One of his Princeton classmate serves as best man. A week ago his first novel, *This Side of Paradise*, was published to glowing reviews. Sales skyrocket, and **the young couple is soon gallivanting all about town**. At clubs, at shows, at restaurants, at parties, they're the incorrigible, insouciant epitome of post-WWI flapper society. After several weeks of dalliance the Biltmore politely asks them to leave, so they switch to the Commodore, then head out to the country for more frolicking. Their alcohol-infused adventures play well for a while, but a sad end's afoot for people who, like the characters in one Fitzgerald short story, have "money and a propensity to dissipation."

April 4 (2008)
Beyoncé Knowles & Jay-Z

Rumors have been flying ever since they took out a marriage license in Scarsdale a few days ago. Today a swarm of media encamped outside his Tribeca apartment building try to get the goods. A tip-off might be arriving shipments of huge silver candelabras and 70,000 white dendrobium orchids flown in from Thailand, and a white tent being constructed atop his 13,500-square-foot penthouse. About 40 family and friends gather for the hush-hush service uniting Jay-Z (Shawn Corey Carter, 38) and Beyoncé Knowles, 26. It's a fitting day given their 4/4 fixation: she was born on Sept. 4, he on Dec. 4, they met in 2002 (which adds up to four), and last year they got matching "IV" tattoos on their ring fingers. While the couple has consistently refused to discuss their relationship publicly, they've conveyed an unmistakable image through songs like **the smash hit "Crazy in Love."** But confirmation of their nuptials remains elusive—even several days later AP stories begin, "It appears that Jay-Z and Beyoncé have finally tied the knot."

April 5 (1955)
Della Beatrice Howard & Ray Charles

Though he lost his sight at age six, blues singer Ray Charles never lost his wandering eye. Just like his nonstop touring, women came and women went. Last year in Houston he met a young woman from a gospel group, the Cecil Shaw Singers, a down-to-earth Southern gal who neither smoked nor drank. She **quickly fell for the blues singer's wily charms**, and before not too long found herself pregnant. Today, Charles, 24, and Della Beatrice Howard (whom he calls "B") are married in Houston by a female minister in the cluttered back room of a lawyer's office. They rent a modest one-story frame house on a tree-lined block in South Dallas, where he thoughtfully establishes credit at a grocery across the street for the missus since he'll be away a lot. And still with the ladies. And heroin too.

His second, lasts 22 years

"Being a musician and a jive-ass celebrity meant that I was exposed to girls every night. That was all right, but I was beginning to want something better—a sweeter, more sensible life...Something deeper. Something permanent. Something solid."

RAY CHARLES

April 6 (1979)
Alana Hamilton & Rod Stewart

Millions of women would enthusiastically answer affirmatively to the question posed by his latest single, **"Do Ya Think I'm Sexy,"** which topped the charts last month in 11 countries. But only one maneuvers him down the aisle: Alana Hamilton, 33, ex-wife of actor George Hamilton. And so ends (temporarily) his bachelor string of romances with long-legged blondes like Liz Treadwell, Dee Harrington and Britt Ekland. They met last year at a party at the house of legendary agent Irving "Swifty" Lazar. Tonight at Tina Sinatra's house before a handful of guests including Ol' Blue Eyes himself, Alana wears a lace and chiffon, off-the-shoulder cream dress. Rod, 34, sports a double-breasted cream suit, pink tie and pink (what, blue wasn't available?) suede shoes. The hot ticket's for the reception afterwards at L'Ermitage in Beverly Hills that attracts folks like Marissa Berenson, Tony Curtis, and Michelle Phillips. The couple then hits the road for his latest concert tour, where it soon becomes obvious that the new Mrs. Stewart is with child. In August she gives birth to daughter Kimberly.

> His first of three, her second, lasts five years

"Marriage worked like the click of a switch. It wiped away all doubts, cleared away all fears." **ROD STEWART**

April 7 (2003)
Danielle Spencer & Russell Crowe

In keeping with the adage that **the groom shouldn't see his bride's gown before the wedding**, he'd worn a blindfold when his intended chose fabric with designer Giorgio Armani in his Milan studio. Today, his 39th birthday, Russell Crowe first lays eyes on the dress of Danielle Spencer, 32, at the site of the festivities: his 560-acre ranch in Nana Glen, Australia. It's a figure-hugging, floor-length satin gown daringly slashed to the thigh at the front and covered in cream lace embroidery with ivory and silver pearls. He wears an Armani tuxedo and waistcoast emblazoned with the Spencer and Crowe family crests. The couple met 13 years ago on a low-budget Australian movie, *The Crossing*. Since then he's crossed over into superstardom, linked romantically with leading ladies including Meg Ryan and Sharon Stone. But Spencer's hold on his heart endured and triumphs on this day, purposely far from Hollywood's bright lights. Their plans for his fatherhood before age 40 come true in December with the birth of son Charles.

April 8 (1995)

Patricia Arquette
& Nicolas Cage

Three years ago he was **celebrating *Honeymoon in Vegas***. This fall he'll star in a far more downbeat tale, *Leaving Las Vegas*, that'll leave him with a slew of Best Actor awards including the Golden Globe and Oscar. But today it's a real-life wedding in Las Vegas for Nicolas Cage, 31, and Patricia Arquette, 27, though press reports only confirm a private ceremony in an undisclosed location. Keeping the film references flying, will it shape up as *Wild at Heart* (his David Lynch outlaw adventure) or *True Romance* (her Tarantino-penned outlaw adventure)? Either way, each brings a son to the table, er, union: her Enzo, four, from a relationship with rocker Paul Rossi, his Weston, six, by actress Kristina Fulton.

His first of three, her first of two, lasts six years

April 9 (2005)

Camilla Parker Bowles & Prince Charles

It'd be pretty nigh impossible to top the worldwide spectacle of his first wedding (July 29) to Lady Diana. And besides, the Church of England frowns upon divorcees remarrying. So Prince Charles, 56, and Camilla Parker Bowles, 57, opt for a small civil service before 30 guests at a modest town hall. Then it's **off to a blessing in a towering gothic chapel** in Windsor Castle, where they pledge their undying love and confess to "manifest sins and wickedness," a phrase lifted from the church's *Book of Common Prayer*. That service attracts a sizeable, diverse crowd of 750 including his parents, Queen Elizabeth II and Prince Philip, plus Prime Minister Tony Blair, Phil Collins, Joanna Lumley and Joan Rivers (July 15). A tea and finger food reception culminates with the couple slicing an organic fruitcake with a sword that belonged to his great-grandfather, King George V. Then it's off to a honeymoon at a Scottish castle in a Bentley decorated with red, white and blue balloons.

April 10 (1971)

Penny Marshall & Rob Reiner

Each has a performing pedigree. Each is starring in a sitcom. Hell, they even grew up on the same block in New York until his family relocated to California. Today Rob Reiner, 23, and Penny Marshall, 28, marry **in the garden behind his parents' Beverly Hills home.** The reception repast? Takeout Chinese. Rob's stepping out from the long shadow cast by his writing/acting/directing father Carl. He's co-starring as the longhaired, freeloading son-in-law on CBS's game changer, *All in the Family*, affectionately (or perhaps otherwise) referred to as "Meathead" by his belligerent father-in-law. She's got a supporting role in ABC's *The Odd Couple*, playing Oscar's secretary. A few years later she lands her own primetime hit, *Laverne & Shirley*, which supplants *All in the Family* as television's #1 show for several years. The couple even combines for a sappy, semi-autobiographical TV movie, *More Than Friends*, which airs a few months before they divorce.

His first of two, her second, lasts ten years

April 11 (1981)
Valerie Bertinelli & Eddie Van Halen

From a wholesome, bubbly teenager on *One Day at a Time* to hard-rockin', hard-living rock'n'roll babe, she's had quite a ride. Today Valerie Bertinelli, 20, strolls down the aisle with Eddie Van Halen, 26, whom she'd met backstage at a Van Halen concert. She wears a traditional white gown with a lace mesh, high-collar front, he wears a traditional tux. To solve the problems of who to invite, **they chuck it all and simply invite everyone**, so 400 pack the ceremony in the cavernous St. Paul the Apostle Church in Westwood. (Forty out-of-town guests even camped out in their 2000-square-foot, three-bedroom home.) Maid of honor Nicolette Larson sings a French love song, but the couple opts against Van Halen performing at the reception at the Beverly Hills mansion where *A Star is Born* filmed. Valerie ends the night in their Beverly Hills Hotel suite passed out on the bed in her gown, while Eddie falls asleep in the bathroom.

> Her first of two, his first, lasts 25 years

April 12 (1986)
Arianna Stassinopoulos & Michael Huffington

A glorious society wedding between the perfect couple: **a filthy rich oil industry heir and a naked social climber**. At St. Bartholomew's Church in Manhattan, Arianna Stassinopoulos, 35, marries R. Michael Huffington, 38, in an Episcopal service with portions of the Greek Orthodox service incorporated. The dizzyingly dazzling guest list includes bridesmaid Barbara Walters (Dec. 8), society doyenne Helen Gurley Brown, Henry Kissinger, Norman Mailer and developer Mort Zuckerman. Settling comfortably into a life of plenty, Arianna begins hosting exclusive salons attracting the best and brightest conservative minds. Michael leaps into politics, spending (a record) $5.4 million to win a seat in the U.S. House of Representatives. Two years later he drops $28 million in an unsuccessful effort to unseat Senator Diane Feinstein. He later comes out of the closet and she reverses political stripes.

Her first, his first, lasts 11 years

April 13 (2002)
Talisa Soto & Benjamin Bratt

The tabloids buzzed incessantly during his near four-year attachment to Julia Roberts. But today there's nary a nosy reporter in sight as easy-on-the-eyes Benjamin Bratt, 38, and Talisa Soto, 35, marry at **a private service on a lush San Franciscan hillside** overlooking the Pacific. Peruvian flute music plays as the bride, one month pregnant, wears an off-the-rack satin chiffon dress with flip-flops. He opts for a black Calvin Klein suit and open-necked shirt. His mother, who is deputized to perform weddings, officiates before a small group of friends and family. The couple met after co-starring in last year's movie *Pinero*, about the hard-living Puerto Rican poet/playwright Miguel Pinero. Two months from now his celebrated ex Roberts marries cameraman Dan Moder, and to date both couples are living happily ever after. In December, Soto gives birth to daughter Sophia Rosalinda.

April 14 (1968)

Veronica "Ronnie" Bennett & Phil Spector

Be his, be his, **be his little baby**, his one and only... The words have been whispering in her ear since wunderkind producer Phil Spector applied his trademark Wall of Sound to the Ronettes' smash single "Be My Baby." Five years later sultry lead singer Ronnie Bennett, 24, and increasingly reclusive Spector, 27, marry in an office at Beverly Hills City Hall, which he somehow convinces the city fathers to open on a Sunday. Only her mother and a couple of his flunkies attend. Afterwards they attend a Mahalia Jackson concert, not her first choice for a post-wedding celebration. Then he heads off, alone, to *his* mother's house—to give her the news. That night the erratic groom arrives back at his mansion, raving that his new bride's only after his money. She spends her honeymoon night curled up on the bathroom floor of her mother's room, safely locked away from Phil.

His second of four, her first of two, lasts six years

"In my fantasy marriage, I'd have the greatest little family to love me and play with me and keep me from ever getting lonely again. The reality wasn't quite so good." **RONNIE SPECTOR**

April 15 (1978)

Danielle Steel & Bill Toth

Ladies love outlaws, goes a hit country song, and a prolific romance writer seems to fit the bill. Married (in a ceremony in prison) to a man serving time for rape, Danielle Steel planned to move to a new San Francisco home. Sparks flew when she met the mover, a recovering heroin addict. Today, **one day after her divorce becomes final**, Steel, 36, marries Bill Toth, 37, at a little church perched halfway up Russian Hill with a spectacular view of Alcatraz Island. Eight and a half months pregnant, she wears an oversized green flower-print dress and a simple string of pearls. About 30 friends and family attend the small service, then head off to a local French restaurant for the reception. Later tonight the groom reportedly disappears to get a fix. Three weeks later Steel gives birth to son Nicholas, and again that day her new hubby departs to shoot up. Personal tragedies notwithstanding (Nicholas commits suicide at 19), Steel endures through times as tempestuous as the fictional heroines in her nonstop bestsellers that elevate her to the title of world's best-selling living author.

Her third of five, lasts three years

April 16 (1994)

Jill Goodacre & Harry Connick, Jr.

Love and marriage, horse and carriage, literally. In his hometown of New Orleans, smooth crooner Harry Connick, Jr., 26, weds model Jill Goodacre, 29, at the St. Louis Cathedral aside Jackson Square. The bride wears a white short-sleeved Valentino satin gown with raised polka dots and a full-length veil. She also dons white opera gloves, and holds a bouquet of pale peach roses tied with an ivory-colored ribbon. Post ceremony the groom whisks his Texas bride on **a rose-bedecked horse and buggy** ride en route to the famed Greek Revival-style Gallier Hall for a traditional festive New Orleans feast. Afterwards the couple jets off on a Caribbean honeymoon. The first of their three daughters arrives two years and one day later.

April 17 (2009)

Brooklyn Decker & Andy Roddick

Lots of guys **go wild over *Sports Illustrated* swimsuit models**. Few of them ever get close to their dreamy fantasies. But when you're a handsome hunky pro tennis player, it's a different world. So when Andy Roddick spotted Brooklyn Decker in the 2007 issue, he promptly had his agent track her down. Today Roddick, 26, and Decker, 22, marry in an intimate twilight candlelit ceremony at his Austin, Texas mansion before a handful of friends and family. Dinner follows at a local country club for some 250 guests including tennis greats Andre Agassi and Steffi Graf, and Billie Jean King. The groom's connections also extend to the musical world, as sounds are provided by another pal, Sir Elton John, whom he met doing charity work. "It was beyond awesome of him to make time for us, " said Roddick, "and needless to say it was beyond amazing."

April 18 (1995)

Kathryn Spath & Stanley Tucci

These are busy days for versatile actor Stanley Tucci. Last week he opened in the comedy *Jury Duty*, and next week he's got a supporting role in the crime thriller *Kiss of Death*. Today he sandwiches in a wedding at his parents' home in Westchester County to social worker Kate Spath, 32. Around 150 family and friends attend the outdoor gala that a cousin likens to **the independent film awards or something**." Come this fall Tucci, 34, gains wider fame playing an enigmatic villain in Steven Bochco's *Murder One*, a role that lands him an Emmy nomination. But it's his unconventional independent film persona that brings him unprecedented success with next year's *Big Night*, a culinary adventure ("sometimes the spaghetti likes to be alone") for which he co-stars, co-writes and co-directs. Though the movie took awhile to happen, he never gave up. "I saw how much [Kate] could accomplish in one day," says Tucci, "and I realized I'd better finish writing this film or I was always going to be kicking myself."

> **His first, her second, lasts 14 years until her death**

"You marry someone with two kids, it's exciting. You get a whole family at once."

STANLEY TUCCI

April 19 (1956)
Grace Kelly & Prince Rainier III

The world holds its collective breath as the **"Wedding of the Century"** begins, with radiant Grace Kelly giving up her cinematic career for a life with the man she loves, Prince Rainier III of Monaco. Chartered buses carry the mix of royalty and Hollywood stars, some of whom are horrified at the plebian mode of transport, to the Cathedral of St. Nicholas, high on the cliffs above the Mediterranean. Kelly, 26, wears a magnificent ivory gown of rare silk taffeta and antique lace, a gift from MGM fashioned by designer Helen Rose, who handled the actress's screen wardrobe. The Prince, 32, wears a Napoleonic uniform of his own design: black tunic with gold leaf on the cuffs, sky blue trousers and a midnight blue bicorne with white ostrich feathers. Film cameras requiring bright klieg lights capture the scene, as the nervous Prince needs his bride's help in slipping the ring on her finger. At the subsequent formal luncheon for 600 at the palace, the couple uses his sword to cut their five-tiered cake.

Her first, his first, lasts 26 years until her death in a car crash

April 20 (2008)
Tia Mowry & Cory Hardrict

On a beautiful spring California day, rather early given the season, **everything's coming up roses**. First there's an archway of pink, fuchsia, lavender and cream-colored roses. Then there are the multi-hued rose bouquets of the bride and bridesmaids. And finally there's a five-tiered, vanilla and red velvet cake ornately festooned with pink rose confections. Resplendent in a one-shoulder, ivory Kevan Hall silk tulle gown with an empire waist, paired with Jimmy Choo platform pumps and diamond earrings, Tia Mowry, 29, weds Cory Hardrict, 28, who sports a satin Hugo Boss suit with a white (what, no pink?) tie and red rose boutonniere. Around 175 guests witness the ceremony at the scenic Biltmore Hotel in Santa Barbara, which begins with her walking down the aisle as singer Kenny Lattimore croons "For You," and ends rather appropriately as the guests shower the couple with rose pedals. Her twin sister Tamera, in a purple gown by Tadashi, serves as maid of honor.

April 21 (2001)
Toni Braxton & Keri Lewis

Smooth, soulful or sultry, chart-topping R&B diva Toni Braxton delivers a varied array of sweet sounds. Though she's never quite sung the blues, that's the predominant color today. Braxton, 34, marries Mint Condition keyboardist Keri Lewis, 30, at the sumptuous, neoclassical Dean Gardens outside Atlanta where **table linens, chair covers and the carpet are dyed robin's egg Tiffany blue**.

Prominent Atlanta native son Andrew Young, an ordained minister, officiates at the late afternoon garden ceremony where tight security helps assure privacy. Braxton wears an ivory Vera Wang (June 22) gown of duchess satin with a notched crystal-beaded bodice and cathedral train with matching veil. Lewis sports an ivory tuxedo jacket and black pants by Ralph Lauren. The wedding cake's a four-tiered creation custom crafted to look like a perfect stack of four Tiffany boxes in that distinctive light blue hue.

April 22 (1912)
Sarah Roth & Daniel Iles

For the last week, one event has gripped the world—the shocking sinking of the ocean liner RMS *Titanic* on her maiden voyage from England to America. Tales of grief and woe abound as more than 1,500 people, two-thirds of the passengers and crew, perished. Yet today **a rare glimmer of hope** emerges as newspapers trumpet the news: TITANIC SURVIVOR MARRIED IN HOSPITAL. Third class passenger Sarah Roth, 26, a tailor, had been en route to marry Daniel Iles, who'd emigrated last year and found work as a department store clerk. "They'd played together as children," wrote *The New York Times*, "in the shadow of the Tower of London." Able to scramble into a collapsible lifeboat, Roth lost all her possessions including the wedding dress she'd made. A relief committee steps up to buy her a new outfit: a blue silk gown and straw hat trimmed with blue velvet. Fellow survivor Emily Badman, "a sturdy, pink cheeked English girl," serves as bridesmaid at the service at St. Vincent's Hospital which attracts many survivors, some in wheelchairs.

April 23 (2008)
Jenny Mollen & Jason Biggs

His goofy *American Pie* persona culminated with *American Wedding*, and he just wrapped filming *Wedding Daze*. Today Jason Biggs, 30, **trades make-believe for the real thing** as he marries actress Jenny Mollen, 28, at City Hall in Los Angeles. It's a private, low-key affair with no friends or family members attending. Then they're off on a Hawaiian honeymoon. A more formal affair happens in July when they exchange vows for a second time at a snazzy winery/vineyard in Napa. There she wears a strapless Monique Lhuillier gown with a feathered train, set off with diamond and platinum art deco-style jewelry. He opts for a cream-colored suit with a pale pink tie. The ceremony ends to the sounds of Guns N' Roses' "Welcome to the Jungle." No word on whether apple pie is among the desserts.

April 24 (1954)
Patricia Kennedy & Peter Lawford

Thousands of **screaming women and bobbysoxers crowd the streets** around the Church of St. Thomas More in Manhattan, the bridal family's second choice after St. Patrick's Cathedral, which was unavailable since the groom isn't Catholic. But it's that groom the ladies are swooning over: handsome British movie star Peter Lawford, 30. And oh yes, a Kennedy is involved too: Patricia Kennedy, 29, whose brothers Jack, Bobby and Ted serve as ushers. She wears a pearl-white satin dress by couturier Hattie Carnegie with a portrait neckline and tight-fitting bodice, full in the back with a long train. After a short ceremony it takes the police half an hour to clear the way for the couple's limo to proceed to a lavish reception at the Plaza Hotel. The newlyweds stand in the receiving line for 90 minutes to welcome their 300 glittery guests before segueing to the dance floor where they whirl to the strains of "Stranger in Paradise." The couple settles in L.A., where next March she gives birth to son Christopher on the same day, and in the same hospital, where good friend Judy Garland gives birth to her son Joseph.

His first of four, her first, lasts 12 years

April 25 (1962)
Loretta Martin & Dick Clark

A good seven years before the Beatles sang about "sweet Loretta Martin," **eternal teenager Dick Clark married her**. This Loretta Martin is a Canadian secretary in the booking agency that handles his *Caravan of Stars* road shows. Savvy Clark, 32, whose flagship *American Bandstand* backbones a burgeoning musical empire, and Martin, 25, marry in a simple ceremony at the Calvary Methodist Church in Philadelphia. It's only a few months since Clark's separation and divorce from his first (and unfaithful) wife, a union that had been showcased as a peachy keen All American family. Perhaps now he's living the lyrics of Motown star Mary Wells' latest hit; she appeared on *American Bandstand* last April Fools' Day singing "The One Who Really Loves You."

His second of three, her first, lasts nine years

April 26 (1986)
Maria Shriver & Arnold Schwarzenegger

A Kennedy wedding, always a major attraction, elevates today to a world stage as CBS news anchor Maria Shriver, 30, weds Austrian-born movie star Arnold Schwarzenegger, 38, in St. Francis Xavier Church in Hyannis, Mass. She wears an elaborate white silk and lace gown by Marc Bohan, who's among the 500-strong guest list that's heavy on media types from Tom Brokaw to Oprah Winfrey (who reads Elizabeth Barrett Browning's sonnet, "How Do I Love Thee?"). Among the strangest sights: **a life-size papier-mâché statue of the couple** in native Austrian dress, from ex-U.N. secretary-general Kurt Waldheim. Among the classiest guests: Jacqueline Onassis, who invites the groom's peasant stock mother Aurelia—as elegant as any of the Kennedy women, in a violet dress, pearls and mink coat—to her Hyannis Port house for a visit. Arnold, who met Maria at a celebrity tennis event in 1977, proposed to her on a rowboat in the middle of a lake in his native village of Thal.

His first, her first

Let's invite Brando to our divorce too.

April 27 (1996)
Robin Wright & Sean Penn

They're together, they're apart, they're quarrelling, they're lovebirds. It's hard to keep track of this passionate pair, who'd met while filming *State of Grace* six years ago and are parents to a young son and daughter. Today they're definitely together, as **a spur-of-the-moment decision sends their tempestuous courtship to the altar**.

In the backyard of the Santa Monica home of a longtime producer pal, Sean Penn, 35, marries Robin Wright, 30, before a small select crowd that includes Warren Beatty, Marlon Brando, Robert De Niro and Jack Nicholson, who calls it a "rousing Irish wedding." Nicholson adds to the festive flair, delivering a poem to the newlyweds while Brando is unzipping his trousers, so he ends up finishing his remarks with his pants around his ankles.

His second, her second, lasts 14 years

April 28 (1990)
Erin Everly & Axl Rose

With a relentless reputation for bad behavior, heavy metal rocker Axl Rose, 28, takes an unexpectedly traditional path today: down the aisle with longtime girlfriend Erin Everly, 24. It's an early morning quickie service at Cupid's Wedding Chapel in Las Vegas, which they visited twice earlier tonight before finally returning for the five-minute service. The limo driver serves as witness. Everly, a fledgling model and daughter of Don Everly (of the smooth-crooning '50s stars, the Everly Brothers), had inspired Guns N' Roses only #1 single, "Sweet Child O'Mine," a surprisingly sweet departure from the band's trademark pounding sound. Pounding perhaps also could describe Axl's treatment of his bride, who files for divorce less than a month later after years of abuse.

His first, her first, annulled after ten months

April 29 (2011)
Catherine Middleton & Prince William

The frenzy has reached fever pitch, with some 2,000 lucky (and elegant) souls jammed into historic Westminster Abbey. A million well-wishers crowd London's streets, and several billion more watch live coverage worldwide. The impeccably choreographed event unites Prince William, 28, dapper in his red Irish Guards tunic offset with a blue sash, with poised, popular Kate Middleton, 29. During the hour-long ceremony he turns to his future father-in-law and says, **"We were supposed to have just a small family affair."** At least that's what's reported by a lip-reader hired by a British newspaper. Of the endless speculation about the royal spectacular, the most scrutinized element has been the bridal gown. Last night, her head largely obscured by a furry trapper hat, the designer tried to sneak into the bride's hotel but intrepid reporters sussed her out: Sarah Burton, creative director of Alexander McQueen. Her modern, structured long-sleeved gown features an ivory satin gazar bodice narrowed at the waist and padded at the hips to echo Victorian corsetry. Its wide skirt includes arches and pleats to evoke the opening of a flower, with a nine-foot train and a veil held in place by a Cartier diamond halo tiara lent by Queen Elizabeth.

"About having Prince William's picture on the wall? He wishes. No, I had the Levi's guy on my wall, not a picture of William. Sorry."

KATE MIDDLETON

April 30 (1988)
Rita Wilson & Tom Hanks

He's about to hit it *Big*, as in the feel-good fantasy film that turns into a summertime box-office smash. But first **he's got love on his mind**. Today Tom Hanks, 31, marries Rita Wilson, 31, at L.A.'s majestic St. Sophia Greek Orthodox Cathedral. During the traditional service, the same golden crowns previously worn by her parents are held over their heads. Then it's off to a downtown art deco café for a reception that includes a starry tinseltown turnout: old *Bosom Buddies* mates plus Dan

Rita Wilson and Tom Hanks, plus Kate Capshaw and Steven Spielberg and his mother Leah

Aykroyd, John Candy, John Lovitz, Penny Marshall, Roger Moore, Bob Saget and Kathleen Turner. Guests pose alongside a life-sized cardboard cutout of the happy couple. The newlyweds spend the night at the swank Bel-Air Hotel before jetting off to a honeymoon on St. Barts.

© Associated Press

May

Priscilla Beaulieu
& Elvis Presley
May 1, 1967

May 1 (1967)
Priscilla Beaulieu & Elvis Presley

While serving in the army in Germany, the rock'n'roll pioneer who'd shook up the world met a pretty 14-year-old brunette. He didn't exactly endear himself to her parents by getting her home late after their first date, but he was hooked. Seven years later the courtship by **one of the most eligible bachelors on earth** ends in Las Vegas. With his domineering manager Colonel Tom Parker handling the arrangements, Elvis Aaron Presley, 32, and Priscilla Beaulieu, 21, fly in this morning from Palm Springs and limo direct to the Aladdin Hotel. In its owner's primo suite, a handful of guests gather including her sister Michelle, maid of honor, and dual Presley assistants as best men. Priscilla wears a white chiffon gown embroidered with pearls, with lace sleeves and a full chiffon veil. The King sports a black brocade tuxedo. A state Supreme Court justice performs the brief ceremony, followed by a champagne buffet breakfast for 100 with all the fixings. A wandering string ensemble serenades the newlyweds with, not "Viva Las Vegas" but "Love Me Tender."

> His first and only, her first and only, lasts five years

"Once home he carried me over the threshold as he sang "The Hawaiian Wedding Song."

PRISCILLA PRESLEY

May 2 (2009)
Maggie Gyllenhaal & Peter Sarsgaard

Catching the star-maker machinery off guard, a classy couple ties the knot at a romantic getaway in southeastern Italy, **far from the madding Hollywood crowd**. The most the press gets is a brief, after-the-fact statement from their publicist confirming that the wedding of Maggie Gyllenhaal, 32, and Peter Sarsgaard, 38, took place at the Grand Hotel Masseria Santa Lucia, a four-star, oceanside resort described as having an atmosphere that's "relaxed and peaceful." The only known guests are her younger brother Jake and his girlfriend Reese Witherspoon. Together since 2003, the newlyweds have a 2 ½-year-old daughter, Ramona.

May 3 (2003)
Melissa McKnight & Matt LeBlanc

Celebrities are gathering in Hawaii for a wedding, the media reports, but no one's quite sure **who's tying the knot**. All becomes clear at sunset on a cliff overlooking a beach in Kauai as Matt LeBlanc, 35, marries model Melissa McKnight, 38. In matching black suits with double ginger leis, Matt and his bride's 12-year-old son Tyler walk halfway down a gardenia-lined path. The groom walks the rest of the way with McKnight, who wears an off-the-rack white slip dress with a chiffon overlay, identical to that of her eight-year-old daughter Jacquelyn. Some 75 well-tanned guests, including *Friends* cast mates Jennifer Aniston, Courteney Cox and Lisa Kudrow, witness the half-hour, nondenominational service. The reception under a nearby tent features island music, hula dancers and Samoan fire dancers.

His first, her second, lasts three years

May 4 (1969)
Anne Byrne & Dustin Hoffman

And here's to you, missus… Hoffman? Once struggling actor Dustin Hoffman burst to fame two years ago as the title character in *The Graduate*, a nebbishy college grad who beds his father's business partner's wife—an affair memorialized forever by the Simon & Garfunkel tune, "Mrs. Robinson." With his financial future finally secure, Hoffman, 31, marries longtime girlfriend Anne Byrne, 25, a ballerina with a young daughter, at Temple Beth El in Westchester County, N.Y., before 35 friends and family. Then they're off on a honeymoon to Asia. Later this month his next movie (he took his sweet time choosing roles) opens, and Hoffman's reputation soars even higher playing the greasy, long-haired small time con man Ratzo Rizzo in *Midnight Cowboy*. Despite his burgeoning career, the couple maintains a purposefully low profile until a rude awakening: next March, a Greenwich Village townhouse next to their apartment explodes, bringing extensive and unwanted publicity in the wake of the left-wing revolutionaries' makeshift bomb factory gone awry.

His first of two, her second, lasts 11 years

May 5 (2000)

Angelina Jolie & Billy Bob Thornton

Weeks after he ditched fiancée Laura Dern, and she finalized her divorce from Jonny Lee Miller, impulsive lovebirds Billy Bob Thornton, 44, and Angelina Jolie, 24, jet to Las Vegas for **the quintessential quickie wedding**. Today at the cozy, well-trod (6,000 weddings a year) Little Church of the West, they walk down the aisle to the strains of the Righteous Brothers' "Unchained Melody:" she in faded jeans and a lilac-colored sleeveless sweater that exposes the recent "Billy Bob" tattooed on her upper arm, he in jeans, a long-sleeved black shirt and baseball cap. He gives her a $29 ring bought from a woman in a bar. The tight-fisted movie stars opt for the least expensive wedding package: the $189 "Beginnings" covering the chapel fee, music, a rose and carnation bouquet, a boutonniere, one 8"x10" portrait and six 4"x6"s.

His fifth, her second, lasts three years

May 6 (1965)

Marianne Faithfull
& John Dunbar

Spotted by the Rolling Stones manager at a swingin' London soiree, she's become an overnight ("As Tears Go By") sensation. A rail thin blonde with an ethereal voice, the big time partier has since bedded male musicians including Gene Pitney and at least three (Brian Jones, Keith Richards, Mick Jagger) Rolling Stones. Today, Marianne Faithfull, 18, marries granny-glassed poet John Dunbar, 22, in Cambridge. She **carries a bouquet of wildflowers picked from the surrounding fields**. They honeymoon in Paris, strangely enough, with drug-addled beatnik poets Allen Ginsberg and Lawrence Ferlinghetti. Though three months pregnant, Faithfull quickly veers into the fast lane of drugs, drink and dissipation. Shortly after her son Nicholas is born in November, she ditches her career, such as it was, and her hubby, attaching herself to Jagger and embracing the hedonistic heyday of sixties rock debauchery.

Her first of three, lasts one year

"I was unable in those days to say no to anybody."

MARIANNE FAITHFULL

May 7 (2006)
Tori Spelling
& Dean McDermott

First time around, her lavish formal wedding drew 350 guests and cost a reported million dollars of daddy's money. Today Tori Spelling, 32, daughter of mega-producer Aaron Spelling (*Charlie's Angels*, *Beverly Hills 90210*) opts for **a far less opulent and populated affair**. After enjoying breakfast in bed and matching massages, she and Dean McDermott, 39, walk the aisle barefoot on a beach in the Fiji islands. She wears a white eyelet Dolce & Gabbana dress with a pink sash, he a white D&G suit. Tori holds a bouquet of white orchids set with small photos of his deceased parents and her former nanny. Guests? Zero. After a short ceremony they build sand castles, feast on a six-course meal, dance to Lonestar's "Amazed" and frolic in the waves while toasting with champagne. Upon returning from their honeymoon they distribute a video of their low-key festivities to family and friends, and Dean gets two tattoos: "Truly, Madly, Deeply, Tori" and a portrait of Tori.

May 8 (1967)
Ann-Margret & Roger Smith

Sex kitten Ann-Margret had ended her highly publicized romance with Elvis Presley, which heated up when they shot the movie *Viva Las Vegas* (left). One week after he married in Vegas, she's back in Sin City with her new beau: handsome TV idol Roger Smith (*77 Sunset Strip*), 34, for a wedding in a smoky hotel room at the Riviera packed with photographers and reporters. It's **far from the church wedding she'd envisioned as a girl**, a rather unhappy day she later calls "a family catastrophe" since her parents disapproved. Ann-Margret, 26, wears a white pique micro-miniskirt and matching fluffy white shorts. When she starts crying the minister hands her a napkin from the buffet table. Afterwards the bride and groom bolt back to L.A., leaving the food and cake for the media. One month later she's back at the Riviera, headlining a five-week cabaret stint to adoring public. Elvis sends a huge bouquet of flowers shaped like a guitar.

"I was released, in some degree, from my childhood and ready to be a married woman. Roger and I stayed together that night, and every night since." **ANN-MARGRET**

May 9 (2005)

Renée Zellweger & Kenny Chesney

You had me at hello. That line worked both in the movies (*Jerry McGuire*) and in song (a #1 country hit for Kenny Chesney). So when the heartthrob singer and the movie's Oscar-winning co-star met at a tsunami relief concert last January, they immediately followed the script. Four breathless, love-at-first-sight months later Renée Zellweger, 36, and Chesney, 37, marry at sunset on a hilltop overlooking the Caribbean in front of his Spanish-style, Virgin Islands retreat. On her father's arm, she strolls barefoot in a strapless, floor- (sand?) length bamboo-twill gown by Carolina Herrera, clutching a bouquet of cream-colored roses. He goes with a white button-down shirt, khakis and his trademark black cowboy hat. Alas, the Oscar meets Opry fairy tale soon crashes, a May-to-December union ended by annulment just before year's end.

Her first, his first, lasts seven months

May 10 (2005)
Heidi Klum & Seal

He proposed in an igloo built atop a 14,000-foot glacier in British Columbia. For the wedding, they opt for warmer climes. At **sunset on a beach near Puerto Vallarta, Mexico**, the British pop star and the German supermodel marry to an assemblage of two: the officiator and the bride's year-old daughter. Five months pregnant, Heidi Klum, 31, wears an ivory Chantilly lace gown by Vera Wang, and her daughter wears an identical miniature version. Seal, 42, serenades his bride with a song he'd written especially for the occasion. Afterwards they celebrate with 40 guests at his nearby home in Costa Careyes, decorated in orange accents that echo the house's colors. A miniature of the striking couple in wedding attire stands atop the cake.

Her second, his first, lasts seven years

May 11 (1974)
Mary Wilson & Pedro Ferrer

She's sung it thousands of times, but today it's strictly **an instrumental version of "I Hear a Symphony"** that plays as Mary Wilson, one third of the original Supremes, marries in Las Vegas. Wearing a Spanish-style dress trimmed in white lace and pearls, Wilson, 30, weds Pedro Ferrer, in a non-denominational service. That night the group, long past its prime and minus diva Diana Ross, opens for Joel Grey at the Riviera. But their Motown name still carries a certain nostalgic cachet, and Wilson and Ferrer spend their honeymoon on the road as the group plays in Hawaii, Hong Kong, Australia and Japan.

Her first, lasts seven years

May 12 (1971)
Mick Jagger & Bianca Perez-Mora Macias

So much for it being a secret. Paparazzi, reporters, Beatles, Stones and assorted friends and family descend upon legendary Saint-Tropez for **the celebrity dream wedding** of Mick Jagger, 27, and Nicaraguan beauty Bianca Macias, 26. She wears a chic, low-cut tailored white jacket, floppy-brimmed hat with a veil and gloves, he sports a three-piece suit and floral shirt. First comes a civil service at town hall, followed by a religious ceremony at a nearby chapel, both conducted entirely in French. An organist plays Bach's "Wedding March" and then, much to Mick's chagrin, his wife's choice—the schmaltzy theme song from *Love Story*. A reception at the très chic Café des Arts kicks off with a reggae band playing a rather odd choice, the Stones' "It's All Over Now, " and later Mick and friends deliver a rousing, half-hour soul medley. The bulging bride, trading in her virginal white outfit for a transparent gown and sequined turban, attends for only a few minutes. Five months later she gives birth in Paris to daughter Jade.

His first of two, her first, lasts eight years

"When Mick first saw me, he had the impression he was looking at himself. I know people theorize that Mick thought it would be amusing to marry his twin. But actually he wanted to achieve the ultimate by making love to himself." BIANCA JAGGER

'Love made me do what I have done, prompted by the noblest intentions that a man could have. I loved deeply, but in loving I may have erred.'

VALENTINO

May 13 (1922)

Natacha Rambova & Rudolph Valentino

He exerts **a fierce, almost unfathomable hold upon womankind**. So when the silent screen's smoldering Latin Lover marries today, it's bound to cause a stir. Yet even the penultimate sex symbol and international star of *The Sheik* can scarcely imagine the uproar. This morning a small party motors to the home of the mayor of Mexicali, Mexico, where a military brass band blares a wedding march and a string orchestra serenades the celebrants. A judge officiates at the short ceremony that unites Rudolph Valentino, 27, in a tan sports jacket and an open-collared shirt, and designer Natacha Rambova, 25, in a white-and-black checked knit ensemble. But immediately dark clouds set in as authorities rule that the divorce from his previous wife, Jean Acker, requires one year to become effective. Next month a judge "cuts the chains that fastened a charge of bigamy to Rudolph's neck and turns him loose to the adoration of a mob of girls." One year later they remarry.

May 14 (1994)
Sydney Biddle Barrows & Darnay Hoffman

She wears a princess-style gown with a chapel-length train, in a hue of blush pink. "With my age and my history, **wearing white would have been ludicrous**," says the bride. Welcome to the rather traditional wedding of Sydney Biddle Barrows, 42, whose exploits as the Mayflower Madam captivated the world a decade ago. At Manhattan's Cathedral of St. John the Divine, she weds colorful lawyer Darnay Hoffman, 46, to the strains of Handel. The couple met after he'd spotted her on a talk show. The steamy story of the descendent of pilgrims who ran an exclusive call girl ring had it all: gorgeous young women, sex, money and whispers of high-powered clients including Arab sheiks, foreign diplomats, Wall Street titans and sports stars. Candice Bergen (Sept. 27) portrayed her in a TV movie. Soon Barrows reinvents herself as a consultant, with the tag line "From Her Lips to Your Bank Account."

Her first, his third

May 15 (1965)
Angie Dickinson & Burt Bacharach

Newlyweds Dickinson and Bacharach are all smiles alongside Loew's Hotel president Robert Tisch

What's new, pussycat? An elopement. One of Hollywood's swingin' party gals, Angie Dickinson, 33, met dashing composer Burt Bacharach, 36, only a few months ago. Smitten, she accompanied him to London where he was completing the score for the zany romantic comedy, *What's New, Pussycat?* Back in her hometown of L.A., the lovebirds impulsively elope to Las Vegas where they marry in a simple, 3:30 a.m. ceremony at the Silver Bell Wedding Chapel. Actor David Nelson and his wife June serve as best man and matron of honor, respectively. A honeymoon's out as she's too busy filming *The Chase* with Marlon Brando, but their jet-setting lifestyle zips along in high style as he turns out a steady stream of hits for top singers like Dusty Springfield and Dionne Warwick. The handsome couple amplifies their glossy, glamorous image with trendy commercials for Martini vermouth.

His second of four, her second, lasts 15 years

"[Burt] woos without every trying. Not only is he devastating looking, but he has this gentility about him, with lots of strength but also softness, like a prizefighter carrying flowers." ANGIE DICKINSON

May 16 (1987)
Jan Dance & David Crosby

Given their history of assorted drug addictions and convictions, today's **a day that few of their friends ever dreamed possible**. Founding Crosby Stills Nash & Young member David Crosby and longtime girlfriend Jan Dance met nearly a decade ago at a recording studio where she was working. (Their first date? At an IHOP.) Recently they've done their best to get straight, attending weekly drug counseling sessions and reporting regularly to their respective probation officers. For the first time in his life, Crosby, 45, wears a formal cutaway coat with striped trousers as he marries Dance, 36, at the Church of Religious Science on Sunset Boulevard. Alongside them, bandmate Graham Nash and his wife Susan renew their 10-year-old vows. The select rock'n'roll crowd includes Howard Hesseman, Chris Hillman, Roger McGuinn, Bonnie Raitt, Grace Slick and Joe Walsh. At a joint reception afterwards at the Nash's home in Encino, both couples impulsively take the plunge—into the pool.

"Marrying her is one of the smartest things I ever did." DAVID CROSBY

May 17 (1923)
Marlene Dietrich & Rudolph Sieber

At an open casting call in Berlin for extras, a dapper production assistant quickly singled out a struggling actress for a bit comedic role in a silent film entitled *Tragedy of Love*. Their blossoming relationship, though never exclusive, was anything but. Today smoldering beauty Marlene Dietrich, 21, and Rudolph Sieber, 26, marry in a short civil ceremony at the Kaiser Wilhelm Memorial Church in Berlin. Her dress fits poorly, his borrowed bowler hat is several sizes too big. Despite the birth of a daughter next year, she zealously pursues her career dreams by frequenting the Weimar Republic's naughty nighttime scene. She haunts lounges, cabarets and jazz clubs in a variety of gender-bending outfits designed to attract attention. "**Take some pictures of me that will make me a star**," she tells one photographer. In 1929, her wish comes true when she's cast as Lola-Lola, a cabaret singer who causes the downfall of a respected schoolmaster in director Josef von Sternberg's classic, *The Blue Angel*.

Her first, his first, lasts 53 years until his death

"I was totally in love. Every girl should have that experience once. Then you know what it is, what it feels like, the real thing. You can never be fooled once you have known true romance, true passion, true love!" MARLENE DIETRICH

May 18 (2007)
Amy Winehouse & Blake Fielder-Civil

They're just a couple of kids in luuv. He's a gofer for music video productions, she's the retro-styled, mega-successful singer/songwriter known as much for her drug, alcohol, assault and mental health problems as her music. Just two months ago multi-Grammy award winner Amy Winehouse, 23, made her U.S. TV debut on the *Late Show with David Letterman*, singing her red-hot anthem "Rehab." Today, groom Blake Fielder-Civil, 25, reportedly strolls down a corridor of the Shore Club Hotel singing to himself, "**They tried to make me sign a prenup but I said no, no no.**" At their brief ceremony at the Miami-Dade Country Marriage License Bureau accompanied by a handful of friends, she wears a short floral-patterned sundress; he wears a retro gray suit. Afterwards it's off to the Big Pink Diner for a celebratory meal. "I hope to be with him for the rest of my life," enthuses Amy. Instead, she heads to rehab and he goes to jail for assault.

Her first, his first, lasts two years

May 19 (1997)
Sarah Jessica Parker & Matthew Broderick

A vacant synagogue on Manhattan's Lower East Side in a dilapidated building with no electricity: a rather unlikely site for a celebrity wedding. But it's simply perfect for the couple dreaming of **an unconventional, candlelit event**. And with the press misled by false stories, Sarah Jessica Parker, 32, and Matthew Broderick, 35, marry quietly before 150 family and friends in a secular service performed by his sister, an Episcopal minister. The quintessential New Yawk bride wears black, a choice she later regrets, the groom a simple dark suit. The Peter Duchin orchestra plays at the reception, serenading the stage and screen crowd with old favorites like "Someone to Watch Over Me." *A National Enquirer* reporter who sneaks in and snaps photos is caught, forced to turn over his film and booted. The honeymoon's delayed as Sarah's back at work in Broadway's *Once Upon a Mattress*, while Matthew begins filming *Godzilla*. Next year stardom beckons as she lands her signature role in *Sex and the City*.

May 20 (1995)
Sharon Summerall & Don Henley

Welcome to the wed-ding California, such **a lovely crowd, such a starry crowd**, celebrating loud... Days after the Eagles' phenomenally successful U.S. leg of their *Hell Freezes Over* tour wraps, five hundred guests gather at a Malibu ranch where Don Henley, 47, marries model Sharon Summerall, 33. The entire band attends but doesn't play, but they and guests including Clint Black and Lisa Hartman-Black, Jimmy Buffett, David Crosby, Randy Newman and Jack Nicholson do hear some all-star sounds. Performers include Tony Bennett, Jackson Browne, Sheryl Crow, John Fogerty, Bruce Hornsby, Billy Joel, Bob Seger, Sting, J.D. Souther and Bruce Springsteen. The groom gets into the act too, singing the jazz standard "Come Rain or Come Shine" and dedicating the Beatles' "In My Life" to his new bride.

May 21 (1945)
Lauren Bacall & Humphrey Bogart

Ten days after his divorce from his third wife, the increasingly unhinged Mayo Methot, Humphrey Bogart, 45, strolls down the aisle with 20-year-old blonde Lauren Bacall. As headlines trumpet World War II battles the couple, **fresh off their triumphant cinematic pairing in *To Have and Have Not***, ops for a quiet ceremony far from the Hollywood scene—but still makes front-page news. Media hordes encamped outside the Ohio country house of Pulitzer Prize-winning novelist and best man Louis Bromfield force the wedding inside. Bacall wears a tan skirt with a short, matching button-up jacket with flared shoulders. Bogie wears a gray flannel suit with a white shirt and maroon tie. A handful of friends and family witness the short, double ring ceremony performed by a local judge. After a night at Bromfield's spacious Malabar Farm, the newlyweds board a train for Los Angeles and work: him back to *The Two Mrs. Carrolls*, her to *Confidential Agent*.

"Bogie and I were ridiculous, holding hands like teenagers. We mooned and swooned—there has never been a more perfect time. **LAUREN BACALL**

His last of four, her first of two, lasts 12 years until his death

May 22 (1993)

Robin Ruzan & Mike Myers

Saturday Night Live and *Wayne's World* have made him a mega-star, and soon he'll be co-starring in *So I Married an Axe Murderer*. But today Mike Myers, 29, goes a more traditional marriage route with a far more affable spouse, walking down the aisle with actress Robin Ruzan, whom he met at a Chicago Black Hawks/Toronto Maple Leafs game. **She becomes his muse, and then some**: he bases one of this most popular *SNL* characters, the Yiddish-spouting *Coffee Talk* hostess Linda Richman, on his New Yawk mother-in-law. Ruzan later nudges him to turn another zany creation, the spy send-up Austin Powers, into a groovy box-office winner. Yeah, baby!

His first of two, lasts 14 years

"With relationships it's more about what you bring to the table than what you're going to get. It's very nice if you sit down and the cake appears. But if you go to the table expecting cake, then it's not so good."

ANJELICA HUSTON

May 23 (1992)

Anjelica Huston & Robert Graham

The headstrong daughter of a Hollywood legend, Anjelica Huston was romantically linked with a somewhat younger Hollywood legend, Jack Nicholson, for many years. Several years after their breakup, at the magnificent Bel-Air Hotel, Huston, 40, marries Robert Graham, 53. The unusual pairing of the **captivating if elusive screen goddess** (*Prizzi's Honor, The Grifters*) and celebrated sculptor (noted massive bronzes of FDR, Joe Lewis and Charlie Parker) attracts a Who's Who of celebrities: Lauren Bacall, Annette Bening and Warren Beatty (Mar. 12), Carrie Fisher, David Hockney, Lauren Hutton, Mick Jagger and Jerry Hall, Penny Marshall, Joe Pesci, Arnold Schwarzenegger and Meryl Streep. The couple honeymoons in Mexico City, and Graham's soon at work designing their extraordinary Venice Beach home: an enormous, fortress-like complex. "He gave me a very beautiful shell," says Huston of their manse, "in which to place my oyster."

Her first, his second, lasts 16 years until his death

May 24 (2003)
Kate Winslet & Sam Mendes

On holiday in the West Indies, a prominent British cinematic couple decides to tie the knot. So on the scenic isle of Antigua, actress Kate Winslet, 27, and director Sam Mendes, 37, marry. Only several friends and her two-year-old daughter Mia, by her former husband, director James Threapleton, attend. Though she's received five Oscar nominations in little over a decade, Winslet is **eternally remembered as the girl in the bow of the ship with arms extended beside Leonardo DiCaprio in *Titanic*.** Mendes has already won an Oscar for his directorial debut, *American Beauty*. By year's end they're celebrating the birth of son Joe, and settling down to family life in downtown Manhattan. Later he directs her in *Revolutionary Road*, where she reteams with DiCaprio, and the following year, as the "older woman," she takes home the Oscar for *The Reader*.

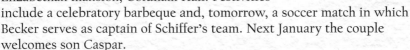

Her second, his first, lasts seven years

May 25 (2002)
Claudia Schiffer & Matthew Vaughn

Fashion models usually crave attention. But striking blonde supermodel Claudia Schiffer, **discovered in a disco in Düsseldorf**, exits her hotel surrounded by handlers holding up blankets—much to the dismay of a hundred curious onlookers. Why the modesty? She's off to her wedding, and wants to keep her "fairy-tale" dress by Valentino a surprise. Schiffer, 31, and producer Matthew Vaughn (*Lock, Stock and Two Smoking Barrels*), 31, marry at the 14th century St. George's Church in Shimpling, England before guests including Valentino, Boris Becker and Guy Ritchie (sans Madonna). The crowd swells for the reception at the couple's newly acquired nearby Elizabethan mansion, Coldham Hall. Festivities include a celebratory barbeque and, tomorrow, a soccer match in which Becker serves as captain of Schiffer's team. Next January the couple welcomes son Caspar.

May 26 (1995)
Teresa Heinz & John Kerry

Springtime on Cape Cod: what a perfect setting for a wedding. This morning Senator John Kerry, 51, announces that later today he'll marry Teresa Heinz at her summer home in Nantucket. It's **a family affair, including his two daughters and her three sons.** Under a canopy on the flowering grounds, Heinz, 56, wears a peach gown by Oscar de la Renta, and Peter Yarrow (of Peter, Paul & Mary) performs. Having previously dated actresses like Morgan Fairchild and Catherine Oxenberg, Kerry met his future bride at an Earth Day Rally in 1990. After her husband, Senator John Heinz, died in a plane crash the following year, they renewed their friendship. Worth an estimated $650 million, thanks to her inheritance of her late husband's family food fortune, Heinz soon resorts to humor to offset talk that she'll help bankroll Kerry's forthcoming reelection battle. Asked by Kerry at a rally how she likes Massachusetts, she replies, "I love Massachusetts—how much is it?"

His second, her second

May 27 (1994)
Marta Fitzgerald & Rush Limbaugh

Supreme Court Justice Clarence Thomas famously, and proudly, rarely asks a question in his day job on the nation's highest court. But today in his Virginia home, he does ask **a familiar one: "Do you take..."** For he's officiating at the wedding of conservative radio personality Rush Limbaugh, 43, and Marta Fitzgerald, 35. The unlikely twosome, the multimillionaire media motormouth and an aerobics instructor, met through an online service. The handful of guests includes their respective mothers, the bride's two children from a previous marriage, plus couples Mary Matalin and James Carville (Nov. 25) and former Secretary of Education William Bennett and his wife Elayne. Finally the world gets to see the "Jacksonville Jaguar" Rush has been dropping tidbits about to his listeners for months.

His third of four, her third, lasts 10 years

May 28 (1988)

Teresa Barrick & Steven Tyler

In the amped-up, coked-out world of rock stars, is it really any surprise that the future wife of Aerosmith's lead singer Steven Tyler was the twin sister of his dealer's girlfriend? Tyler first met Teresa Barrick in Hawaii, where she was waitressing after high school. A couple years later they reconnected when she accompanied her sister to one of the band's recording sessions. His first marriage was on the rocks, and the two became an item. A budding clothing designer, Barrick made him his first of many outfits: a silk unicorn jacket. Today, **in the midst of a purple haze of drugs, detox and repeat**, the quintessential bad boy rocker (his motto? "wretched excess in dandified duds") takes time out to tie the knot. Tyler, 40, and Barrick, 31, marry in her hometown of Tulsa, Oklahoma. The party rages on. Three months later his ex-girlfriend Bebe Buell takes their daughter Liv (Mar. 25) to a concert, where she figures out Steven's her father. In an extended family kind of way, the video for next year's "Love in An Elevator" features both Teresa and her twin sister Lisa.

His second, her first, lasts 18 years

May 29 (1998)
Cindy Crawford & Rande Gerber

She's made a handsome living posing in places like this. On this sultry Bahamian evening, though, it's not work. On a beach aside the exclusive, elegant Ocean Club Resort on Paradise Island, stunning supermodel Cindy Crawford, 32, weds restaurateur (and ex-model) Rande Gerber, 36. She wears a spaghetti-strapped, beige lace miniskirt by Galliano that she bought —gasp—off the rack, setting it off with a Valentino shawl, and holds a cluster of orchids and frangipani. The short service includes Bruce Roberts crooning "**Have a Little Faith in Me**." Afterwards the newlyweds and 100 guests feast on seafood, pasta and roast beef in a clubhouse patio. Dessert? A three-tiered carrot cake. The relaxing, stylish affair is a far cry from her '91 Las Vegas quickie to Richard Gere, a marriage that stirred so many tabloid headlines that the couple took out a full-page ad in a London newspaper several years later, proclaiming: "We got married because we love each other and we decided to make a life together. We are heterosexual and monogamous and take our commitment to each other very seriously." Months later that marriage was over.

Her second, his first

May 30 (1992)
Edie Brickell 𝄞 Paul Simon

A rocky start, a happy ending. This couple has been an item since shortly after a *Saturday Night Live* episode several years ago when he playfully distracted her while she was singing "What I Am," her lone Top Ten hit with the New Bohemians. "He made me mess the song up when I looked at him," she said later. "**That's when we first laid eyes on each other.**" Today Paul Simon, 50, and Edie Brickell, 26, marry at his estate in Montauk, Long Island, and six months later she gives birth to their first child, Adrian. A couple weeks ago Simon reunited for the first time in more than a decade with most famous other half, Art Garfunkel, at a benefit performance in New York. Next year Paul and Edie perform together in person at Willie Nelson's "Big Six-O," joining the birthday boy on a version of "Blue Eyes Cryin' in the Rain."

His third, her first

"After one evening with someone, even someone this wonderful, I had no business deciding I'd found my soul mate. And yet that was what I was feeling... It's just the greatest thrill in the world to find somebody that you want to be with every day." JANE LYNCH

May 31 (2010)

Jane Lynch & Lara Embry

Trading in her trademark tracksuit for a wedding gown, Sue Sylvester (Jane Lynch) memorably married herself in an episode of *Glee*. **Happily, in real life, she has found a mate.** Today Lynch, 49, weds clinical psychologist Lara Embry, 41, at a restaurant in Sunderland, Massachusetts, the first U.S. state to legalize same-sex marriage. Jeannie Elias, a friend who became a Universal Life minister for the special event, performs the service before 20 guests. Lynch wears a cream wrap blouse and black slacks, Embry dons a harmonizing cream and black cocktail-length dress. A jazz combo performs at the reception before Lynch and Embry's eight-year-old daughter Haden take to the floor to show off dual Madonna "Vogue" moves. At home Lynch had practiced the steps with her new stepdaughter for an episode of *Glee*. The couple met a year ago at a San Francisco fundraiser where Lynch was a presenter and Embry an honoree.

Letting the day unfold. Observing, rather than orchestrating the festivities. Creating beautiful, spontaneous images that capture both the intimacy and the essence of your wedding day. Amy and Stuart, a married couple who have been shooting weddings for more than a decade, use digital and film cameras to capture those perfect moments that you'll cherish for years to come.

For more information, please visit amyandstuart.com.

June

Crown Princess Victoria
& Daniel Westling

June 19, 2010

June 1 (1941)
Gene Tierney & Count Oleg Cassini

As the phone rings incessantly at the Las Vegas home of the justice of the peace, the bride pleads with him not to answer. On the ceremony goes, but when he asks the groom to repeat, "With this ring, I thee wed," the groom freezes: **he forgot to buy a ring!** Luckily the bride substitutes one of her gold hoop earrings, so actress Gene Tierney, 20, and Count Oleg Cassini, 28, are happily married. Then she answers the phone and, as expected, it's the director of publicity from 20th Century Fox, urging her not to wed. Informed that it's a fait accompli, despite the vehement opposition of both the studio and her parents, he jets in from L.A. with a stream of reporters and photographers. Front-page headlines trumpet the union of the dark-haired, fast-rising Hollywood star filming her first starring vehicle, *Belle Starr*, and the French fashion designer with the exotic name. Until his U.S. citizenship papers are processed a few months later, she enjoys brief status as a countess.

> Her first of two, his second of three, lasts 11 years

June 2 (1989)
Sarah Owen & James Woods

As they say in the movies, **they met "cute"**—at a gas station on Sunset Boulevard. He, the edgy actor, was gassing up his black Porsche. She, a horse trainer, was doing likewise for her old pickup truck. Soon they were an item, though their rocky relationship barely survived his fling with co-star Sean Young, (*The Boost*), who generated a media frenzy by launching a vitriolic reign of terror after Woods dumped her. Last January, dining at a Morton's restaurant, he slipped a three-carat diamond ring into Owen's glass of champagne and proposed. Today Woods, 42, and Owen, 26, marry in a small ceremony at the historic Greystone Mansion in Beverly Hills. Guests include Robert Downey, Jr., James Garner, Don Henley, Sarah Jessica Parker and Bob Seger. But her dress designer later reveals that the bride had black-and-blue marks on her back, and soon it's the groom—not jilted ex-lover Young—who's accused of abusive behavior.

> His second, her first of two, lasts four months

June 3 (1937)
The Duke & Duchess of Windsor

Years of controversy and feverish international gossip culminate in simple, back-to-back civil and religious services. In a mere 17 minutes it's over, as the most celebrated couple on earth, the Duke and Duchess of Windsor, are married in a French chateau. The love of King Edward VIII, 42, for twice-divorced American socialite Wallis Simpson, 40, overrode his royal position, and he abdicated the throne last December. The royal family boycotts the event, rapturously described by the press: "A picture of graceful loveliness in her floor-length bridal dress and the little, blue veil hanging from her hat, the bride was composed and stately as she stood at Edward's side for both the civil and religious ceremonies." As **the lovers of the storybook "romance of the century"** drive off to a honeymoon in Austria, they toss long-stemmed red and white roses to the cheering French villagers who line the streets.

His first, her third, lasts 35 years until his death

"I'll make my life with you outside the boundaries of a nationality. Nothing is going to crush me – not the British empire, not the American press. You and I will make a life together, a good life."

WALLIS SIMPSON

June 4 (1951)
Janet Leigh & Tony Curtis

They're both attractive, fast-rising Hollywood stars under contract to rival studios. Flush with the success of his first starring role, *The Prince Who Was a Thief*, he's pressured by Universal to marry co-star Piper Laurie. But in a surprise ceremony at Pickwick Arms, a hotel in Greenwich, Conn., one day after his 26th birthday, Tony Curtis **marries his true love**, Janet Leigh, 23. She wears an aqua linen dress, trimmed with tartan plaid at the neckline and in the skirt's fishtail back. Jerry Lewis and wife Patti serve as best man and matron of honor, respectively. Afterwards it's back to N.Y.C. and dinner at a trendy eatery, Danny's Hideaway. Their short four-day honeymoon at the Waldorf-Astoria Hotel is interrupted by interviews and TV show appearances. Within a few years they have two daughters, Kelly and Jamie Lee, and matching, successful careers: him with hits like *Sweet Smell of Success* and *Some Like It Hot*, her with the ultimate screen screamer, *Psycho*.

His first of six, her third of four, lasts 11 years

"I have to admit that had I not met Janet, I might have taken the money to marry Piper. It certainly was tempting. And truth be told, I was so broke that if someone had actually riffled the cash money right under my nose, I might have taken it, Janet or no Janet. But no one ever did. And I'm really glad I didn't." TONY CURTIS

June 5 (1993)
Mariah Carey & Tommy Mottola

All she did when beginning her career was rewrite the record books by delivering five straight #1 singles. On this misty New York day Mariah Carey, 23, marries the man who masterminded that launch: Sony Music honcho Tommy Mottola, 43. At the cavernous Saint Thomas Church on Fifth Avenue, the star-studded guest list includes Billy Joel and Christie Brinkley (Mar. 23), Bruce Springsteen and Patti Scialfa (June 8), Michael Bolton, Dick Clark, Tony Danza, David Geffen, Hall and Oates, and an unlikely tuxedoed Ozzy Osbourne. The bride wears an off-the-shoulder jeweled bodice gown with a 27-foot train, and a precious stone-encrusted tiara. Afterwards **50 flower girls lining the church steps toss handfuls of flower petals** as fans behind police barricades strain for a glimpse of the swell crowd. This fall Mariah's back atop the charts with "Dreamlover," the year's biggest single that reigns for two months. And those first five #1's? "Vision of Love," "Love Takes Time," "Someday," "I Don't Wanna Cry" and "Emotions."

Her first of two, his second of three, lasts four years

June 6 (1992)
Iman & David Bowie

'My father taught me how to be a parent and gave me a positive connection with men because he is a gentleman. And that is what attracted me to David. He is a gentle soul.' IMAN

Mere mortals tremble at the improbable news of today's wedding of the impossibly good-looking runway goddess and the god of fashion and music. They'd met when a hairdresser set them up on a blind date, and despite the age gap and omnipresent media glare, they clicked. He **proposed on a rainy Parisian moonlit cruise on the Seine**, but to throw off the press they leaked a false story of impending church vows on the West Indian isle of Mustique. David Bowie, 45, and stunning Somalia native Iman, 36, marry at an Episcopal church in Florence, Italy, with a brief ceremony featuring original music composed by the groom. She wears a white Herve Leger halter gown and white opera gloves, he dons a Thierry Mugler tuxedo with a white bow tie. The small gathering of the rich and famous includes Bono, Brian Eno, Eric Idle of Monty Python and Yoko Ono. Despite the subterfuge, word spreads and a thousand locals surround the church, necessitating a police escort back to the 400-year-old Villa Massa hotel for dinner, dancing and fireworks.

His second, her second

June 7 (2003)
Christy Turlington & Edward Burns

In the wake of 9/11, the couple decided to postpone their plans to wed that October. Then, the actor/director and entrepreneurial supermodel broke up. **And reconciled—and how!** Today Edward Burns, 35, and Christy Turlington, 34, finally marry at the dual-spired Saints Peter and Paul Church in San Francisco. The pregnant bride wears a cap-sleeved, silk and lace Galliano gown plus a (borrowed) $250,000 diamond Riviera necklace and drop earrings. News reports suggest that U2 frontman Bono gave Christy away, but she walks the aisle alone. (Her father died in 1997.) The traditional Catholic ceremony features two flower girls, four ring bearers and a seven-person choir. A reception at the Asian Art Museum attracts A-listers including Sting and Vin Diesel. Despite the heavy musical talent in attendance, the couple shares its first dance to Bruce Springsteen's "If I Should Fall Behind" (written to Patti Scialfa, see below). Then it's off to a quiet Mexican honeymoon. Daughter Grace arrives in October.

June 8 (1991)
Patti Scialfa & Bruce Springsteen

It's **a private ceremony**, not all that surprising since the couple's been together for a few years—and oh yes, she's also several months pregnant. First brought front and center during his *Tunnel of Love* tour in '88, backup singer and archetypal Jersey girl Patti Scialfa, 37, marries The Boss, a.k.a., Bruce Springsteen, 41, at their Beverly Hills home before a handful of friends and family. As his marriage to actress Julianne Phillips crumbled, tabloids had pumped up the volume on his affair with Scialfa, who'd grown up ten miles from Springsteen and broke barriers as the first female member of the E Street Band. Next month their son Evan turns one, and in December she gives birth to daughter Jessica Rae.

"When you're married to someone famous, people know you but they're not really seeing you."

PATTI SCIALFA

June 9 (2001)

Angie Harmon & Jason Sehorn

When *Law & Order*'s Angie Harmon appeared last year on *The Tonight Show with Jay Leno*, she sat chatting with the host alongside guest Elton John. As Leno quizzed her about her love life, out came a surprise guest, Jason Sehorn of the N.Y. Giants, who **got down on bended knee and proposed** to the stunned actress. For good measure her father also appeared to give his permission. Today they tie the knot at Highland Park Presbyterian Church in her native Dallas with 400 guests looking on. As trumpets sound Harmon, 29, enters in a strapless satin gown by Vera Wang (June 22) and an antique tiara by Neil Lane. Sehorn, 30, wears a Zegna tuxedo he'd accidentally forgotten in New York that got flown in only hours before. Three bridesmaids and three "bridesmen," close male friends, round out the party. The reception's held at the home a longtime family friend, where guests dine on a menu featuring beef tenderloin and chicken with mango relish.

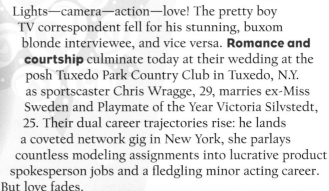

June 10 (2000)
Victoria Silvstedt & Chris Wragge

Lights—camera—action—love! The pretty boy
TV correspondent fell for his stunning, buxom
blonde interviewee, and vice versa. **Romance and
courtship** culminate today at their wedding at the
posh Tuxedo Park Country Club in Tuxedo, N.Y.
as sportscaster Chris Wragge, 29, marries ex-Miss
Sweden and Playmate of the Year Victoria Silvstedt,
25. Their dual career trajectories rise: he lands
a coveted network gig in New York, she parlays
countless modeling assignments into lucrative product
spokesperson jobs and a fledgling minor acting career.
But love fades.

> His first, her first, lasts seven years

June 11 (2002)
Heather Mills & Paul McCartney

Just **an innocent game of ring toss** gone awry, said the
happy couple. A furious argument, claimed the tabloids.
Regardless of the truth, facts show that a diamond sapphire
engagement ring—from betrothed Sir Paul McCartney,
59, to ex-model Heather Mills, 34—flew out of their hotel
window last month at the chic Turnberry Isle Resort &
Club in Miami. Days later a nighttime security guard,
searching with a flashlight, found and returned it for an
undisclosed reward. Today Mills strolls down the aisle of
a remote, lakeside Irish castle to the strains of "Heather,"
composed by Paul. She wears a self-designed, fitted ecru
lace dress and carries a bouquet of peonies and pink
McCartney (named for Paul, natch) roses. The beaming
couple marries to a wedding march he wrote for a 1966
British movie, *The Family Way*. The 300-strong invitees,
including Pink Floyd's David Gilmour, Chrissie Hynde
(July 10), Beatles producer George Martin, Ringo Starr and
Twiggy, enjoy a vegetarian Indian feast afterwards under
huge tents. The gala affair costs an estimated $3 million.

> His second of three, her second, lasts six years

There Goes the Bride

June 11, 1991: Soundstage 14 on the 20th Century Fox lot presents a garden paradise, with flower-bedecked trellises and freshly laid sod. But it's not for a movie, silly, it's for **Hollywood's most magical wedding of the decade**. Until today, that is, three days before the main event, when **Julia Roberts** jilts her intended, **Kiefer Sutherland**. A tongue-wagging frenzy erupts as tabloids stalk the participants, feeding the public's voracious appetite for juicy bits. Terse statements from publicists won't do, so friends on both sides trash the other, anonymously. "She dumped him," offers one insider, amid stories of his recent dalliance with a go-go dancer. Roberts jets off to Ireland with hunky actor Jason Patric, igniting even more breathless coverage.

People's Sexiest Man Alive, **Brad Pitt**, called girlfriend **Gwyneth Paltrow** "the love o' my life, my angel" after they met while filming the thriller *Seven* in 1995. The engaged "it" couple ended things two years later.

Several days before their reported $2 million wedding in Santa Barbara in Sept. 2003, the dazzling duo known universally as Bennifer (**Ben Affleck** and **Jennifer Lopez**) called the whole thing off, blaming the intense media spotlight and negative publicity.

Kiefer
Sutherland

Julia
Roberts

Three high-profile celebrity hookups that dissolved before reaching the altar

June 12 (1999)

Kate Kreider & Jon Gosselin

Splashed all over the news today is the chi-chi wedding of actors Courteney Cox and David Arquette in San Francisco before a starry array of 200 guests including Brad Pitt and Nicolas Cage. Thousands of miles away in the small town of Wyomissing, Pa., the wedding of an unknown couple—a registered nurse and a network engineer—attracts **nary a blip of coverage**. Having met at a picnic several years ago, Kate Kreider, 24, and Jon Gosselin, 22, marry in a friend's backyard and honeymoon at Disney World. Fame remains elusive until they begin fertility treatments that produce twins, sextuplets and media superstardom. The TLC reality series *Jon & Kate Plus 8* turns the burgeoning family into household names. Jon and Kate renew their vows in a made-for-television Hawaiian spectacular, complete with a conch shell blower, dancer and drummer, their children placing white leis around their parents' necks, and a native version of "Somewhere Over the Rainbow." Unfortunately, somewhere over their rainbow is adultery and divorce.

His first, her first, lasts ten years

June 13 (1970)
Peggy Fleming & Greg Jenkins

On their first date they saw the blockbuster musical *The Sound of Music*. Two nights later they **shared their first kiss during a fireworks display on New Year's Eve**. Today America's favorite skating champion Peggy Fleming, 21, weds medical student Greg Jenkins, 24, once a skating student, at the Bel Air Presbyterian Church. Afterwards 350 guests enjoy the reception at the swank Bel-Air Country Club. Two years ago she captivated millions while winning a gold medal at the Olympics, where even a competitor called her "a skater without weaknesses… a pure ballerina." Despite her world-class talent and the adulation of millions, she's still under mama's thumb. Her mother nixes including the groom's brother from the wedding party because he has a beard. But the bride declines mom's offer to pick out her dress, shopping herself and choosing a traditional one with a long train and veil, but with short sleeves that she feels makes it sporty. After a Hawaiian honeymoon, she's back on the skating circuit with Ice Follies.

June 14 (1980)
Jane Pauley & Garry Trudeau

Her best work can be seen on television. His, in newspapers—**on the funny pages**, to be exact. Jane Pauley, 29, host of NBC's *The Today Show*, marries Pulitzer prize-winning *Doonesbury* creator Garry Trudeau, 31, at their home on Governor's Island, a tiny, exclusive island off the coast of Long Island Sound. Not surprisingly, given the groom's well-known aversion to publicity, it's a small, simple outdoor ceremony. Their planned Parisian honeymoon is delayed after the groom realizes his passport isn't up to date, so tonight it's off to see *Star Wars: The Empire Strikes Back*.

'*Ordinary New Yorkers greeted her as if she actually were the girl next door. 'Hi ya, Judy!' a truck driver might shout.*'

GERALD CLARKE ON THEIR NYC HONEYMOON

June 15 (1945)
Judy Garland & Vincente Minnelli

A beloved American icon who never puts on airs solidifies her girl-next-door reputation by marrying in a simple ceremony—on the front lawn of her mother's house in Los Angeles. One week after her divorce from bandleader David Rose, Judy Garland, 23, weds director Vincente Minnelli, 32. MGM honcho Louis Mayer gives away the bride, resplendent in a high-necked, softly draped gray jersey gown with pink pearl beading (to match her pearl engagement ring) by costume designer Irene Gibbons. Confidante Betty Asher serves as bridesmaid, and Ira Gershwin as best man. Afterwards the couple boards a train for a three-month honeymoon in New York, a city flush with excitement in the wake of Germany's surrender last month. MGM rewards its premiere contract player with a Tiffany's bracelet of square diamonds and emeralds; hubby gets a fine gold wristwatch. By the end of the happy honeymoon she's pregnant, and next March gives birth to her first child: Liza.

Her second of five, his first of four, lasts six years

June 16 (1943)
Oona O'Neill & Charlie Chaplin

His iconic silent screen performances as The Tramp remain legendary. Though now it's nearly a quarter century since his debut in the blockbuster, *The Kid*, gossip columnists are feasting on his personal predilections—especially a 23-year-old aspiring actress's claim that he fathered her unborn child. Today indomitable Charlie Chaplin, 54, takes his fourth bride, Oona O'Neill, 18, daughter of playwright Eugene O'Neill. A justice of the peace marries them in tranquil Carpinteria, Ca., in a three-minute ceremony "**without fuss, feathers or folderol**," says the justice. They enjoy the privacy only due to the driving skills of his chauffeur who successfully shook several carloads of pursuing reporters at speeds approaching 80 m.p.h. Chaplin soon appears in court to deny the pending paternity charge, an allegation fanned by news reports that report his accuser grew "hysterical" after learning of the wedding. Blood tests later exonerate Chaplin.

His fourth, lasts 34 years until his death

"Most women are charmed by Dad, but in Oona's case it was different. She worshipped him, drinking in every word he spoke whether it was about his latest script, the weather or some bit of philosophy." CHARLIE CHAPLIN, JR.

June 17 (1997)
Grace Hightower & Robert De Niro

Big name, low profile. That's how Robert De Niro likes to play it when it comes to his private life. But mama said there'd be days like this, and his mother Virginia added some advice: "Grace is the one for you—**don't let her get away.**" So at his upstate estate in Marbletown, N.Y., the 53-year-old actor marries companion Grace Hightower, 38, a tall black former flight attendant, at a quiet affair that includes guests Harvey Keitel and Joe Pesci. Though his NYC digs have been a traditional bachelor pad, De Niro's been remaking it into a more family-friendly environment for the two-year-old twin boys he fathered via a surrogate mom with his former companion Toukie Smith. Before year's end the busy actor stars in three movies, *Cop Land*, *Jackie Brown* and *Wag the Dog*, and next spring goes the daddy route once more when Hightower gives birth to their son Elliot.

June 18 (1953)
Coretta Scott &
Martin Luther King, Jr.

She's a headstrong country gal from rural Alabama, attending college in Boston with dreams of becoming a concert singer. He's an eloquent preacher's son, about to carve his name into American history, and a flagrant philanderer. On their first date, arranged by a fellow student, she found her pudgy suitor rather conceited but charming. His imperious father wanted his son to marry a woman from a proper (i.e., elite) black Atlanta family, but his stubborn offspring had other plans. Today Martin Luther King, Jr., 23, and Coretta Scott, 26, in a pastel blue gown with lace and net, marry on the front lawn of her parents' house. His father performs the ceremony. Her sister Edythe Bagley serves as maid of honor, his brother Rev. A.D. King as best man. Since no local hotels will rent bridal suites to African-Americans, they spend their wedding night at the home of a family friend who's an undertaker, and later joke that **they honeymooned in a funeral parlor**.

"Having made that decision [to marry] – the most important in my life – is what made all the rest possible, the amazing and wonderful and terrible things that came later in our lives. CORETTA SCOTT KING

June 19 (2010)
Crown Princess Victoria
& Daniel Westling

It's the story of **the princess and her personal trainer**, or as one royal watcher declares, Sweden's 15 minutes in the limelight. A jubilant crowd of a half-million jams Stockholm's streets to catch a glimpse of Crown Princess Victoria, heir to her country's throne, and Daniel Westling, the bespectacled owner of the gym she joined eight years ago. On the same date that her father King Carl XVI Gustaf married Queen Silvia 34 years ago, the 32-year-old princess wears an off-the-shoulder, floor-length ivory-colored gown with a seven-foot train, and a long veil held in place by the same tiara her mother wore. Her beaming groom, 36, now becomes Prince Daniel, Duke of Vastergotland. Their only sign of nerves during the ceremony occurs when they briefly fumble the exchange of rings. Guests number 1,200 including royalty from around the globe and the groom's humble parents: she a clerk in the Swedish post office, he a manager of a municipal social services center.

June 20 (1975)
Anne Murray & William Langstroth

She seems to have it all: money and fame thanks to a successful career that's included Top Ten hits "Snowbird," "Danny's Song" and "You Won't See Me." Last year at the Grammy awards, when she won her first for "Love Song," John Lennon told her that her version of "You Won't See Me" was his favorite Beatles' cover ever. But what's been missing in the mellow crooner's life is **her dream to start a family**. She spends today, her 30th birthday, in a Toronto recording studio. But tonight, at home, her dream comes true as Anne Murray marries boyfriend William Langstroth, 45, who she'd met several years ago when auditioning for the CBC's *Singalong Jubilee*. Murray wears a green muumuu, plucked from her closet, and goes barefoot. It's a quiet, private affair with only a handful of family members and friends attending. About the biggest excitement is when the photographer backs into one of many lit candles and sets his jacket afire. Afterwards they enjoy a lobster dinner in the garden, and celebrate with a chocolate cake courtesy of Sara Lee. Next year they welcome son William.

Her first, his second, lasts 29 years

June 21 (1998)
Rachel Miner & Macaulay Culkin

Well they were just 17, you know what I mean, and the way he earned was way beyond compare-air... That oh-so-cute tyke Macaulay Culkin, a mega-multi-millionaire thanks to the smash *Home Alone* movies, marries actress Rachel Miner in the 19th century Stone Church in rural Washington, Connecticut. She wears a sheer, ecru-colored full-length gown with ruffled straps flowing into a scooped neckline, with a cathedral-length veil attached to a coronet of white baby's breath. The select group of 50 guests doesn't include his pushy stage father Kit, who along with Macaulay's mother (the two never married) has been famously feuding over the earnings of **the highest paid child star in film history**. Miner's currently appearing on Broadway as Anne Frank's sister Margot in *The Diary of Anne Frank*, but Macaulay's star has dimmed as he's grown and starred in a series of duds that nevertheless pay him high seven figure salaries.

His first, her first, lasts two years

June 22 (1989)
Vera Wang & Arthur Becker

Shopping for a wedding dress, the bride discovered that bridal wear hadn't evolved all that much. Everything she saw seemed too old-fashioned. **Where was the flair?** Working for Ralph Lauren, she knew a thing or two about design, so she created her own and hired a tailor to construct the 45-pound, hand-beaded white duchesse satin gown. Vera Wang, less than a week away from turning 40, and stockbroker Arthur Becker, 38, marry in an interfaith service (a Baptist minister and a rabbi) at New York's snazzy Pierre Hotel before 400 guests. For the reception she slips into a simple pink slip dress. Soon thereafter, Wang quits her job and ignores the entreaties of Calvin Klein to come work for him. Vera Wang's Bridal House Ltd., bankrolled by her father, opens next year at the Carlyle Hotel. The risky proposition pays off as she makes her name as *the* designer of some of the dreamiest bridal fashions to ever float down the aisle.

"A dress must be tailored to the hows, wheres and whens. Then you try to marry the fantasy to the reality." **VERA WANG**

June 23 (1966)
Meredith Baxter & Bob Bush

They're just a couple of aimless kids hanging around, working menial jobs and getting high. In their tiny apartment just off Laurel Canyon, they **glue pieces of colored tissue paper to the windows to mimic stained glass**. The neighborhood's home to hipsters like Sonny and Cher (Oct. 27), Joni Mitchell and Frank Zappa, none of whom they know—though they do pal around with musician Lowell George, later to form Little Feat. Today Meredith Baxter, 19, in a sleeveless, floral print cotton dress, and Bob Bush, 21, marry before two friends at a small Unitarian church in North Hollywood. Next spring she gives birth to a son, followed by a daughter two years later. With money always short, she taps family connections (her mother was a longtime bit actress, her stepfather a producer) to land a guest part in an episode of *The Interns*. The marriage fades as her career heats up, leading to a title role in *Bridget Loves Bernie* opposite future husband David Birney, and small screen prominence with *Family* and *Family Ties*.

Her first of three, lasts three years

'Jo and Duke were madly in love with each other, but they were poles apart in society. She came from a sophisticated and cultured background, while he was a former homesteader who had changed from being a shy, awkward, and anxious young man to a fun-loving man's man.' LORETTA YOUNG

June 24 (1933)

Josephine Saenz & John Wayne

Society gal meets starry-eyed college boy. With his USC fraternity brothers, 19-year-old Marion Michael Morrison headed north to a beach party in Balboa, California, a sleepy fishing village. Afterwards he **took his blind date home and became smitten with her younger sister**. Over the next six years he ground out dozens of quickie, Poverty Row westerns until he finally signed a long-term contract with Monogram Pictures. Today John Wayne, 26, marries Josephine Saenz, 25, daughter of the envoy of the Panamanian Consulate, in the garden of Loretta Young's home in Bel Air. Young serves as maid of honor, his brother Robert as best man. The bride wanted a church wedding, but since Wayne wasn't Catholic she settled for a civil ceremony. Religion becomes a thorny issue, perhaps not as much as his womanizing. The stormy union produces four children, two girls and two boys, before imploding a decade later.

His first of three, her first of two, lasts 12 years

June 25 (1983)
Pauletta Pearson & Denzel Washington

They were just a couple of unknown, budding actors appearing in their first major credit: *Wilma*, a TV biopic in which he portrayed the boyfriend of Olympian Wilma Rudolph (played by Cicely Tyson). The night it debuted, he wasn't watching but bussing tables. Several years but not much professional success later, they met again at a party in Manhattan. As she later told Oprah, "I thought he was cute, but I fell in love with his spirit. And then I thought, **'Hmm, not a bad package.**'" Then he finally got his big break: noble Dr. Phillip Chandler on *St. Elsewhere*. Today Denzel Washington, 28, and Pauletta Pearson, 32, marry, and it's truly a family affair. Their son John David, born two months ago, portrays a baby in a maternity ward scene and earns a $400 paycheck. Washington stays with *St. Elsewhere* for its six-year run, parlaying his stature into leading man cinematic status.

"There are only four women in the world. The one you marry, your mother, your daughter and all the rest of them. As long as you keep that perspective, you'll be all right." — DENZEL WASHINGTON

June 26 (1970)
Patty Duke & Michael Tell

She soared to stardom as a teen, winning an Emmy award at 16 (the youngest champion to date) for portraying Helen Keller in *The Miracle Worker*, a part she'd previously played on Broadway. Her subsequent TV hit *The Patty Duke Show* made her a household name, and playing identical twins with opposite personalities wasn't all that far from her real life disorder, manic depression. Today Duke, 23, **impulsively marries her tenant**, rock promoter Michael Tell, in Las Vegas. Thirteen days later, following a raging, throwing-things fit in their hotel suite, the marriage is annulled, but not before Duke blurts out on *The Dick Cavett Show* that she's pregnant. She thinks the father is former boyfriend Desi Arnaz, Jr., and her future husband John Astin adopts the boy (Sean Astin). DNA testing later reveals Tell to be the father, an interesting turnabout since Duke received the annulment by claiming the marriage had never been consummated.

> **Her second of four, lasts 13 days**

June 27 (1994)
Anna Nicole Smith & J. Howard Marshall II

Take one besotted billionaire, add in a devious gold digger, and what do you get? The culmination of **the quintessential May/December romance**. Despite a yawning 64-year age gap, oil tycoon J. Howard Marshall II, 89, marries Anna Nicole Smith, 25, at Houston's White Dove Wedding Chapel. Everyone in the sparse crowd wears white: the buxom bride bursting out of her puffy fairy-tale dress; the groom in his wheelchair; ring bearer Daniel, her eight-year-old son by a previous marriage; her aunt and uncle; Marshall's secretary and one of his nurses. It's a slapdash, secret affair, since she fears his son Pierce would sabotage the event if he knew about it. Best known previously for her provocative poses for Guess jeans and *Playboy*, Anna soon springs some news upon her hubby: she's jetting off that afternoon for a photo shoot in Greece, though she actually flies to L.A. with her hunky bodyguard/lover.

Her second, his third, lasts one year 'til his death

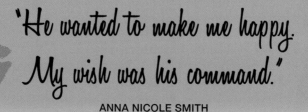

"He wanted to make me happy. My wish was his command."

ANNA NICOLE SMITH

June 28 (1963)
Judy Carne & Burt Reynolds

Sock It To Me.

A mustachioed macho man and a free-spirited waif. They're an unlikely pair, these headstrong, struggling actors: Burt Reynolds, 27, and Judy Carne, 24. They'd met while on promotional tours for their television shows, *Gunsmoke* and *Fair Exchange*, respectively. After **a whirlwind six-month courtship**, the brawny Burt and British transplant Judy marry at a church in Burbank, which the groom chose after other churches in the San Fernando Valley wanted too much money. Even Burt, known for his frequent brawls and boisterous behavior, was shocked by her devil-may-care ways. "I'd never heard a woman say the 'f' word before," he said, "but she said it in every sentence and made it sound as if she'd said 'flower.'" But opposite personalities and dueling career aspirations doom the marriage. She finds brief success first as the "Sock It To Me" girl on *Rowan and Martin's Laugh-In*, while he steers surprisingly from wooden supporting TV player to enduringly popular cinematic leading man.

His first of two, her first of two, lasts two years

"*Sometimes the things that attract you in the first place are the things that drive you crazy in a marriage... When reality settled over our romance, we saw two nice, completely incompatible people.*" **BURT REYNOLDS**

June 29 (2005)
Jennifer Garner & Ben Affleck

After the spectacular implosion of his tabloid-crazed Bennifer relationship with Jennifer Lopez, Ben Affleck went **decidedly low key**. Thankfully off the paparazzian radar, he jets off to the luxurious Parrot Cay resort in the British West Indies. Today Affleck, 32, marries his *Daredevil* co-star Jennifer Garner, 33, in a secret beachside ceremony with a lone guest: her *Alias* co-star and on-screen papa, Victor Garber. Four months pregnant, Garner wears a white empire waist Vera Wang gown with a green sash and carries a single calla lily. Ben sports a cream-colored suit by Hugo Boss. After exchanging Harry Winston rings and personal vows in a brief non-denominational service, the newlyweds crash for a few days at the nearby shorefront villa of (absent) Bruce Willis. Then it's off to Vancouver, B.C., where she resumes filming *Catch and Release* though to date, they're still happily on the "catch" part. Daughter Violet Anne arrives in December.

June 30 (1975)
Cher & Gregg Allman

After four days **the ink's barely dry on her divorce
papers** from Sonny Bono. But there she goes again, that
impulsive man-hungry diva Cher, marrying... another
musician. A far hunkier, hipper one, at least: longhaired
rocker Gregg Allman. In her lawyer's suite at Caesars Palace
in Las Vegas, a dozen guests witness the short ceremony.
Cher, 29, wears a two-piece blue satin gown with a white
camisole top while Allman, 27, wears a white shirt and
white scarf. Little more than a week later she files for
divorce, claiming "I've always believed it best to admit
one's mistakes as quickly as possible." Then, they reconcile
only to split again, eventually staying together long enough
to become parents to a son, Elijah Blue.

Her second, his third, lasts three years

*"I had to have known it was the wrong thing to do,
but there was something about Gregory. He was handsome
and wild. He was rock'n'roll, the definitive Bad Boy,
but he was also tender and sensitive."* CHER

July

Prince Charles &
Lady Diana Spencer
July 29, 1981

July 1 (1961)
Martha Kostyra & Alexander Stewart

They **met on a blind date, set up by his sister**: a handsome Yale law student and a Barnard coed juggling part-time jobs as a housekeeper and model for clients including Lifebuoy and Breck. In fairy-tale fashion, it was love at first sight. But the short courtship wasn't without its problems, especially the bitter opposition of her Catholic father to her Jewish boyfriend, whose nonobservant father had changed the family name to the wasp-ish Stewart. Love triumphs. With only immediate family members watching, Martha Kostyra, 19, and Alex Stewart, 23, wed in St. Paul's Chapel at Columbia University. Martha wears an elaborately embroidered dress she and her mother made from Swiss organdy, plus a pillbox hat now so in vogue thanks to First Lady Jackie Kennedy, and carries a bouquet of daisies. Lunch is a simple affair for 18 at the Berkshire Hotel, ending with an ice-cream cake. Next month's *Glamour* features Martha as one of the ten best-dressed college gals of the year. Her career as a lifestyle goddess extraordinaire is still several decades away.

> Her first, his first of two, lasts 28 years

July 2 (1939)

Ann Landers & Julius Lederer

Abigail van Buren & Morton Phillips

The twins were inseparable, and having each accepted marriage proposals, happily went off shopping for their trousseaux. But then a rather strange thing happened: **a handsome young millinery salesman at the department store asked one of them out on a date**. She accepted, and soon the double wedding was on—only with one new groom. On a blisteringly hot day in Sioux City, Iowa, 20-year-olds Esther Friedman (later Ann Landers) and Pauline Friedman (Abigail van Buren) marry Julius Lederer (the salesclerk) and Morton Phillips, respectively. The brides wear ornate, old world-style gowns and headpieces reflecting the heritage of their Russian immigrant parents. It's a major family affair, with 11 bridesmaids accompanied by 11 groomsmen, 750 guests, and three rabbis: one Orthodox, one Conservative, one Reform.

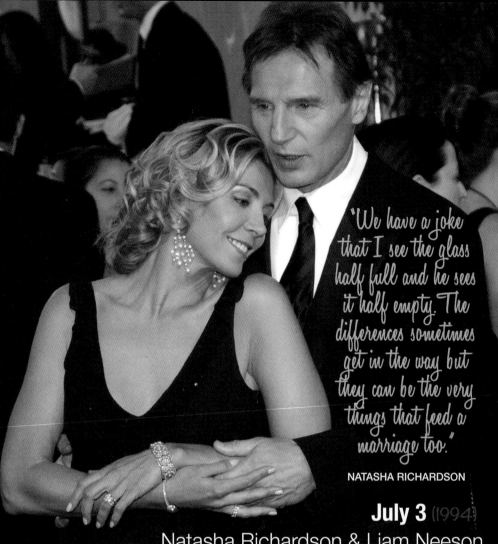

"We have a joke that I see the glass half full and he sees it half empty. The differences sometimes get in the way but they can be the very things that feed a marriage too."

NATASHA RICHARDSON

July 3 (1994)
Natasha Richardson & Liam Neeson

They fell in love on Broadway but **married far from the bright city lights**. At their rural upstate estate, the scion of a distinguished British acting dynasty weds a working-class Irish bloke. Actor Franco Nero, subbing for the bride's mother Vanessa Redgrave (in Italy, shooting a movie) gives away Natasha Richardson, 31, to Liam Neeson, 42, in an outdoor sunset service featuring mass and a choir singing "Morning Has Broken." The hush-hush event attracts a glittery array of stars including Steven Spielberg and wife Kate Capshaw (Oct. 12), Lauren Bacall, Mia Farrow, Ralph Fiennes and Emma Thompson. The couple met while performing in a Broadway revival of Eugene O'Neill's *Anna Christie* (for which each received a Tony nomination), though she had to extricate herself from her then husband, producer Richard Fox. Neeson, red hot after playing the title role in last year's multi (seven) Oscar-winning *Schindler's List*, departs a bachelorhood once studded with a succession of lovely lasses including Brooke Shields, Barbra Streisand, Julia Roberts and Helen Mirren.

Her second, his first, lasts 15 years until her death

July 4 (1999)
Victoria Adams & David Beckham

When the deep purple falls, over rustic castle walls... The Bishop of Cork wears purple robes, matching the wedding's Robin Hood theme of burgundy, forest green and aubergine accents. And on his feet he sports Man U socks since he's a huge fan of Manchester United—and afterwards earns the nickname Purple Spice from his fellow bishops. It's **a wedding of worldwide distinction and lavish excess**, 14 months in the making, co-starring incomparable soccer star David Beckham, 24, and Victoria Adams, 25, a.k.a. Posh Spice, at a remote Irish castle. *OK! Magazine* snags exclusive photo rights, adding a heavy layer of security to eliminate competitors and commoners. Victoria wears a champagne-coloured Vera Wang original that she dubs "sexy in a kind of virginal way." Ever the dandy, David wears a cream outfit by Timothy Everett with a knee-length jacket, gold and cream waistcoat and top hat. The couple drips with jewelry, including matching Asprey & Garrard diamond rings set in 18-carat yellow gold bands. Adding a family touch is four-month-old son Brooklyn, who inopportunely throws up on his father during the reception.

"You can always count on your kids to make sure nobody's in danger of taking things too seriously." DAVID BECKHAM

July 5 (1943)
Betty Grable & Harry James

The **girl with the million dollar legs** and the handsome, mustachioed stud acclaimed as the greatest trumpet player on earth. At 4 a.m. in a little church adjoining the Last Frontier Hotel in Las Vegas, Betty Grable, 26, weds bandleader Harry James, 27. After a quick reception the couple drives back to L.A. where she begins shooting *Pin-Up Girl*, and he continues his tri-weekly radio show. America's #1 box-office star, Grable receives 10,000 fan letters a week, and her over-the-shoulder cheesecake photo has become the #1 pinup for America's wartime soldiers. At last fall's opening of the Hollywood Canteen, the servicemen's special place, Grable jitterbugged the night away, changing partners 46 times during a 10-minute "tag" dance. Marriage doesn't dim her star, as Fox famously insures her shapely gams for a million bucks with Lloyd's of London, and features her in films opposite heartthrobs like Victor Mature, Tyrone Power and Cesar Romero.

Her second, his second, lasts 22 years

'If it hadn't been entered into in haste, it might have worked. But then if it hadn't been entered into in haste, it wouldn't have happened.'

DIANA RIGG

July 6 (1973)
Diana Rigg & Menachem Gueffen

The producers had wanted a character with "man appeal," which got shortened to "m-appeal" and begat her most famous role—lithe crime-fighting Emma Peel in *The Avengers*. Today beautiful, talented Diana Rigg, 34, marries Israeli artist Menachem Gueffen, 43, in a private service at the registry office in Richmond Upon Thames. They met only a few months before at a London dinner party, and several weeks ago Rigg had told a magazine that **she saw no reason to ever get married**. That bit of misdirection notwithstanding, they soon relocate their whirlwind romance to a rented house in Los Angeles where she begins filming her gone-in-a-flash NBC sitcom, *Diana*. Its short run presages the impulsive marriage, as he bristles at the perception of being Mr. Diana Rigg. She files for separation 11 stormy months later.

Her first of two, his third, lasts three years

July 7 (2001)
Drew Barrymore & Tom Green

The sacred **vows of marriage rarely include passages about drag racing**, but today's wild and crazy couple delights in bizarre behavior. After having fibbed for months about having already gotten married, or suggesting they might do it on *Saturday Night Live*, Drew Barrymore, 26, and wacky comedian Tom (*Freddy Got Fingered*) Green, 29, actually tie the knot on a Malibu beach. Starry guests including Cameron Diaz and Lucy Liu (her fellow Charlie's Angels), Courtney Love, Adam Sandler and Molly Shannon witness what her publicist calls "a beautiful, low-key event." Low-key, as in passing out pamphlets about drag racing and having guests read back paragraphs. But Drew thoughtfully invites her formerly estranged mother Jaid, who once sold her daughter's baby clothes on eBay. No need for baby clothes now, since Tom's recent announcement on *The Tonight Show* that she's pregnant is another hoax. What's true is that the marriage is over by Christmas.

July 8 (1942)
Barbara Hutton & Cary Grant

Heiress, princess, countess. Today, call her Mrs. Cary Grant. One of the richest women on earth, Woolworth's heiress Barbara Hutton, **hopes to shed being unlucky in love, again**—like with husband #1, a money-grubbing Russian prince, and #2, a Danish count. At high noon, under a towering oak at the Lake Arrowhead mountain lodge of his agent, Grant, 38, and Hutton, 29, marry. She wears a navy blue silk moiré suit, pink blouse and a tiny hat that resembles a bowl overflowing with pink roses. He wears a dark gray pinstriped suit. Papers dub the couple "Cash and Cary," and a society columnist haughtily calls him a "former Coney Island hot dog salesman." The truth, revealed years later, is that he signed a pre-nuptial agreement relinquishing any claim to her millions if they divorced. The movie star with a decidedly working class background never hits it off with her high society friends. "If one more phony noble showed up," said Grant later, "I would have suffocated." His next film, seriously: *Once Upon a Honeymoon* opposite Ginger Rogers.

After years of searching, after hundreds of heartaches, dozens of mistakes and a quest that has taken her all over the world, she has found the right man at last – a man who will never, never be known as "Mr. Barbara Hutton." **MODERN SCREEN**

His second of five, her third of seven, lasts three years

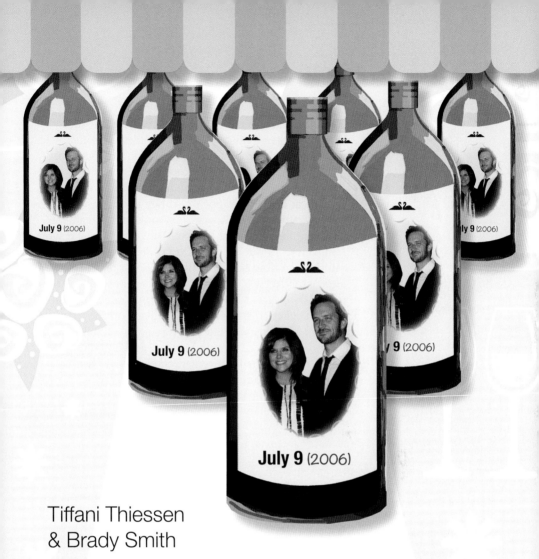

July 9 (2006)

July 9 (2006)

July 9 (2006)

July 9 (2006)

July 9 (2006)

ly 9 (2006)

y 9 (2006)

Tiffani Thiessen & Brady Smith

An hour up the coast from Beverly Hills 90210, **a fairy-tale Hollywood wedding** unfolds in sunny Santa Barbara for Tiffani Thiessen, 32, and Brady Smith, 34. At a posh estate overlooking a lake dotted with swans, the couple shares their vows in front an antique gate woven with geraniums, yellow roses and olive branches. She wears a strapless French tulle and lace gown by Vera Wang, he wears a khaki Kenneth Cole suit. The 135 guests, including her *90210* co-stars Lindsay Price, Jason Priestley and Tori Spelling (May 7) walk through a vine-covered arbor to the reception at an upper garden. As a violinist plays Edith Piaf tunes, the French Provincial-themed dinner features arugula salad with white truffle oil, filet mignon with potatoes au gratin, and a New York-style cheesecake. After dancing late into the night, the couple wraps with a Perrier-Jouët Champagne toast before heading to their honeymoon night at the nearby Hotel Andalucia. Guests take home bottles of hand-pressed olive oil.

July 10 (1997)
Chrissie Hynde & Lucho Brieva

Wearing jeans to a low-key civil ceremony at the Westminster Register Office in London, iconoclastic rocker Chrissie Hynde, 46, and Columbian sculptor Lucho Brieva, 32, tie the knot. Afterwards they and a small group of friends, including Annie Lennox, dine at a pizza shoppe on Abbey Road, and **then the newlyweds stroll home**. Just another typical, anti-establishment move for the Midwest (U.S.) gal who moved to London in '73 and became a seminal figure in the dawning punk revolution. Front and center, her alternately aching or throbbing vocals propelled The Pretenders to great heights with "Stop Your Sobbing," "Brass in Pocket (I'm Special)" and "Back on the Chain Gang." Along the way she dated two rockers—Ray Davies of the Kinks and Jim Kerr of Simple Minds—and had children by each. Of the first, with Davies, she later remarked she went "from rock'n'roll goddess to straight-A student, from greaseball to mother's pride in 15 seconds. I never even picked up a baby before I had one."

Her second, lasts six years

"He was the first person I met who spoke of marriage in a real sense." **KARLA DeVITO**

July 11 (1982)
Karla DeVito & Robby Benson

Opposites attract: **the squeaky clean heartthrob and the steamy bad girl**. Robby Benson, 26, and Karla DeVito, 29, marry today in her sleepy hometown of Mokena, Ill. There's nary a dry eye in the house when they sing a duet he'd written called "Believe in Fate." The unlikely couple met while co-starring in a Broadway revival of Gilbert and Sullivan's *The Pirates of Penzance*, where they succeeded Rex Smith and Linda Ronstadt, respectively. After a honeymoon in Hawaii, they're back reprising their roles in a Midwest tour. Born to a theatrically inclined family, Benson has seen his career as a sensitive boy-next-door stall since hits like *Ode to Billy Joe*. With a musical background, DeVito drew considerable acclaim as one of the two hot chicks beside Meatloaf in the steamroller *Bat Out of Hell* album and tour, lip-synching the words to the horny anthem "Paradise By the Dashboard Light." Despite naysayers' doubts, the marriage lasts and produces daughter Lyric and son Zephyr.

'I was obsessed with Steve from the moment he stepped into my world, and there was never enough air for me to breathe to change that feeling.' ALI MacGRAW

July 12 (1973)
Ali MacGraw & Steve McQueen

Neither of them have even the remotest connection to Cheyenne, Wyoming, but **the name has a very cowboy/romantic feel**. Plus it has the decided advantage of being far away from Hollywood and prying paparazzi. So Ali MacGraw, 35, and Steve McQueen, 43, pulled into town last night with him behind the wheel of a rented truck. This morning he phones a justice of the peace who's out playing golf. When the pro shop relays the message, he trades in his clubs for a bible and marries the high-profile couple in a park under a spreading cottonwood tree. MacGraw wears a long-sleeved tee shirt and madras skirt, identical to the outfit of the groom's teenage daughter Terry, one of three witnesses besides her brother Chad and MacGraw's infant son Josh. The budding starlet of *Love Story* and *Goodbye, Columbus* fame soon shelves her career to raise the kids, while hard-charging McQueen stays hot with *Papillion* and *The Towering Inferno*.

His second of three, her third, lasts five years

July 13 (1925)
Lillian Bounds & Walt Disney

The struggling filmmaker never appeared all that interested in women; his work came first. But **he gradually became attracted to one of his first employees**, a cartoon cel inker earning $15 a week. She took the job at Disney Bros. primarily because she could walk to work from her sister's apartment and thus save on bus fare. An attraction grew between the thin, ambitious man (already sporting a neat toothbrush mustache, which made him look older) and this compact, attractive woman with a broad smile and fashionably bobbed dark hair. Today Lillian Bounds, 26, marries Walt Disney, 23, at her brother's rural home in Lewiston, Idaho. They spend their honeymoon at Mount Rainier National Park, but the wedding night is rather a disappointment. Timorous Walt, suffering from a toothache, spends the night helping a porter at the hotel shine shoes 'til morning, when he finds a dentist to pull his bad tooth.

> His first, her first, lasts 41 years until his death

> *"I have never known a man like him. I feel mad, serene, wonderstruck. I have arrived at the end of a long journey."* BRIDGITTE BARDOT

July 14 (1966)
Brigitte Bardot & Gunter Sachs

Even sex kittens should get the chance to strut down the aisle, oui? Early this morning, shapely French actress Brigitte Bardot, 31, ties the knot in Las Vegas with wealthy German "industrialist" (or "playboy" or "sportsman," gush the press) Gunter Sachs, 33. When he was wooing her, Sachs had a helicopter fly over her Saint-Tropez estate and shower it with hundreds of red roses. The jet-setting pair flew in unexpectedly yesterday from Paris for a post-midnight service timed to coincide with Bastille Day. The judge who performs the short ceremony at the home of a lawyer who made the arrangements says, **"This afternoon I sentenced a murderer to death, tonight I'm marrying Brigitte Bardot."** She wears a short purple shift dress and holds a single chrysanthemum, he sports a black mohair blazer, white flannel slacks and silk shirt, Gucci loafers and no socks. A decade removed from her star-making turn in *...And God Created Woman*, shot by her then husband Roger Vadim, Bardot still creates a stir. Her wedding makes front-page news at home, overshadowing Charles de Gaulle's participation in a parade and reportedly making the president furious.

> Her third of four, his second of three, lasts three years

July 15 (1965)

Joan Rivers & Edgar Rosenberg

She's a mouthy broad with an unmistakable New Yawk accent. He's a courtly producer with a refined, British public-school accent. Today in a Bronx courthouse, **this outwardly unlikely couple** marries with minimal ceremony. Budding comedienne Joan Rivers, 32, wearing a black dress with cream lace bought at Bloomingdale's for $26, weds Edgar Rosenberg, 40. She later recalls in her inimitable comedic style that the couple ahead of them were "Filipinos escorted by the whole Philippine Navy." Tonight she performs her usual two shows at the Bitter End in Greenwich Village. Soon, thanks to appearances on *The Tonight Show* orchestrated by her husband/manager, Joan's career—and her "Can We Talk?" persona—takes off.

Joan Rivers (center) in an early NYC performance

Her second, his first, lasts 22 years until his suicide

"His emotional reticence never bothered me, though, because our relationship was not about passion, it was about friendship, support, protection—and business. At the best times in our marriage, we were loving partners." JOAN RIVERS

"While the helicopters above and the media presence outside were not an inconvenience to us, we know that they were to the neighboring communities of Arlington and Manchester, Vt., and for that we are truly apologetic."

FOX FAMILY STATEMENT

July 16 (1988)
Janet Jones & Wayne Gretzky
Tracy Pollan & Michael J. Fox

Two of **the world's most famous Canadian bachelors** tie the knot today. In the closest thing to a Canadian royal wedding, hockey superstar Wayne Gretzky marries minor actress Janet Jones, both 27. Thousands line the streets outside St. Joseph's Basilica in Edmonton, where 650 guests witness the ecumenical service. His wedding present to her? A cream and tan Rolls-Royce Corniche. But rumors about extravagance reached such a fever pitch that the groom previously held a press conference: no, her satin dress didn't cost $40,000, though it did have 40,000 sequins; no, the champagne wasn't $3,000 a bottle, it was free. So too was the beer, courtesy of both Molson and Labatts. Meanwhile, across the border, *Family Ties* co-stars Michael J. Fox, 27, and Tracy Pollan, 28, marry in a super stealthy ceremony at a Vermont country inn. Their private security firm thwarts all invasive attempts, even ferreting out paparazzi disguised as lamas attempting to blend in with the innkeeper's pet livestock. Around 75 close friends and family members enjoy an intimate, media-free event, marred only by the whir of helicopters overhead. Next month she's pregnant (with Sam, their first of four children), and he's back filming *Family Ties* and *Back to the Future II*.

JANET JONES AND WAYNE GRETZKY

TRACY POLLAN AND MICHAEL J. FOX

July 17 (1954)
Eden Hartford & Groucho Marx

He's been tossing out one-liners about marriage for years, like "Marriage is a wonderful institution, but who wants to live in an institution?" and **"Hollywood brides keep their bouquets and throw away the grooms."** Yet today renowned funnyman Groucho Marx, 63, marries Eden Hartford, 24, in a Sun Valley, Idaho hotel suite. A justice of the peace performs the small service attended only by his seven-year-old daughter Melinda and two lodge officials. Back in L.A. his son Arthur, whose well-received bio *Life With Groucho* appears this fall, reads about the wedding in the paper and then receives a telegram: "If you've heard about this, please refund the price of the telegram. Love from both of us, Groucho." Enjoying immense popularity with his quiz show *You Bet Your Life*, Groucho met his future bride on the set of a movie, *A Girl in Every Port*, in which her sister Dee Hartford had a supporting role.

His third, her second, lasts 15 years

"*A man is only as old as the woman he feels.*" GROUCHO MARX

July 18 (1992)

Whitney Houston Bobby Brown

The whispers about eating disorders, drug abuse and sexual preference have turned into shouts, but show must go on. Today pop diva Whitney Houston, 28, and R&B bad boy Bobby Brown, 23, tie the knot in **a gazebo adorned with 8,000 roses and hundreds of orchids** aside her multi-million dollar New Jersey mansion. The bride wears a formfitting, floor-length gown of French Lyon lace with iridescent beads, white pearls and sequins, and a matching beaded skullcap. She doesn't wear heels so not to appear taller than the groom, decked out in a white suit with tails and cowl-collared shirt with a silver jewel at the throat. The ceremony climaxes with the release of seven white doves and a long, passionate kiss during which he lifts her into the air to jubilant applause from the star-studded crowd including Gloria Estefan, Patti LaBelle, Gladys Knight and Dionne Warwick. This fall Houston's career soars with the release of *The Bodyguard* and her #1 hit, "I Will Always Love You," a song that won't quite describe their subsequent stormy marriage.

Her first, his first, lasts 15 years

"*I've got a good man. He takes care of me. I don't have to be scared of anything because I know he will kick every ass... Disrespect him and you've got a problem.*" WHITNEY HOUSTON

July 19 (1966)
Mia Farrow & Frank Sinatra

The answer to that eternal question **"What were they thinking?!"** is clear: they weren't. Yet whatever the Chairman of the Board wants, he gets, and today he wants a waiflike 21-year-old who's younger than two of his three children. Frank Sinatra, 50, marries Peyton Place star Mia Farrow in a suite at the Sands Hotel in Las Vegas. She wears a simple two-piece white silk faille dress with diamond-shaped buttons. Old Sinatra pal William Goetz, a producer, and his wife serve as best man and matron of honor, respectively, at the five-minute civil ceremony. The handful of guests includes no family members but comedian Red Skelton, whose wife Georgia accidentally shot herself here last night. Off the newlyweds jet to Palm Springs for a blowout bash featuring a Who's Who of Hollywood: Hepburn and Tracy (arriving separately, of course), Dean Martin, Edward G. Robinson and more. Everyone on earth collectively shares one thought: it can't last. Everyone's right.

> His third of four, her first of two, lasts 14 months; his lawyer infamously serves her divorce papers on the set of *Rosemary's Baby*

"We understood ourselves and each other so little, and whatever comprehension we may have had, we could not convey. Blindly we sought completion in each other." MIA FARROW

July 20 (1991)
Chelsea Noble & Kirk Cameron

Fairy tales can come true. Not for the 1,000 screaming, and some **undoubtedly heart-broken fans** jammed outside Our Lady Help of Christians Catholic church in suburban Buffalo, N.Y. But certainly for the newlyweds, impossibly cute Kirk Cameron, 20, and model-turned-actress Chelsea Noble, 26, whose scripted romance on *Growing Pains* blossomed into the real deal. Noble wears a white gown with a pearl-embroidered bodice and floor-length veil. The religious, family-oriented couple reads self-composed vows before a small crowd of family but no TV costars. Trying to capture the moment, an inventive photographer dresses as a priest and another tries hiding in the church's confessional. Though it's a sacred day, the couple has dabbled in rather impish behavior previously. Before their first on-screen kiss, for example, Kirk coated his lips with an ointment used to numb pain, and Chelsea recalled that within 30 seconds her whole mouth went numb: "And I had this dialogue scene to do!"

July 21 (2010)
Miranda Kerr & Orlando Bloom

Even by today's over-the-top celebrity hype standards, the coverage has been excessive. Last April *People* trumpeted, "Orlando Bloom Meets Miranda Kerr's Parents," followed in June by **"Orlando Bloom and Miranda Kerr Are Engaged!"** Alas, tomorrow all the media can report is that the couple secretly married today in an undisclosed place. Bloom, 33, the red-hot *Lord of the Rings* and *Pirates of the Caribbean* star, and Australian model Kerr, 27, met backstage at a Victoria's Secret lingerie show in New York in 2006. Next month the breathless coverage grinds on as *People* reports, "Miranda Kerr: Yes, I'm Pregnant!" and in January an Australian paper bestows a one word hyphenate with "It's a baby boy for KerrBloom." Among the first to hear the news are the residents of her hometown of Gunnedah. "I was walking through town to pick up the papers," says the mayor, "and discovered Miranda's terrific news had already, very quickly, made it into the local coffee shops."

July 22 (1991)
Sheryl Berkoff & Rob Lowe

He's still the handsome Brat Packer and all, but let's face it: sex tapes shot with underage girls don't exactly help one's career. With the tabloids circling, Rob Lowe signs up for the movie *Bad Influence*, and ironically meets someone who has the exact opposite effect. His makeup artist, Sheryl Berkoff, had been a blind date years ago, but **this time sparks really fly**. Then he heads off to rehab to address a longtime drinking problem. Today, telling family and friends that they're attending a wedding-themed charity luncheon, Lowe, 27, and Berkoff, 30, marry at the magnificent home of friends in Hancock Park, a chichi L.A. neighborhood. Their under-the-radar plan works to perfection as zero media intrude upon the event and its small, select crowd including Emilio Estevez, Garry Marshall and Steve Tisch. For their first dance, the newlyweds take the floor to John Barry's theme from *Out of Africa*.

'I feel like, together, we will blaze a new trail of love, hope, and possibility.

ROB LOWE

July 23 (1986)
Sarah Ferguson & Prince Andrew

SARAH FERGUSON SMOOCHING WITH SIR ELTON JOHN

Though it can't hold a candle to his older brother Charles's lavish nuptials five years ago (July 29), the royal marriage must go on. So today **another commoner, albeit with some blueblood ancestry, marries into the royal family**. Sarah Ferguson and Prince Andrew, both 26, wed at the flower-bedecked (some 30,000 flowers) Westminster Abbey before a crowd of 2,000 that includes First Lady Nancy Reagan and British Prime Minister Margaret Thatcher. The bride wears a puff-sleeve, scooped-neck ivory duchess satin gown by London couturier Lindka Cierach, with a bead-embellished A (for Andrew) at the bottom of her 17-foot train that flows from beneath a large, dramatic bow on the gown's back. The groom wears ceremonial naval attire. Afterwards the Duke and Duchess of York ride past cheering crowds to Buckingham Palace in the open-top, horse-drawn 1902 State Landau especially built for King Edward VII's coronation.

His first, her first, lasts ten years

"Since I met Mariana, there is more to my life than tennis, tennis, tennis. I can take a loss better than I could before, because now I have someone to go home to and the defeat is not so lonely."

BJORN BORG

July 24 (1980)
Mariana Simionescu & Bjorn Borg

Raise a salute with, what else, tennis racquets? Fifty members of the Romanian Tennis Federation hold racquets and red and white gladiolas aloft as the world's #1 male star takes a bride. A civil ceremony at a Bucharest district town hall weds Bjorn Borg, 24, and Mariana Simonescu, 23, the latter **a picture of a medieval princess** in a glittering, floor length Ted Tinling gown bedecked with jewels, silk embroidery and a sweeping train (at a reported cost of $8,000, four times the average Romanian's annual salary). The gentlemanly blond Swedish giant, who last month won a record fifth straight Wimbledon title, wears a navy blazer and light slacks. Then it's off to a 17th century lakeside monastery for a religious service to fulfill the bride's orthodox faith. The medieval architecture and spires make for an inspiring, ancient backdrop, but just beyond its gates a teeming mass of photographers and reporters provide a modern counterpoint and reality check.

His first of three, lasts three years

July 25 (2008)

Amy McCarthy & Dan Hinote

There's **quite the turnout** for this wedding at the Keystone Ranch in Colorado: Fidel Castro, Marilyn Monroe, Elvis Presley, Groucho Marx and more. The celebs are actually guests dressed in '50s costumes per the unusual request of the bride and groom. (Fidel is none other than Jim Carrey, who's dating the bride's big sister Jenny.) Ex-Playboy playmate Amy McCarthy, 32, and St. Louis Blues right winger Dan Hinote, 31, wed under threatening skies. One NHL teammate gamely dons a blond wig and *Seven Year Itch* white dress and heels to portray Marilyn. After the cake cutting, the bride and groom get into the act by changing from their traditional wedding garb into '50s characters from *Grease*. They got chills, they're multiplying...

July 26 (1995)
Lynn Frankel & Mick Fleetwood

That was then, this is now. Nearly 20 years ago, at the height of their considerable musical powers, Fleetwood Mac posed in bed for a memorable *Rolling Stone* cover as co-founder Mick Fleetwood recalled the hedonistic scene: **"Tales of flamboyant infidelity and dementia** circulated like polluted air. So rampant were the rumors that we sometimes heard them fifth-hand." Today, at NYC's Tavern on the Green, Fleetwood, 48, marries longtime girlfriend Lynn Frankel. The wedding had originally been slated for last April in Laughlin, Nevada, aboard a paddlewheel boat with thousands of Harley-Davidson bikers cheering them on, but got postponed after the bride's father died of a heart attack the night before. Today, the couple hosts a post nuptial reception at club Downtime where the star-studded, hearty partying crowd includes Pat Benatar (Feb. 20) and REO Speedwagon, both part of Fleetwood Mac's current *Can't Stop Rockin'* tour, plus the Beastie Boys and Ione Skye.

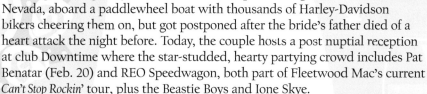

His third, her first

"Some love is seemingly just not put together in the stars, but I believe rare moments do occur where stars align just so, and two magnetisms combine into once conscious and unconscious force." **NANCY WILSON**

July 27 (1986)
Nancy Wilson & Cameron Crowe

Rock into film. Nancy Wilson of the hard rockin', singin' sister act Heart made a cameo appearance in *Fast Times at Ridgemont High* as **"beautiful girl in car."** Wearing a pink sweater, she pulled up alongside Judge Reinhold in a convertible and flashed a flirtatious smile. But she really only had eyes for screenwriter Cameron Crowe, whom she'd met on the set of the late-night ABC sketch comedy show *Fridays*. The rock goddess, having just ended a longtime relationship with ex-Heart drummer Michael Derosier, and the budding writer clicked. Today Wilson, 32, and Crowe, 29, marry at her sister Ann's house in their hometown of Seattle. Light comes via hundreds of white candles, scattered about amidst 600 dusty rose (her favorite color) roses. With love comes a musical rejuvenation too, as Heart scores its only #1 singles just before ("These Dreams") and after ("Alone") the wedding.

Her first, his first, lasts 22 years

July 28 (1973)
Farrah Fawcett & Lee Majors

He's a major TV star, she's a new girl in town described in the papers as "a blonde frequently seen in toothpaste and cigar advertisements." Their first date, arranged by his agent, didn't go so well, but the next day he sent her a baker's dozen of yellow roses, the state flower of her native Texas. Today, **on the fifth anniversary of that awkward first date**, Lee Majors, 34, and Farrah Fawcett, 26, marry in a garden ceremony at the Bel-Air Hotel. Noted costume designer Theodora Van Runkle (currently working on *The Godfather: Part II*) creates original outfits for the entire bridal party, which includes Majors' father, the best man, and her sister, the matron of honor. He casts his wife in occasional episodes of his popular series, *The Six Million Dollar Man*, but their world changes overnight several years later when the drop dead gorgeous blonde poses for a poster. It sells millions of copies, kicking her career into overdrive and leading to her co-starring role in ABC's jiggly hit *Charlie's Angels*. Soon Farrah's career and fame far eclipses that of her hubby.

Her first, his second of four, lasts nine years

"The stuff of which fairy tales are made."

ARCHBISHOP OF CANTERBURY
ROBERT RUNCIE

July 29 (1981)
Prince Charles & Lady Diana Spencer

A year ago she was simply another teacher, albeit a strikingly beautiful one, working in a kindergarten in London. Today all eyes throughout the world focus on 20-year-old Diana Spencer and her 32-year-old suitor, Prince Charles. Several million spectators line the route, policed by 4,000 cops and 2,200 soldiers, as they pass in a glass coach. Inside St. Paul's Cathedral 3,500 guests witness the historic ceremony as **an estimated 750 million people watch live** TV coverage. Her meringue silk wedding dress with puffed sleeves, frilly neckline and 25-foot train features hand embroidery, lace, sequins and 10,000 pearls. Prince Charles, heir to the British throne, wears his full dress naval commander's uniform. Instantly crowned the "people's princess," Diana offers a smiling, approachable counterpart to her stuffy, aloof husband. The marriage produces Princes William and Harry, but dissolves in a glare of publicity and recriminations of adultery. Her fairy-tale ride ends infamously in a 1997 Parisian car crash, and her funeral again commands an international audience.

July 30 (1976)
Natalie Cole & Marvin Yancy

These are the good times for Natalie Cole, daughter of
the late, silky smooth-toned balladeer Nat King Cole.
Her debut album, *Inseparable*, has produced two hit songs,
the title track and "This Will Be." Last February she won
two Grammy awards, including the prestigious Best New
Artist. Today, Cole, 26, and co-producer/songwriter Marvin Yancy,
25, marry in Chicago, where Yancy does double duty as an ordained
Baptist minister. They **wed while driving down Lakeshore Drive in the
backseat of a white Cadillac Eldorado**, a minister friend performing
the ceremony while his wife drives. The couple keeps it a secret until
next Valentine's Day, when they announce not only that they're married,
but that she's pregnant. Son Robbie is born the following October.

> Her first of three, his first, lasts four years

July 31 (2010)
Chelsea Clinton & Marc Mezvinsky

It's not every day that you see a former U.S. President
precariously hoisted on a chair above a surging crowd.
Or dancing with his only daughter to the strains of "The Way You
Look Tonight." But that's the scene as Chelsea Clinton, 30, and Marc
Mezvinsky, 32, marry at the magnificent Astor Courts in Rhinebeck,
N.Y. at a sunset interfaith service officiated by a rabbi and Methodist
reverend. Clutching a bouquet of gardenias, she walks down the aisle
in a strapless ivory Vera Wang gown featuring a silk tulle diagonally-
draped bodice, raw-edged swirling silk organza ball skirt and train. He
wears a custom-made wool and mohair tuxedo by Burberry, while the
dozen (!) bridesmaids wear strapless lavender chiffon gowns. At the
reception for 400 guests in a huge tent, Chelsea slips into a Grecian-
inspired Vera Wang gown with a black ribbon belt at the waist and
crisscross straps in back, before taking to the dance floor for **a tango to
Etta James' classic, "At Last."** Guests leave with gift bags that include
a bottle of Clinton Vineyards wine, chocolates, pastries and lip balm.

August

Gloria Hatrick McLean & Jimmy Stewart

August 9, 1949

August 1 (1986)
Tatum O'Neal John McEnroe

Some enchanted Hollywood evening, **two strangers' eyes meet across a crowded room**. And somehow they know, they know even then... Amidst movie stars galore, the youngest winner to date of an Oscar Award (at age 10 for *Paper Moon*) and the infamously temperamental bad boy of tennis chat away in a quiet corner, and steal an occasional kiss. Several tabloid-chronicled years (and one baby, Kevin, last May) later, John McEnroe, 27, and Tatum O'Neal, 22, marry today at St. Dominic's Church in Oyster Bay, N.Y. Tennis player Peter Rennert serves as best man, and McEnroe's doubles partner Peter Fleming ushers alongside the groom's brothers Mark and Patrick. Conspicuously absent is her father Ryan O'Neal. The honeymoon's delayed as McEnroe re-hits the tennis circuit after a six-month sabbatical. At Christmastime they honeymoon in Hawaii, where on New Year's Day she announces she's pregnant again.

> His first of two, her first, lasts eight years

"I think we were a good match. We were both shy, but we each also put up a tough front – although as I got to know her, I realized her toughness was more real than mine. She had been through a lot more than I had." JOHN McENROE

August 2 (1978)
Pegi Morton & Neil Young

One of the most influential, enigmatic singer/songwriters of his time settles down today, **far from the madding rock'n'roll crowd**. He's ended his seven-year, live-in arrangement with actress Carrie Snodgrass, with whom he had a son. Today at his 15,000-acre Broken Arrow ranch in Northern California, Neil Young, 32, marries Pegi Morton, 26, who'd waitressed at a nearby hangout and lived for awhile down the road in a teepee. Afterwards they enjoy a quiet honeymoon on his yacht *WN Ragland*, 101-foot schooner built in 1913. In November he releases the folk/rock album *Comes a Time*, two years in the making, and welcomes his first child with Morton, son Ben, who is later diagnosed with cerebral palsy. A daughter, Amber Jean, arrives in 1984.

"I remember thinking Pegi would always be a beautiful girl, even when she was a hundred years old." NEIL YOUNG

August 3 (2007)

Tameka Foster 𝄞 Usher

Last week tongues began a'wagging when they abruptly cancelled a ritzy Hamptons wedding for which the invitations alone cost a reported $10,000. Today, at his lawyer's office, sexy R&B star Usher Raymond, 28, quietly marries stylist Tameka Foster, 37, in a short civil ceremony. Next month the couple does it up in style with **a snazzy wedding at a luxurious, faux 16th century French chateau** set on 3,500 acres outside Atlanta. Foster, five months pregnant, wears a strapless satin gown by Vera Wang with an empire waist. Usher opts for a natty black Giorgio Armani tux with an ivory bow tie and gardenia boutonniere. The 200 guests don't include his mother, who's apparently not pleased with her son's choice. Mother knows best: the union doesn't last.

His first, her second, lasts two years

August 4 (1973)
Naomi Sims & Michael Findlay

Running with a glamorous celebrity crowd that included the likes of Salvador Dali (Jan. 30) and Andy Warhol, the barrier-breaking black model once attended a party where LSD guru Timothy Leary tried to hit on her. "She dissuaded him," recalled another guest, Michael Findlay, "in a **charming but definitive** way —with such aplomb." Today Naomi Sims, 25, the first black model to grace the cover of *Ladies' Home Journal*, marries Findlay, a noted art dealer, at NYC's Roman Catholic Church of the Blessed Sacrament. She wears a crepe and lace, mid-calf length dress by Norma Kamali. A large lace kerchief covers her hair, drawn back in her usual style and rolled into a chignon, with white lilies with specked red centers pinned over the kerchief. Her attendants include fellow model Charlene Dash and Museum of Modern Art curator Kynaston McShine. Often called the first black supermodel, the long-limbed, elegant Sims has come to epitomize the Black is Beautiful movement. But she rejects blaxploitation, turning down the title role in the movie *Cleopatra Jones* because she deemed the script racist.

"Naomi was the first. She was the great ambassador for all black people. She broke down all the social barriers." HALSTON

August 5 (1956)
Shirley Jones & Jack Cassidy

They've been getting married night after night. Onstage. Today, before the evening performance of *The Beggar's Opera*, they wed for real in a church in Cambridge, Mass. Fresh-faced Shirley Jones, 22, and suave Jack Cassidy, 29, who'd met in a touring show of *Oklahoma!*, do their usual evening performance and proceed to a reception at the Ritz Carlton. Tonight the bride lays out on a hotel bed her wedding eve outfit: see-through black lace pajamas and matching black high heels. The groom spots them and promptly puts them on, along with a shower cap. Then he goes to the door and greets her agent, who they'd ill-advisedly invited up for a nightcap. **A strange honeymoon, that**. As their family (stepson David, from his first marriage, plus Shaun, Patrick and Ryan) grows, he grows bitter. His career stalls while hers heats up as the matriarch of *The Partridge Family*, co-starring heartthrob David. Cassidy turns down a role based on him: vain, shallow newsman Ted Baxter on *The Mary Tyler Moore Show*.

Her first of two, his second, lasts 18 years

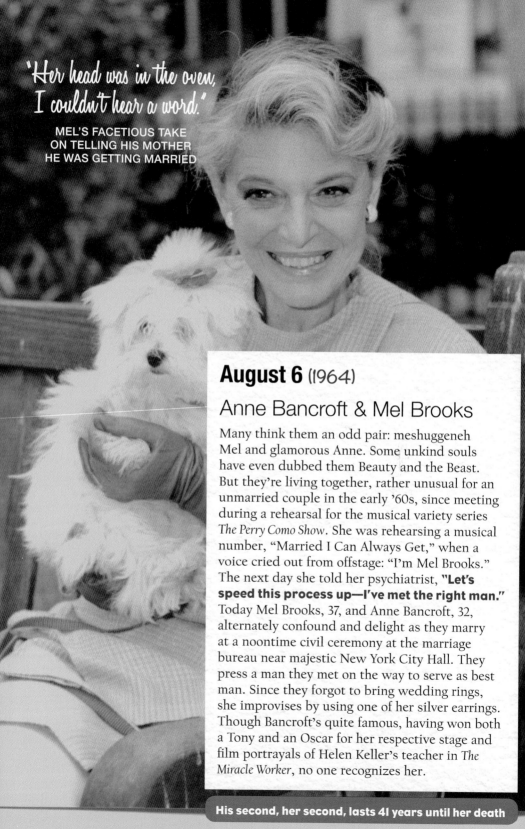

"*Her head was in the oven, I couldn't hear a word.*"

MEL'S FACETIOUS TAKE ON TELLING HIS MOTHER HE WAS GETTING MARRIED

August 6 (1964)

Anne Bancroft & Mel Brooks

Many think them an odd pair: meshuggeneh Mel and glamorous Anne. Some unkind souls have even dubbed them Beauty and the Beast. But they're living together, rather unusual for an unmarried couple in the early '60s, since meeting during a rehearsal for the musical variety series *The Perry Como Show*. She was rehearsing a musical number, "Married I Can Always Get," when a voice cried out from offstage: "I'm Mel Brooks." The next day she told her psychiatrist, **"Let's speed this process up—I've met the right man."** Today Mel Brooks, 37, and Anne Bancroft, 32, alternately confound and delight as they marry at a noontime civil ceremony at the marriage bureau near majestic New York City Hall. They press a man they met on the way to serve as best man. Since they forgot to bring wedding rings, she improvises by using one of her silver earrings. Though Bancroft's quite famous, having won both a Tony and an Oscar for her respective stage and film portrayals of Helen Keller's teacher in *The Miracle Worker*, no one recognizes her.

His second, her second, lasts 41 years until her death

Everlasting Love

1934   **Bob Hope & Delores DeFina** (69 years until his death)

1944   Charlton Heston & Lydia Clarke (64 years until his death)

1948   **Ruby Dee & Ossie Davis**

1954   **Kirk Douglas & Anne Buydens**

1958   **Paul Newman & Joanne Woodward** (50 years until his death)

1961   Paula Prentiss & Richard Benjamin

1961   **Martin Sheen & Janet Templeton**

1962   Olympia Dukakis & Louis Zorich

1964   **Mel Brooks & Anne Bancroft**

1969   Paul McCarthy & Linda Eastman (29 years until her death)

1975   **Ron Howard & Cheryl Alley**

1975   **Patrick Swayze & Lisa Niemi** (33 years until his death)

1977   **Jeff Bridges & Susan Geston**

Patrick Swayze
& Lisa Niemi

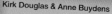

Kirk Douglas & Anne Buydens

August 7 (1974)

Faye Dunaway & Peter Wolf

Sleek, cool and always seemingly in total control, Faye Dunaway finds herself today **in Beverly Hills, surrounded by wolves**— but not to worry. She's in the chambers of Judge Leonard Wolf alongside her fiancé, Peter Wolf, 28, lead singer of the Boston-based, hard rockin' J. Geils Band. Dunaway, 33, wears a pale peach dress of jersey and chiffon, he sports a yellow linen suit, black silk shirt and scarf. Only her makeup man and hairdresser attend, and afterwards the foursome enjoys lunch. It's an unlikely union, the screen goddess with an offstage reputation as a demanding diva, and the bohemian musician with his shades, close-cropped beard and beret. After a bit of a dry spell, Dunaway has come back strong with *Chinatown*, gracing magazine covers, drawing rave reviews and an Oscar nomination. His band's on the rise, too, with its biggest hit to date coming this fall: "Must Have Got Lost."

Her first of two, his first, lasts five years

"We were there for each other, without an effort. We were two warriors standing shoulder to shoulder... There was no ego clash between us, though we were both always ambitious." **FAYE DUNAWAY**

August 8 (1998)

Christine Amanpour & Jamie Rubin

They **met on the job** last year in Bosnia, where she was covering a visit by Secretary of State Madeleine Albright. After a 15-month trans-Atlantic romance, CNN's chief international correspondent Christine Amanpour, 40, marries assistant secretary of state for public affairs Jamie Rubin, 38, in back-to-back ceremonies in Bracciano, Italy: a Roman Catholic service at the medieval Church of Santo Stefano; and a Jewish ceremony at Castello Orsini-Odescalchi. The wedding, attended by notable guests including John F. Kennedy, Jr. and diplomat Richard Holbrooke, was nearly derailed by yesterday's terrorist bombings of the U.S. embassies in Tanzania and Kenya. Fortunately both the reporter and the official manage to avoid having to cover and/or manage the response. "Can you imagine," Amanpour says later, "a government official and a journalist on the eve of their wedding having to deal with Osama bin Laden?"

August 9 (1949)
Gloria Hatrick McLean & Jimmy Stewart

Relieved that his movie star son won't be marrying an actress, Alex Stewart still had some reservations about his future daughter-in-law. Yes, she was independently wealthy: her family owned the Hope Diamond, but she was divorced and a smoker. And when he asked if she was a regular churchgoer, she replied, **"Only for funerals and weddings."** Nevertheless all goes well today at the Brentwood Presbyterian Church as affable everyman Jimmy Stewart, 41, marries socialite Gloria Hatrick McLean, 31. She wears a cocktail-length gray satin dress and carries white orchids and a white prayer book. The nervous groom's lines are barely audible, but he does firmly slip a plain gold band inscribed "Gloria and Jimmy 8-9-49" onto her finger. Many of the 50 guests, including Gary Cooper, Henry Fonda, David Niven, Ann Sothern and restaurateurs Dave Chasen and Mike Romanoff, cause quite a stir outside amidst a crowd of some 500 well-wishers.

> His first, her second, lasts 45 years until her death

"The crowd began gathering in the mid-afternoon... Many came from the nearby beach in bathing suits and one girl watched astride a horse." REPORTER BOB THOMAS

August 10 (1962)
Tarita Teriipia & Marlon Brando

There was **trouble in paradise** as tabloids worked overtime to chronicle the misbegotten 1960 remake of *Mutiny on the Bounty*—star Marlon Brando's off-set shenanigans and gluttony, a revolving door of writers and directors, massive delays and budget overruns. But there was also **love in paradise** in the form of 20-year-old Tahitian beauty Tarita Teriipia. A waitress who won both a small film role and the attentions of its over-the-top headliner, she'd never even heard of Brando—and he loved her naiveté. Today Brando, 38, marries Teriipia shortly after his quickie divorce from Mexican actress Movita Castenada, who had ironically played a small role in the 1935 version of *Mutiny* that featured Clark Gable. Brando's love affair extends to all of Tahiti, where he buys a small island and builds a house. Next year their son Simon is born, followed by a daughter, Cheyenne, in 1970. Brando later ill advisedly pours millions into building a hotel on his heavenly island retreat.

> His third, lasts ten years

August 11 (1978)

Charo & Kjell Rasten

She's carved out quite a career for herself as a bubbly, buxom Latina. Her maiden name is María Rosario Pilar Martínez Molina Baeza, but the world knows her simply as Charo—with her trademark, hip-shaking catchphrase **"Cuchi-cuchi!"** In an outdoor ceremony at a private home in Lake Tahoe, Charo, 37, marries producer Kjell Rasten, before 30 friends and family members. While many actresses often shave a few years off their age, Charo went the other direction. She added ten years to appear older than 15 when she married 66-year-old bandleader Xavier Cugat in 1966. A trained and respected classical guitarist, Charo has made her name and garnered much fame as a voluptuous performer who appears frequently on talk shows (*The Tonight Show*), game shows (*Hollywood Squares*) and series (*The Love Boat*).

"Around the world I am known as a great musician. But, in America I am known as the cuchi-cuchi girl. That's okay because cuchi-cuchi has taken me all the way to the bank." CHARO

August 12 (1988)
Cassandra Delaney & John Denver

Tonight's truly **a Rocky Mountain high for this down-home country boy** as John Denver, 44, marries Cassandra Delaney, 27, at his mountaintop Aspen estate. They've been an item ever since meeting in Australia two years ago when the fledgling actress/singer was performing in a hotel bar where the homespun troubadour ("Sunshine on My Shoulders," "Annie's Song") was staying. "She was a breath of spring air," says Denver. "Bright, funny, irreverent." He called her his protégé and took her along on tour, even inviting her to sing with him sometimes. Almost immediately after the wedding Denver jets off, not on a honeymoon but to the Soviet Union, solo, where he reportedly offers its space program $10 million to include him on a future launch to the Mir Space Station. (It never happens.) Soon, back at home wonderful news dawns: Cassandra is pregnant, an especially happy development since he'd been undergoing painful fertility treatments to treat his impotence. Next year he helps a midwife deliver daughter Jesse Belle, but the marital bliss doesn't last.

His second, her first, lasts six years

"When I first met John, I really did think I was the luckiest girl in the world... I was falling in love with a spiritual man who was on the same path as me." **CASSANDRA DELANEY**

August 13 (1937)
Gypsy Rose Lee & Bob Mizzy

You might think that being **a stripper and a wife** would be an incompatible combination. You would be right. Nevertheless, noted naughty Gypsy Rose Lee, 23, gives it a whirl (rather than a twirl) by marrying businessman Bob Mizzy, 25, on a chartered water taxi off the coast of Long Beach, California. It's at the behest of screen mogul Darryl Zanuck, who feels the burlesque queen needs to tone down her image to appeal to moviegoers and appease the powerful censoring Hays Office. Questions about the legality of their sea marriage surface, so the couple reties the knot in a more conventional ceremony a week later. Not only is Gypsy not cut out for the role of housewife, but her overbearing stage mother Rose proves to be the quintessential mother-in-law from hell. Gypsy's movie career is a moderate success, and she even writes a murder mystery that's made into *Lady of Burlesque* starring Barbara Stanwyck (Aug. 26), but this stormy marriage ends after three years.

"A gal has to know something besides wearing a jewel-studded G-string if she's going to hold her husband." **GYPSY ROSE LEE**

August 14 (1993)
Geraldine Oliver & William Masters

Half a century is **a long time to carry a torch**—but he was busy most of that time with the sex business. Renowned sex researcher William Masters, 77, marries his former childhood sweetheart, Geraldine Oliver, 76, in a church near Lake Placid, N.Y. After he plants a chaste peck on his bride's lips, the minister admonishes him: "C'mon, Bill, you can do better than that!" After ending his 21-year marriage to famed co-researcher Virginia Johnson, Masters reconnected with the love of his life after her husband died. He learned that, more than 50 years ago, she'd never received the roses he'd left for her during a brief hospitalization. Each figured the other had lost interest, and went their separate ways—until now.

His third, her third

"[Sex] goes on until we die. But what's romantic to me is to sit across the breakfast table and look at her— she's a beautiful woman." **DR. WILLIAM MASTERS**

August 15 (2009)
Alyssa Milano & David Bugliari

Once charmed, now hitched, actress Alyssa Milano ties the knot today with agent David Bugliari, 24, at his family's estate in New Jersey. The bride, 31, wears an ivory organza and tulle gown by Vera Wang, a headpiece by Maria Elena, and holds a bouquet of lilies of the valley. They stroll down a grassy aisle strewn with cream-colored rose petals to the tune of John Lennon's "Imagine," and exchange vows under a wrought-iron gazebo decorated with calla lilies, roses and willow.

An Episcopalian minister performs the service that includes a reading by actor Bradley Cooper. Their rustic theme continues with a reception in a tent with wood flooring and wrought-iron chandeliers, with hay bales doubling as cocktail tables and wooden farmhouse tables for the family-style dinner. Familiar for TV roles in *Who's the Boss?*, *Melrose Place* and *Charmed*, Milano has previously been linked to a host of high-profile boyfriends including Scott Wolf, Corey Haim and Justin Timberlake.

August 16 (2008)
Ellen DeGeneres & Portia de Rossi

One of entertainment's most outspoken, visible lesbians, whose talk show draws millions of viewers every day, pulls the curtain closed tonight. In a private, intimate affair at her Beverly Hills estate, Ellen DeGeneres marries Portia (yes, at 15 she exchanged her birth name of Amanda for the name of Shakespeare's heroine in *The Merchant of Venice*) de Rossi in front of 20 guests including their mothers. DeGeneres, 50, wears a white vest, blouse and slacks designed by Zac Posen, while de Rossi, 35, wears a pink and white sleeveless v-neck, open-backed floor-length gown also by Posen. The couple **met at a photo shoot** a few years ago when the closeted de Rossi, appearing in *Ally McBeal*, couldn't admit to falling in love with the woman who courageously came out in real life and on her sitcom *Ellen* in 1997. Earlier this year the now out actress showed off a three-carat, pink pavé diamond that DeGeneres had given her in anticipation of their big day.

"Anybody who's married knows there is a difference. It feels like you're home. There's an anchor, there's a safety. I'm going to be with her until the day I die." ELLEN DeGENERES

August 17 (1964)
Linda Emery & Bruce Lee

Born into different worlds, they met on campus and fell in love after she'd tagged along with a friend taking the Mandarin language course he taught. On their first date they went up in Seattle's famed Space Needle. Today the blue-eyed, reddish brown-haired coed and the handsome, intense Asian American boy marry in the chapel at the University of Washington. It's still a few years before **his legend will catch fire** and he'll catapult into renowned martial arts master Bruce Lee. Linda Emery, 19, wears a sleeveless, long white dress with a jeweled neckline while Lee, 23, wears a conventional business suit. Within a year they've relocated to L.A., where he catches the eye of Hollywood producers who cast him as Kato in a rock 'em, sock 'em ABC adventure, *The Green Hornet*. The show fades but Lee leaps into a run of low-budget kung fu flicks like *Fists of Fury* and *Return of the Dragon* that cement his iconic status.

August 18 (1932)

Bette Davis & Harmon "Ham" Nelson

Her career is heating up, but it's nothing compared to today's blazing desert heat. As the thermometer tops 100 degrees in the shade, starlet Bette Davis, 23, marries bandleader Harmon Nelson, 25, before a Methodist minister on an Indian reservation in Yuma, Arizona. "I wore a two-piece beige street dress that resembled the sands of the Arizona desert after the rain it never gets, brown accessories, and two limp gardenias," recalled Davis. The small, sweat-soaked wedding party, which motored in last night from L.A. (to avoid California's mandatory six-week waiting period), includes her stage mother Ruth, sister Bobby, and two poodles. Tonight the traditional bride delights in losing her virginity, recalling, **"I was finally released from my maddening curiosity about physical sex."** But her skyrocketing career, which earns her $1,000 a week, imperils the marriage to her $100-a- week, trumpet-playing hubby.

Her first of four, his first of two, lasts five years

'If only Mother had been wise enough to suggest we have an affair first—but that was too much to expect. She came from another time. I wasn't that smart myself, and Ham had too much respect for me to suggest it.' **BETTE DAVIS**

August 19 (1993)
Kim Basinger & Alec Baldwin

Their off-screen shenanigans drew gossipy headlines two years ago when they co-starred in Neil Simon's *The Marrying Man*. But to throw off reporters, they kept their impending nuptials a secret by faxing out invitations a couple days ago for a whale-watching cruise and pie-eating contest. At sunset on an East Hampton, Long Island beach, inside **a circle of flickering torches,** Alec Baldwin, 35, marries Kim Basinger, 39. She wears a long white gown by designer John Hayles, while he sports a dinner jacket. His younger brothers Daniel, William and Stephen serve as groomsmen. The short ceremony ends with the release of thousands of pink, red and white rose petals, and one guest jokes that the couple's kiss lasted longer than the service. The hundred or so guests, including Christie Brinkley, Billy Joel, Paul Newman and Chynna Phillips (Billy Baldwin's girlfriend and later wife), enjoy dinner under a tent aside the beachfront mansion of fashion designer Josephine Chaus, and a gala fireworks display.

His first of two, her second, lasts nine years

"In marriage, you should never just trundle along – that's when problems start. Remember to go out for dinner if you haven't seen each other all week, and make regular dates." EMMA THOMPSON

August 20 (1989)
Emma Thompson & Kenneth Branagh

The family that plays together, stays together. Well, not quite, but the union of two of England's most respected actors does generate considerable heat. To deal with the naturally nosy press Kenneth Branagh, 29, and Emma Thompson, 30, take a carrot and stick approach. The carrot? A pre-event press release disclosing all the specifics: locale, the stately Cliveden House; best man, actor Brian Blessed; the menu, a breakfast of smoked salmon and roast lamb. The stick? **A full-scale private security contingent to keep away interlopers**. The bride wears a knee-length, multi-hued pastel dress with a pink geometrical lattice bodice and stylish white veil, the groom a double-breasted navy linen suit. The service includes readings of Shakespeare, Samuel Pepys and Sir Philip Sidney by Judi Dench (Feb. 5) and Richard Briers. Tomorrow it's a night of marital strife—on stage that is, as the co-stars return to their West End production of *Look Back in Anger*.

His first of two, her first of two, lasts six years

August 21 (1982)
Alison Stewart &
Paul Hewson (Bono)

In the name of love, a budding musical star marries his
longtime schoolyard sweetheart. It's a modest affair with none
of the rockstar extravagance that's been building for fast-rising
U2. At the Church of All Saints in Raheny, Dublin, a 19th century gothic
granite and limestone church built by the Guinness family, Bono, 22, marries Alison
Stewart, 21. Bandmate Adam Clayton serves as best man at the service attended
by a handful of family members and friends. The couple jets off for a Caribbean
honeymoon at Goldeneye, the island retreat of famed James Bond creator Ian
Fleming (Mar. 24), courtesy of its current owner, Island Records' honcho Chris
Blackwell. Here Bono pens "Two Hearts Beat As One," a love song that strikes a
tender tone alongside the politically strident "Sunday Bloody Sunday" and "New
Year's Day" on U2's forthcoming blockbuster album *War*.

*'I feel I hold on a lot tighter to her than she does to me,
and that slightly bothers me. She's so independent.'* **BONO**

August 22 (1992)

Trudie Styler & Gordon Sumner (Sting)

Yesterday the longtime couple married in a brief ceremony at
Camden Town Hall in London. Today it's **a grand affair at
the nearly 900-year-old St. Andrew's church** in Great
Dunford. Sting, 40, and Trudie Styler, 38, are clad head-to-
toe in Versace. She wears a hand-beaded ivory satin dress
embroidered with arabesques, with a full crinoline skirt and
short-sleeved bolero bodice, he a Beau Brummel-style tailcoat,
striped waistcoat and skintight trousers. (Both outfits are later
auctioned off with proceeds going to the Rainforest Foundation.)
The jet set international crowd of 250 includes musical and movie
royalty from Billy Connolly to Meg Ryan. At the couple's country mansion in Wiltshire,
a Jaguar XJS adorned with a giant bow is parked in the driveway courtesy of his
accountant and co-manager. The bash lasts all night long, a throwback to the good old
days of rock'n'roll, with a reunion of the sloshed Police accompanied by Peter Gabriel
and the newlyweds' six-year-old son Jake.

*'When I met her, she was beautiful. But then I figured
out she was smart, much smarter than me.'* **STING**

August 23 (1942)

Fay Wray & Robert Riskin

Even renowned gossip columnist Walter Winchell got it wrong when he suggested that the high-profile cinematic couple might elope to Las Vegas. The big event happens this afternoon, some 20 blocks **up Fifth Avenue from the Empire State Building**, scene of her greatest screen screams. Courted by that gigantic smitten ape in the blockbuster *King Kong* in 1933, Faye Wray, 34, marries screenwriter Robert Riskin, 45, in the St. Regis Hotel suite of Colonel "Wild Bill" Donovan, founder of the nascent Office Of Strategic Services (that later morphs into the C.I.A.). Only a handful of guests are present, but they're a powerhouse bunch: Mr. and Mrs. Irving Berlin, Mr. and Mrs. William Paley, and David O. Selznick. The groom's many hit scripts include *Mr. Smith Goes to Washington*, *You Can't Take It With You* and *It Happened One Night*.

Her second of three, his first, lasts 13 years until his death

August 24 (2002)
Hilary Quinlan & Bryant Gumbel

He's **an early riser by trade**, a fixture on *The Early Show*, but today his big moment arrives at sunset. Popular anchor Bryant Gumbel, 53, marries financial analyst turned model Hilary Quinlan, 42, on a Mediterranean-styled outdoor terrace of the Breakers Hotel in Palm Beach, Florida. The bride wears a tea-length, bias cut, spaghetti-strapped gown by Ralph Lauren. The groom's son Bradley serves as best man at the service that attracts a couple dozen guests including the groom's older brother, sports announcer Greg, and *Today Show* host Matt Lauer. The lavish reception menu features Kobe beef, quail eggs, Sevruga caviar, rack of lamb Dijonnaise, and ends with a three-tier lavender buttercream cake.

August 25 (1941)
Billie Holiday & Jimmy Monroe

Mama don't like her headstrong daughter's man one bit. And truth be told, he is a two-bit hustler and part-time pimp. But he's handsome and smooth, and as a smitten Billie Holiday later says, "He had taste and class." Today Holiday, 26, and Jimmy Monroe elope to Elkton, Maryland, where they marry. Then she's back singing in NYC clubs with that extraordinary, bluesy vocal style which adds a distinctive rough edge to jazz standards like "God Bless the Child." Still **the livin' still ain't easy**, and he introduces her to one of his favorite pastimes, smoking opium, which leads to her longtime addiction to heroin. One night he comes back with lipstick on his collar, prompting Holiday to pen one of her biggest hits, "Don't Explain." He takes much of her money and splits for California, where he later serves time for possession of marihuana. Hard-luck Lady Day hooks up with more losers and users, spiraling downhill until dying at 44 of cirrhosis of the liver, days after she'd been arrested for drug possession while lying on her hospital deathbed.

Her first of two, lasts 16 years

August 26 (1928)
Barbara Stanwyck & Frank Fay

Meet me in St. Louis, Barbara, meet me, we're a pair. When her beau proposed by telegram, the budding actress couldn't say no. So she **hopped a train from New York to St. Louis**, and early this afternoon Barbara Stanwyck, 21, marries Frank Fay, 31, at the home of the St. Louis recorder of deeds. Then she boards a late afternoon train back east to begin a road tour of *Burlesque*, the Broadway show that's making her a name. Her hubby's got quite the name too, Broadway's Favorite Son. Six months later they're off to Hollywood, where her timing is perfect. Stanwyck's throaty voice makes her an appealing attraction during the gold- rush shift from silent films to talkies. Her talent and affability make her one of the screen's enduring leading ladies, praised by director Frank Capra: "This chorus girl could grab your heart and tear it to pieces. She knew nothing about camera tricks. She just turned it on—and everything else on the stage stopped."

Her first of two, his third, lasts eight years

August 27 (1956)
Gloria Vanderbilt & Sidney Lumet

She's led **a life in the spotlight**. A great-granddaughter of railroad and shipping tycoon Cornelius Vanderbilt, she inherited a mind-boggling $4 million as an infant and became the center of a sensational custody battle between her mother and an aunt. She had an affair with Howard Hughes, married a Hollywood agent and a conductor 40 years her senior. Today heiress Gloria Vanderbilt, 32, weds actor turned director Sidney Lumet, 32, at the Manhattan apartment of playwright Sidney Kingsley. She wears a beige ankle-length gown of French lace with full sleeves and a low bodice, a replica of a Victorian gown from the Metropolitan Museum of Art, and a hat festooned with white orchids. Society, newspapers report, is conspicuously absent from the small service. The couple met when Lumet directed the fledgling actress in a summer stock production of *Picnic*, though she soon abandons acting for the world of fashion. His career soars with next year's *12 Angry Men*, his feature film debut.

Her third of four, his second of four, lasts seven years

August 28 (2004)
Mariska Hargitay & Peter Hermann

Pink was her mother's favorite color, so that's what the bride proudly wears. Mariska Hargitay, 40, daughter of '50s screen siren Jayne Mansfield (Jan. 13), marries *Law & Order: SUV* co-star Peter Hermann, 37, at the historic church of the Unitarian Society of Santa Barbara. She wears a pink strapless Carolina Herrera gown that contains a wealth of sentimental secrets: the groom's initials and the wedding date embroidered into the lining, and a locket containing portraits of Mansfield (who died when Hargitay was three) and the bride's grandmother tucked into the folds of the dress. The groom wears a black Dolce & Gabbana suit and a matching pink tie. She strolls down the aisle on the arm of her father Mickey Hargitay, past the 200 guests that include Jodie Foster and couple Chad Lowe and Hilary Swank (Sept. 28). A choir ends the ceremony with a rousing version of "Ain't No Mountain High Enough."

August 29 (1955)
Mamie Van Doren & Ray Anthony

With every studio in town searching for a blonde bombshell to rival the inimitable Marilyn Monroe, Universal grabbed up curvaceous Mamie Van Doren. Today she jets to Toledo, Ohio, after finishing her latest unmemorable film, to tie the knot with bandleader Ray Anthony. AP describes the scene: **"The 22-year-old bride amply filled a street length champagne chiffon dress**, horizontally from top to bottom, with a low rounded neckline. Anthony, 33, wore a dark gray business suit." A handful of guests, including several reporters and photographers, witness the two-minute ceremony in the bridal suite of the Commodore Perry Hotel. Shots of the bride's busty figure sell many newspapers tomorrow. Mamie (born Joan), who took her first name in honor of President Eisenhower's wife, was one of the so-called three M's alongside Monroe and Jayne Mansfield, the latter of whom starred in a film in which Anthony also played: *The Girl Can't Help It.*

Her second of five, his second of three, lasts six years

August 30 (2008)
Deborah Lin & James Gandolfini

They seem to have a thing for islands. They announced their engagement while on vacation in the Bahamas, and today they marry in Hawaii. While most people are kicking back over Labor Day weekend, the man who played America's favorite mobster, the serially unfaithful Tony Soprano, gets married in his bride's hometown. Tony Gandolfini, 46, weds Deborah Lin, 40, a former Miss Asia World, in a short service at the flower-bedecked Central Union Church. At the reception at a nearby resort, the bride's mother Ruth welcomes all by saying thanks in English, Hawaiian, Japanese, Chinese and Italian. **Instead of tossing the bouquet, Deborah presents it to her mother**, a former hula dancer who performs renditions of the "Hawaiian Wedding Song" and "I'll Remember You." Not to be outdone, a bunch of guys from the groom's side dons hula skirts for a version of "All You Need is Love." Far better dancing comes in the form of teams of Chinese dancers, who cavort in elaborate lion costumes between the tables as guests slip dollar bills into their open mouths for good luck.

His second, her first

August 31 (1986)
Paula Yates & Bob Geldof

Blood red, not the usual color for a wedding dress. But then again, Paula Yates is a rather unusual bride. The star-fixated Boomtown Rats groupie pursued Bob Geldof, the organizer of mega-fundraisers Band Aid and Live Aid, sealing the deal by flying to Paris to surprise him after a concert. Three years ago they welcomed the first of three flamboyantly named daughters, Fifi Trixibelle (the others? Peaches and Pixie). For today's Las Vegas wedding Yates, 26, dons a flowing, red satin ballroom dress with a gargantuan train, and adorns her cropped blonde hair with a row of red rosebuds. Geldorf, 34, opts for a formal black suit, gray top hat and—what else?—a red rose boutonniere. Dave Stewart and Annie Lennox serve as best man and maid of honor, respectively. Guests include Simon Le Bon and David Bowie. In a blaze of tabloid publicity Yates later leaves him for INXS's Brian Hutchence, with whom she has a fourth daughter named, seriously, Heavenly Hiraani Tiger Lily. Devastated by Hutchence's death in 1997, she commits suicide in 2000.

His first, her first, lasts ten years

"I came out of the gig that evening and there she was, standing in the snow with the Eiffel Tower behind her." BOB GELDOF

September

Jacqueline Bouvier & John F. Kennedy

September 12, 1953

September 1 (1946)
Julia McWilliams & Paul Child

Yesterday, en route to a rehearsal dinner, their car collided with a truck that had lost its brakes. Each suffered many cuts, requiring stitches, and bruises, and the car was totalled. But the plucky couple insisted **the wedding must go on**. No formalwear, no bridesmaids, no fuss. In the backyard of the home of an attorney in Stockton, N.J., Julia McWilliams, 34, marries Paul Child, 44. Tall and reed thin, the bride wears a short-sleeved, brown-and-white polka dot pinch-waisted suit—and sports a white bandage on the left side of her forehead. The balding groom uses a cane. The outdoor reception, at a friend's house across the Delaware River in Pennsylvania, is a similarly casual affair. Tables set on the lawn groan with hearty fare for the two dozen friends and family members. As the couple touches wineglasses, Paul cries out "Le carillon de l'amitie" (the bell of friendship). The budding French Chef's cheery cry of "bon appetit" is still more than a decade away.

"We were married in stitches—me on a cane and Julia full of glass." **PAUL CHILD**

September 2 (1997)
Sadie Frost & Jude Law

The older, more established actor of the pair ditched her husband (Spandau Ballet's Gary Kemp) when she fell for this promising, gangly blond. Sadie Frost, 32, and Jude Law, 24, marry on a barge **on the canal in Little Venice, London**. Barefoot and with no makeup, she wears a dress by John Galliano, borrowed from supermodel pal Kate Moss whose boyfriend Jonny Lee Miller serves as best man. Afterwards they celebrate in a penthouse suite at the Covent Garden Hotel in the heart of the theater district. Before the year is out he's bringing the heat with new films *Gattaca* and *Midnight in the Garden of Good and Evil*. With this trendy, tabloid-covered couple the parties stay hearty amidst his soaring career and their growing family. Frost gives birth to their third child in 2002, the same month that Moss has a daughter, but the bloom's off the rose.

His first, her second, lasts six years

"I felt a weight pressing on my heart. It was an unshakable and unwelcome premonition – like being confronted with the juicy apple in the Garden of Eden. I felt it was my fate to spend the rest of my life with Jude." **SADIE FROST**

September 3 (1988)

Kyra Sedgwick & Kevin Bacon

Footloose no more, Kevin Bacon ties the knot today with Kyra Sedgwick in a private ceremony in Connecticut before a handful of family and friends. Nary a word leaks out to the press, even afterwards when the happy couple hosts a reception for 300 guests at a Manhattan club. Bacon, 30, and Sedgwick, 23, met last year while filming the PBS movie *Lemon Sky*. Early this year the budding leading man—whose career has progressed far from an early role as another horny, slain teenager in the original *Friday the 13th*—co-starred (with Elizabeth McGovern) in *She's Having a Baby*, and next year his real-life wife does just that when their son Travis is born. A daughter follows three years later, and Bacon and Sedgwick continue to occupy that rarest of Hollywood perches—a couple that stays happily married. "We always knew that we were each other's 'one,' " says Sedgwick. "**Both of us knew this was forever**, and we were going to work it out no matter what happens."

"He is the person I count on to live and walk through life with. It's a dependency that is there and large and real and profound." **KYRA SEDGWICK**

September 4 (2004)
Shadonna Jones & Juvenile

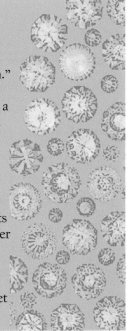

Earlier this year the rapper topped the charts with "Slow Motion." And that's just how his wedding proceeds this evening when his bride arrives more than two and a half hours late. A quick call to a local Popeyes had brought Juvenile and his backstage posse fried chicken to tide them over, but the crowd gathered for the 6 p.m. service at the Victory Fellowship Church in Metairie, Louisiana can only wait, stomachs growling. Finally the service begins for Juvenile (born Terius Grey), 29, and nurse Shadonna Jones. She wears a body-hugging white silk gown with spaghetti straps by Demitrios, set off with a diaphanous, elbow-length veil. He sports a long, formal gold suit with a pink rose boutonniere. Between her sparkling diamond necklace and tiara, and his jewel-encrusted walking stick amidst other gleaming jewelry, **even the minister comments about the overwhelming bling**. Afterwards the crowd finally gets to chow down on no, not fried chicken but filet mignon, topped off by dessert from a chocolate fondue fountain.

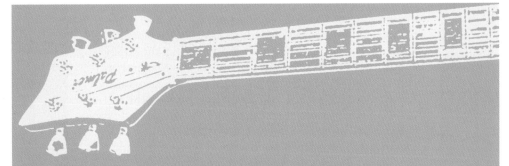

September 5 (1992)
Tracey McQuarn & Kenny "Babyface" Edmonds
Elaine Irwin & John Cougar Mellencamp

Musical marriages with video hooks: the chicken pox kayoed her first appearance in a music video for Babyface's "Whip Appeal." But the multi-faceted producer/performer/songwriter couldn't get a certain young lady out of his mind, so he called her back for the "My Kind of Girl" video—and was she ever. Today Edmonds, 34, and real estate agent Tracey McQuarn, 25, marry in Beverly Hills. Also today, just down route 65 from Edmonds' hometown of Indianapolis, heartland rocker John Cougar Mellencamp, 40, marries model Elaine Irwin, 23, in his hometown of Seymour. They too met via the video route when she appeared in his "Get a Leg Up" video, and she later appears on the cover of his album *Whenever We Want It*.

Babyface's second, Mellencamp's third

September 6 (1942)

Dorothy Dandridge & Harold Nicholas

They met during rehearsals at Harlem's famed Cotton Club, each in an act with a sibling: the tap dancing Nicholas Brothers, who achieved considerable fame, and the singing Dandridge Sisters. Dashing Harold took a shine to shy Dorothy. Moving separately to Hollywood, they shone in a lively rendition of "Chattanooga Choo Choo" in the movie *Sun Valley Serenade*. Today they marry at his mother's house. Elegant and beautiful Dorothy, 19, wears a modestly low-cut white gown and a string of pearls while Harold, 21, wears a dark suit. His brother Fayard serves as best man, her sister Vivian as matron of honor. Soon their modest home is **welcoming a Who's Who of black entertainers** including Count Basie, Sammy Davis, Jr. (Jan. 10) and Louis Armstrong. But his infidelity dooms the marriage. She achieves stardom with an Oscar nomination for *Carmen Jones*, the first in a leading category for a black actor, but her life spirals downward and ends tragically at age 42.

Her first of two, his first of three, lasts nine years

September 7 (1943)

Rita Hayworth & Orson Welles

Is sawing a girl in half the fastest way to her heart? Last month *Citizen Kane* wunderkind Orson Welles, 28, opened a carnival-like live magic show to benefit World War II servicemen with an act that included him sawing Rita Hayworth in half. Today **the master showman wows the world by marrying the glamorous, red-haired beauty**. With traces of makeup still visible under her ears, Hayworth, 24, hurries to Santa Monica City Hall from the Columbia soundstage where she's filming the musical *Cover Girl* opposite Gene Kelly. She wears a beige suit with a ruffled white blouse, oversized hat and veil, he sports a double-breasted, wide pinstripe suit, pink shirt and bow tie. Actor Joseph Cotten serves as best man. Then she's back to work, and he's back to the show where he's now sawing Marlene Dietrich in half nightly. Gossip columnists jeer, dubbing the couple Beauty and the Brain, and lambaste him for stealing the gal previously linked romantically with hunky actor Victor Mature, who's off serving in the Coast Guard.

"Letters passed between [Hayworth and Mature], but what are letters? Letters cannot kiss, they cannot go dancing at nightclubs or for moonlight drives along the shore...The lad in the service, the girl who's left behind, and the other lad who's also been left behind. What should the girl do?" *THE AMERICAN WEEKLY*

September 8 (1926)

Greta Garbo & John Gilbert
Eleanor Boardman & King Vidor

Greta Garbo
and John Gilbert in
Flesh and the Devil

Still reverberating from the sudden death two weeks ago of heartthrob Rudolph Valentino (May 13), **a leading Hollywood couple (or two?) impulsively decides to tie the knot.** Noted director King Vidor, 32, and actress Eleanor Boardman, 28, marry at the Beverly Hills mansion of moviedom doyenne Marion Davies, decorated for the occasion with roses, dahlias and lilies of the valley. The small but starry crowd includes hostess/maid of honor Davies, best man Irving Thalberg (Sept. 29), Samuel Goldwyn, William Haines, Louella Parsons, William Randolph Hearst and John Gilbert, 27, silent film's most dashing and desired lover. But the planned double wedding between him and Swedish screen goddess Greta Garbo, 20, never materializes, as she doesn't show. Earlier today the two, who'd met less than a month ago, filmed torrid love scenes for *Flesh and the Devil*. Their on-screen chemistry turned into off-screen romance that, despite endless rumors, never ended at the altar. Never to marry, the elusive Garbo lived up to her famous line in *Grand Hotel*: "I vant to be alone."

"When they got into that first love scene... Well, nobody else was even there. Those two were alone in a world of their own. It seemed like an intrusion to yell, 'Cut!'"

CLARENCE BROWN, DIRECTOR OF *FLESH AND THE DEVIL*

September 9 (2012)

Blake Lively & Ryan Reynolds

On television she may be gossipy, but in real life her lips are sealed—at least when it comes to **top secret wedding plans**. To ensure that attendees also won't blab (or take photos, either), cell phones are confiscated before the sunset service. Blake Lively, 25, and Ryan Reynolds (*People*'s 2010 Sexiest Man Alive), 35, who met on the set of *Green Lantern*, marry at Boone Hall Plantation in Mount Pleasant, S.C. She walks down a pine needle-strewn aisle in a Marchesa gown by Georgina Chapman, with a hand-draped silk tulle bodice with crystal and rose gold embroidery. He wears a Burberry tuxedo with custom leather suspenders. A children's choir from a nearby church whose parents, like all guests, had to sign non-disclosure agreements, serenade the couple with Frankie Valli and the Four Seasons' "Can't Take My Eyes Off You." Lively's pal Martha Stewart helped orchestrate the events which kicked off with an antebellum, carnival-themed cocktail hour in a room decorated with parasols and balloons.

September 10 (1978)
Joan Lunden & Michael Krauss

Lovers by night, competitors by day. Budding *Good Morning America* reporter Joan Lunden, 27, and *Today* show producer Michael Krauss, 39, tie the knot today. It's the first of a two-part, cross-country affair, a ceremony in Detroit where the groom grew up. Several days later California native Lunden gets her turn at a celebration in Sacramento. Then it's back to work in New York and home life at a cottage in nearby Westchester County. Krauss soon leaves *Today* to begin shepherding his wife's career through syndicated and cable shows alongside her signature ABC morning perch that showcases her friendly, fresh-scrubbed appeal. Her wholesomeness brings fame and fortune with multi-million dollar contracts from companies like Beech-Nut and Vaseline, as viewers eagerly follow her three pregnancies that produce daughters Jamie, Lindsay and Sarah.

> Her first of two, his first, lasts 14 years

September 11 (1960)
Nancy Sinatra & Tommy Sands

What do you call the daughter of the Chairman of the Board? Today you **can call her a bride** as Nancy Sinatra, 20, weds crooner Tommy Sands, 23, at the Sands Hotel in Las Vegas where they'd first met last year when he was headlining. She wears a white street-length dress designed by Don Loper, who'll also design Frank's wardrobe for JFK's inaugural next January, and star-shaped diamond earrings from her proud papa. The groom, a reservist, wears his Air Force uniform. Thirty-five friends and family members attend, including teary-eyed Frank and his ex-wife Nancy Barbato, who gives her daughter a sewing machine as a wedding present. Though Tommy had the million-seller "Teenage Crush" several years ago, his singing career is kaput and his acting career, propelled by Nancy's insistence that her father get him into his pictures, never jells. He walks out on Daddy's girl five years later while she's filming *Marriage on the Rocks* alongside Frank and Dean Martin. The following year she tops the charts with her signature song, "These Boots are Made for Walkin'."

> Her first of two, his first of two, lasts five years

"It was a very spasmodic courtship, conducted mainly at long distance with a great clanking of coins in dozens of phone booths."

JACQUELINE KENNEDY

September 12 (1953)

Jacqueline Bouvier & John F. Kennedy

Two upper crust families, the Auchinclosses of Newport and the Kennedys of Cape Cod—a bit wary of one another, truth be told—join forces today to stage a grand wedding. A crowd of 3,000 encircles St. Mary's Church in Newport, R.I., **straining for a glimpse of the glamorous couple**: Senator John F. Kennedy, 36, and Jacqueline Bouvier, 24. She walks down the aisle on the arm of her stepfather Hugh Auchincloss, since her father "Black Jack" Bouvier is reportedly too soused. Though she'd preferred a more modern gown, Jackie accedes to her intended's wishes and wears an old-fashioned, ornate silk taffeta dress with a portrait neckline, fitted bodice and bouffant skirt with interwoven bands of tucking and tiny wax flowers. At the reception at Hammersmith Farm, her childhood home overlooking Narragansett Bay, it takes two and a half hours for the couple to receive all the well-heeled guests. For their first dance, the band plays Rodgers and Hart's "I Married an Angel." The radiant bride steals the show; on close inspection the groom's face shows scratches and bruises, the result of an early morning football scrimmage with his pals.

September 13 (1963)
Barbra Streisand & Elliott Gould

Luck be a lady today: who cares if it's Friday the 13th? From the gambling town of Lake Tahoe, two young lovebirds drive to nearby Carson City to tie the knot. Before a justice of the peace the visiting east coasters, Barbra Streisand, 21, and Elliott Gould, 25, exchange vows with one slight alteration: she **changes "love, honor, and obey"** into **"love, honor, and feed."** And what's the fast-rising singer doing out west, you ask? Only opening for Liberace at Harrah's resort and casino. After her two-week engagement ends they skedaddle for a quasi-honeymoon at the posh Beverly Hills Hotel, a.k.a. the Pink Palace. The newlyweds frolic poolside, but Barbra's in demand. She tapes a Bob Hope comedy special and makes a tour-de-force appearance on CBS's *The Judy Garland Show*, a spectacular pairing of two singing sensations whose duet of "Happy Days Are Here Again" and "Get Happy" is a timeless, once-in-a-lifetime gem. She's also penciled in to sing at the White House in early December, an engagement that's wiped out by JFK's assassination two months later.

Her first of two, his first of three, lasts eight years

September 14 (2002)
Gwen Stefani & Gavin Rossdale

The perfect union: **man, woman and... sheepdog?** Wild child Gwen Stefani, 32, arrives in dramatically late fashion (one hour) to the 17th century St. Paul's Church in London's Covent Garden in a blue Rolls-Royce. Groom Gavin Rossdale, 36, awaits with his Hungarian sheepdog Winston, sporting a garland of red roses. Eschewing her usual offbeat tastes, the singer wears an antique lace veil and an elegant pink and white silk faille dress by John Galliano for Dior, with the skirt's hem and train dyed a stunning pink. She carries a bouquet of phalaenopsis orchids, rosary beads and her grandmother's Catholic prayer book, he wears a traditional British morning suit. They exchange time-honored Anglican vows before 150 guests. Then it's all aboard double-decker busses to a private club for a six-course Italian dinner. Two weeks later the couple hosts a vow-renewal ceremony in L.A. with celebrity guests including Jennifer Aniston, Brad Pitt and Ben Stiller.

September 15 (1951)
Anne Hayes & Peter Sellers

The Goon Show, BBC Radio's audacious, irreverent comedy program, has been making the young impressionist quite a name since its launch last spring. Today Peter Sellers, 26, and Australian actress Anne Hayes, 20, marry at Caxton Hall registry office in London. The pretty if somewhat naïve blonde had met Sellers at the BBC offices several years ago, and he pursued her assiduously. **He reportedly proposed only after locking her in a cupboard**, and refusing to let her out until she accepted. Despite his unconventionality, and a smothering mother, Anne accepted and they wed —though his parents were conspicuously absent. The rocky union endures for a decade and produces two children, while Sellers' reputation and career soars with hit films like *The Ladykillers* and *The Mouse That Roared*. But by the time he's into his signature role of Inspector Clouseau in *The Pink Panther*, he's also onto wife #2, Swedish blonde bombshell Britt Ekland.

His first of four, lasts ten tempestuous years

"[Peter] was amoral, dangerous, vindictive, totally selfish, and yet had the charm of the devil." ANNE HAYES

September 16 (1967)
Susan Tomalin & Chris Sarandon

He was a grad student, a budding, handsome actor with classically chiseled features who caught the eye of many a Catholic University coed. She was a 20-year-old freshman, reveling in her newfound independence and going to civil rights and anti-Vietnam War rallies. They moved in together, rather shocking to her conservative parents, and soon decided to marry. In **an offhand slap at convention**, a priest who headed the drama department performed today's service uniting Chris Sarandon, 25, and Susan Tomalin, 25. After her graduation they moved to Connecticut and slid into a quasi-bohemian life. He landed several roles at the Long Wharf Theater while she began doing entry-level modeling work in catalogs and magazines. Tagging along on one of his auditions in New York, she read and impressed an agent. A week later she had her first role, the teenage daughter of title character Peter Boyle in *Joe*.

Her first, his first of three, lasts 12 years

"That evening we celebrated alone. We had dinner in our bungalow, by candlelight."

SOPHIA LOREN

September 17 (1957)
Sophia Loren & Carlo Ponti

One of the most voluptuous women on earth, engaged to debonair Cary Grant, gets married today in Juarez, Mexico. Only **she has a beard and mustache, and is actually a he.** A thousand miles away in Los Angeles, Sophia Loren, 22, and Carlo Ponti, 47, learn of their proxy marriage in which his Mexican lawyers stood in for the actress and producer after having his previous marriage voided. It's not exactly the storybook wedding Loren had envisioned growing up in Naples. That happens, ironically, several days later when she films the climactic scene of *Houseboat*, in which she marries costar Grant. "A very unkind quirk of cinematic fate," Loren wrote later. The Vatican refuses to recognize the Loren/Ponti vows, religious conservatives threaten to boycott her films, and his bigamy case languishes for years. On April 9, 1966, they marry in the flesh, in Paris—and thereafter celebrated two wedding anniversaries every year.

Her first, his second, lasts 49 years until his death

September 18 (1984)
Gilda Radner & Gene Wilder

St. Paul de Vence

His baby does the hanky panky. Come to think of it, so does he. That's how these two crazy lovebirds met, filming the romantic comedy Hanky Panky. After a two-year courtship in which she was the aggressor, Gilda Radner, 38, and Gene Wilder, 51, marry in St. Paul de Vence, a mountaintop medieval village in Provence, in a small service attended by a handful of friends. The couple combines pleasure with business, having arrived via Paris after attending the French premiere of their latest film, *The Woman in Red*, in the seaside resort of Deauville. The movie fades fast, but it does deliver a smash song: Stevie Wonder's "I Just Called to Say I Love You," which hits #1 next month. More than anything the famed *Saturday Night Live* comedienne wants a baby, but she has problems getting pregnant. Feeling unwell, she embarks on countless doctors' appointments, hearing misdiagnoses until being informed she has stage four ovarian cancer. Radner passes away in May 1989.

September 19 (1945)
Shirley Temple & John Agar

The world swoons as **America's first sweetheart weds her Prince Charming.** It's a fairy tale come true for bubbly blonde Shirley Temple, 17, the most recognizable and richest teen actress on earth, and John Agar, 24, a blue-eyed, square-jawed All-American soldier who stands a foot taller than his bride. A massive crowd estimated at 12,000 surrounds the Wilshire Methodist Church, where 500 guests witness a ceremony that begins with Mendelssohn's "Wedding March" and proceeds flawlessly like a Hollywood production. When the couple ends with an extended smooch, the audience titters and producer David Selznick later notes it "was longer than the movie censor would allow." Outside a near riot ensues, with hundreds of police reinforcements called in. When a cop inadvertently locks the keys inside the couple's limo, they tear the door off its hinges to get inside. Tomorrow's departure for a honeymoon in Santa Barbara is delayed for two hours until a repairman can reattach the door.

Her first of two, his first of two, lasts five years

September 20 (1948)
Martha Graham & Erick Hawkins

One of the most important, influential dancers in America makes an unexpected move today: she gets married. In the foyer of a Presbyterian church in Santa Fe, N.M., Martha Graham, 54, marries Erick Hawkins, 39, the first male dancer in her groundbreaking troupe. She wears a black taffeta skirt, a coat specked with red, and a little veil over her face. For the church's record book she shaves 15 years off her age, noting: "After all, my wonderful Viennese doctor had said I could get away with it, and **as a doctor's daughter I knew better than not to follow my physician's instruction.**" Off they move to a nearby Indian pueblo, but after having lived together, the thrill is gone. The pioneer of modern dance, the first ever to dance at the White House, shoulders on, an uncompromising individualist who contributes so much that *Time* magazine names her Dancer of the Century.

"After eight years of living together, Erick decided we should marry. I didn't want to but I did it. During that ninth year it all fell apart. It shows. Never try to hold on to anything."

MARTHA GRAHAM

September 21 (1996)
Carolyn Bessette & John F. Kennedy, Jr.

Over rutted roads and through the woods, to a clapboard Baptist Church build by freed slaves goes a fleet of four-wheeled vehicles. On remote Cumberland Island off the Georgia coast, a stealthy wedding—all the help, from ferrymen to waiters, signed confidentiality agreements—unfolds. In the tiny candlelit church, with **the Jesuit deacon needing a flashlight to read the service**, the famous couple weds. Carolyn Bessette, 30, wears a bias-cut, floor-length, pearl-colored silk crepe gown by Narciso Rodriguez. (Snubbed designer friend Calvin Klein never spoke to her again.) JFK, Jr., 35, wears a blue suit with a white pique vest, one of his late father's shirts and a pale blue tie. Gospel singer David Davis sings "Amazing Grace" and "May the Circle Be Unbroken." For the reception the small wedding party gathers at one of the island's few buildings, the Greyfield Inn. Hoodwinked by the secrecy, the press catches up to the honeymooners (traveling as "Mr. and Mrs. Hyannis") in Istanbul.

His first, her first, lasts three years until their death in a plane crash

September 22 (1973)
Rona Barrett & Bill Trowbridge

The old-time gossip columnists are fading away, and upstart shows like *Entertainment Tonight* and *Access Hollywood* are years away. That leaves the field wide open for celebrity journalist Rona Barrett, whose print and broadcast coverage of celebrities has turned her into a celebrity herself. But despite making a fabulous living by spilling the beans on the lives of the rich and famous, **she keeps her home life quite private**. She did give Phil Donahue a scoop by announcing on his show that she was getting married, but today there's almost no coverage as Barrett, 37, marries Bill Trowbridge, 44, a former deejay who now manages singer Eddie Fisher (Sept. 26). A month later, covering a star-studded ball at the Beverly Hilton, Barrett receives a rare moment of press coverage: "Glamourland's Gorgeous Gossip, Rona Barrett and her new hubby got almost as much attention as arrivees Michael Landon and his family."

Her first of two, his second, lasts 28 years until his death

"He was different from every man I'd ever met. A whole new thing. I'd been dazzled before, always disappointed."

RONA BARRETT

September 23 (1996)
Lauren Holly & Jim Carrey

Perhaps, in hindsight, the union of a couple that **met on the set of *Dumb & Dumber*** wasn't exactly fated to last. Nevertheless megastar Jim Carrey, 34, ties the knot today with actress Lauren Holly, 32, whose major role to date was as an ambitious deputy in the quirky CBS series *Picket Fences*. His price tag has skyrocketed, with this past summer's smash *The Cable Guy* moving him into stratospheric, $20 million per movie territory. By next spring they're gutting and renovating a $4+ million home in Brentwood, but before they can move in she's filing for divorce. Perhaps she should have listened when, three months before their wedding, he told a reporter: "It's pretty much impossible to build a nest with me right now."

His second, her second of three, lasts ten months

Celebrity Cash

Since weddings can be so expensive, many media-savvy celebs offset the costs by auctioning off exclusive pix to the highest bidder. The photogenic winners?

$3 million from *Hello!*
Elizabeth Hurley/Arun Nayar (2007)

$3 million from *OK!*
Demi Moore/Ashton Kutcher (2005)

$2 million from *OK!*
Eva Longoria/Tony Parker (2007)

$1.5 million from *People*
Kim Kardashian/Kris Humphries (2011)

$1 million from *OK!*
Michael Douglas/Catharine Zeta-Jones (2000)

$1 million from *People*
Anna Nicole Smith/Howard Stern (2006)
(and it wasn't even a real wedding)

September 24 (2005)
Demi Moore & Ashton Kutcher

Saturday night, at home: what would you like to do, honey? I don't know... why don't we get married? Completing last-minute arrangements, Ashton Kutcher, 27, and Demi Moore, 42, marry tonight in their Beverly Hills home, though doubters wrongly label it a hoax and stunt for his MTV show *Punk'd*. For the traditional Kabbalah service she wears a white, off-the-rack Lanvin gown, he sports a cream-colored Brooks Brothers suit and matching fedora. The 100 guests include her three daughters and ex-husband Bruce Willis, plus Soleil Moon Frye, Lucy Liu and Wilmer Valderrama. They recite self-written vows, and **he (not she) is reportedly moved to tears**. The couple honeymoons in Barcelona, where Demi mixes work with pleasure by shooting a spot for a Spanish sparkling wine.

His first, her third, lasts seven years

September 25 (1954)
Audrey Hepburn & Mel Ferrer

Last summer in Paris, when she stopped by promising designer Hubert de Givenchy's shoppe to chose the wardrobe for her next film, *Sabrina*, an assistant told him that a Miss Hepburn had arrived. He assumed it was Katharine, since he'd never heard of Audrey. Though that somewhat brusque beginning turned in a lifelong friendship, she chose a more established couturier for her wedding dress. For today's marriage to Mel Ferrer, 37, in a 13th century Protestant chapel high in the Swiss Alps, Audrey Hepburn, 24, wears a white Pierre Balmain organdie dress, with a small crown of white roses in her hair. Gregory Peck, who'd introduced the couple, couldn't serve as best man to due his film schedule, so hotelier Fritz Frey steps in. Fresh off an Oscar win for *Roman Holiday* (opposite Peck) and Tony award for *Ondine* (opposite Ferrer), this captivating delight caps a triumphant year—and **a limitless future stretches ahead**. For *Funny Face*, the 1957 musical co-starring Fred Astaire, de Givenchy designs her wedding dress.

"The day I marry a man I'm very much in love with, and he lives in Timbuktu, that's where I'll live."

AUDREY HEPBURN (JAN. 1954), WHO MARRIES IN SWITZERLAND AND MAKES IT HER HOME FOREVER

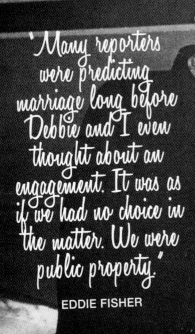

News of crooner Eddie Fisher's marriage breaks young hearts nationwide

September 26 (1955)

Debbie Reynolds & Eddie Fisher

"America's Sweethearts"—the media hangs on their every move. A match made in entertainment heaven, or so it seems, and gossip gallops far beyond Hollywood. After singer Eddie Fisher's Royal Command Performance before the Queen in London last March, Prince Philip shook his hand and asked, **"You're not really going to marry that girl, are you?"** Riding a string of Top Ten hits, pretty boy Fisher, 27, weds budding starlet Debbie Reynolds, 23, at sundown at Grossinger's resort in the Catskills. (Originally scheduled for yesterday, the ceremony was postponed after the groom realized it was Yom Kippur, the holiest Jewish holiday and completely inappropriate for a wedding, let alone to a shiksa.) His manager serves as best man, her high school gym teacher and best friend as maid of honor, with his divorced parents sitting far apart and her stage mom reveling as mother of the bride. The fairy-tale union ends badly when Eddie becomes smitten with Elizabeth Taylor, who becomes his bride #2.

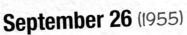

His first of five, her first of three, lasts four years

September 27 (1980)
Candice Bergen & Louis Malle

Like the title of the movie she's about to begin shooting, **the bride is indeed rich and famous**. The groom is making waves too with his latest masterpiece, *Atlantic City*. Today this internationally renowned cinematic couple weds in a tiny village in southwestern France where he owns a mountaintop home called Le Coual ("the raven's cry"). Candice Bergen, 34, wears a Victorian dress of ivory silk and antique lace she'd discovered in Paris. Louis Malle, 48, wears a fawn-colored jacket and light slacks. The townspeople decorate the small, spare town hall with flowering plants and matching French and American flags for a private ceremony for a handful of family and friends. The mayor, usually glimpsed riding his tractor in overalls, wears an old but immaculate suit and speaks movingly of the couple's love and their native countries' noble past. As dusk approaches, the couple hitches up their donkey Nanette to a cart for a leisurely afternoon promenade.

Her first of two, his second, lasts 15 years until his death

September 28 (1997)
Hilary Swank & Chad Lowe

Not only are they married in Beverly Hills, she works there too. Hilary Swank has just joined the cast of *Beverly Hills 90210*, so her **16-hour workdays have cut into wedding planning**. Nevertheless, the 23-year-old actress ties the knot today with Chad Lowe, 29. They've been sweethearts for five years, ever since meeting at a bash at the Hollywood Athletic Club. He's got the more famous pedigree as the younger brother of Brat Packer Rob Lowe (July 22), and has amassed television credits in *Life Goes On* and *Melrose Place*. But she's heading towards far greater fame: an Oscar for Best Actress in *Boys Don't Cry* two years later, and then another for *Million Dollar Baby*. She famously forgets to thank Lowe during the first acceptance speech but makes up for it the second time around.

His first of two, her first, lasts eight years

September 29 (1927)
Norma Shearer & Irving Thalberg

Marrying the boss: rarely a bad career move. Much
to the consternation of every other actress on the MGM
lot (except Greta Garbo, who's in a class all her own),
Norma Shearer, 25, walks down the aisle with filmdom's
Boy Wonder, Irving Thalberg, 28. Ever the workhorse despite
a weak constitution, he conducts a story conference about a new
Ramon Novarro picture with its screenwriter while dressing for the ceremony.
This afternoon, in the garden of his rented (from silent screen star Pauline
Frederick) home at 9401 Sunset Boulevard, studio mogul Louis Mayer serves
as best man for the grand Hollywood event. Shearer wears an ivory-colored,
pearl-studded velvet gown with a yoke of handmade rose lace. Despite having
practiced Hebrew with a local rabbi, she muffs her lines and repeats them
only with the rabbi's whispered help. After a supper enlivened by bootleg
champagne, the couple departs by train for a short honeymoon at the Del
Monte Lodge in Monterey.

> Her first of two, his first, lasts nine years until his death

September 30 (2000)
Bridgette Wilson & Pete Sampras

She's just wrapped *The Wedding Planner*, in which
she'll (sigh) lose Matthew McConaughey to Jennifer
Lopez. But today Bridgette Wilson, 27, celebrates the
real deal as she weds tennis star Pete Sampras, 29.
At the twilight ceremony at his Beverly Hills estate,
she wears an ivory silk georgette bias Vera Wang
gown that arrived yesterday via FedEx, along with
$400,000 worth of diamonds on loan from posh
high-end jeweler Fred Leighton. Sampras' backyard
has been converted into a dreamy setting with white
candles and flowers floating in the pool, plus a tent
erected over the tennis court turned reception hall
decorated with flowers, chandeliers and mirrors.
After dinner the groom pulls off **a major surprise:
Sir Elton John**, who plays 45 minutes of greatest hits,
culminating with "Can You Feel the Love Tonight."
Fresh off his fourth straight Wimbledon title,
Sampras had spotted Wilson at an L.A. movie theatre
last fall. From there the court champion (whom she'd
never seen play) commenced his courtship.

October

Elizabeth Taylor & Spencer Tracey
in Father of the Bride

October 1 (1949)
Jody Wolcott & Johnny Carson

Heeeeeere's Johnny!

An ambitious, fresh-faced college grad walks down the aisle today with his girlfriend, "an All-American girl with artistic ambitions **who looked as if she walked out of an ad for Coca Cola**" (described by Nora Ephron). Johnny Carson, 23, and Jody Wolcott, 22, who'd worked as the assistant in his part-time, small-time magic act that traveled to milkmen's conventions and American Legions halls, wed before 150 guests at an Episcopalian church in North Platte, Nebraska. She wears an ice-blue satin gown with a fingertip veil, changing into a wool gabardine suit with a white orchid for the reception at the nearby Pawnee Hotel, a six-story structure that dominates the town's skyline. Only a few months out of college, Johnny has landed a $47.50 per week gig as a combo deejay/news reader at WOW, one of Nebraska's biggest radio stations that, like the rest of the country, is soon dabbling in the new medium of television. The native son itches to become a star, and he succeeds.

His first of four, lasts 14 years

"There wasn't any equality in our marriage, but I didn't expect there to be. It was all what John wanted. It was all John."

JODY WOLCOTT

October 2 (1941)
Elizabeth McDonald & Dean Martin

When Irish eyes are smiling, and Italian voices are singing, **it must be amore**. Budding crooner Dino Paul Crocetti, 23, strolls down the aisle with Elizabeth McDonald, 18, at St. Ann's Church in Cleveland. She wears a dress made by her future mother-in-law, and her toddler sisters scatter rose petals and sing "I'll Be with You in Apple Blossom Time." Yet it's her hubby, currently pulling in a substantial $50 week, who's got a bright musical future. Dubbed "The Boy with the Tall, Dark Voice," Dino met Betty when she and her father attended a performance of the Sammy Watkins Band in the Vogue Room of Cleveland's Hollenden Hotel. Just to be sure the handsome singer noticed her, Betty wore a big red sombrero. Tonight they honeymoon at the hotel, and tomorrow morning she joins him on the bus for a six-week tour.

His first of three, lasts eight years

October 3 (1992)
Michelle Robinson & Barack Obama

Assigned to advise a summer associate from Harvard Law School, **she refused the young man's entreaties for a month**. Finally she agreed to spend a day with him. They visited the Chicago Art Institute, lunched at an outdoor café, caught a screening of Spike Lee's *Do the Right Thing* and finished off the evening with drinks on the 99th floor of the John Hancock Center. Three years later Barack Obama, 31, and Michelle Robinson, 28, marry at Chicago's Trinity United Church of Christ. She wears a long-sleeved, off-the-shoulder white silk dress with a chiffon overlay and a sweetheart neckline. He wears a traditional black suit and a white rose boutonniere. In keeping with the groom's Kenyan roots, some guests—including his best man, half-brother Malik—wear traditional African dress. Their wedding song? Stevie Wonder's "You and I (We Can Conquer the World)."

"I think it's fair to say that had I not been a Stevie Wonder fan, Michelle might not have dated me. We might not have married. The fact that we agreed on Stevie was part of the essence of our courtship."

BARACK OBAMA

October 4 (1997)
Tabitha Soren & Michael Lewis

She's become a household name among the younger set as MTV's news anchor and host of its *Choose or Lose* political coverage. Today she chooses to walk down the aisle in **a decidedly offbeat ceremony** at a friend's estate in Garrison, New York. Tabitha Soren, 30, wears an off-white velvet Morgan Le Fay dress ("very King Arthur") opposite the groom, writer Michael Lewis (*Liar's Poker*), 36, who believes his rented dark brown Edwardian suit makes him look like Count Chocula. Their cocker spaniel Vegas serves as ring bearer. The eclectic crowd of 100 guests includes REM's Peter Buck and Senator John McCain. While the celebration isn't quite the midnight wedding in Transylvania that the bride had envisioned growing up, it does elicit sparks. "We had lots of candles and torches," says Soren, "and some people got drunk and accidentally set the tablecloths on fire. I was charged for it."

His third, her first

October 5 (2004)
Elin Nordegren & Tiger Woods

Money may not be able to buy you love, but **it can buy plenty of privacy**. Renowned golfer Tiger Woods has rented out all the rooms at Sandy Lane, an idyllic resort in Barbados. He has also rented all rooms at two adjoining properties, plus every helicopter on the island that he orders grounded. Airplanes are still flying, however, bringing in 200 guests including basketball greats Michael Jordan and Charles Barkley. Stunning Swedish bride Elin Nordegren, 24, whom he met at the 2001 British Open when she was working as a nanny for a fellow golfer, wears a white sleeveless floor-length gown by Vera Wang (June 22). Woods, 28, wears a beige suit and white shirt. The sunset wedding on the 19th hole is held under a white-netted pagoda decorated with 500 long-stemmed red roses. A lavish reception features past-their-prime Hootie and the Blowfish, and culminates with a $75,000 fireworks display. The newlyweds spend their honeymoon on his 155-foot, $22 million yacht, appropriately named "Privacy."

His first, her first, lasts six years

"What makes our marriage work amid all the glare is that my husband is my best friend. He inspires everything in my life and enables me to do the best that I can. I want to hang out with him more than anyone."

FAITH HILL

October 6 (1996)
Faith Hill & Tim McGraw

Invitees think they're coming for a softball game and benefit concert, but the hosts have other ideas. Country superstars Tim McGraw, 29, and Faith Hill, 29, marry in his hometown of Rayville, Louisiana in a noontime outdoor service. She wears a white dress and goes barefoot while he opts for jeans and a black sports coat. Though the crowd doesn't know it, the timing underscores the title of his breakout album (and single) *Not A Moment Too Soon*, since Hill's three months pregnant. Or, **the happy event might personify the bride's debut too: *Take Me As I Am*.** Last year the couple hooked up for their *Spontaneous Combustion* tour, which she began engaged to another man but ended in the arms of the headliner. McGraw clinched the deal by inviting her over one night for some home cooking. "I was thinking, 'Yeah, right, homemade...' " admits Hill, who was bowled over by his chicken, dumplings and corn bread. "It tasted just like my mom's."

October 7 (1995)

Mary Steenburgen & Ted Danson

They're getting to be such regular visitors—three summers running —that the locals on Martha's Vineyard, this laid-back island five miles off the coast of Cape Cod, don't pay all that much attention. Nevertheless President Bill Clinton and First Lady Hillary (Oct. 11) flew in last night on Air Force One. Today, despite the rain, the prez attempts a round of golf before heading off for **the main event**: the wedding of Ted Danson and Mary Steenburgen. At their refurbished farmhouse overlooking the Atlantic, Danson, 47, and Steenburgen, 32, an Arkansas native and longtime friend of the First Family, marry before a starry array that includes Laura Dern, Jeff Goldblum, Tom Hanks and Rita Wilson (April 30), James Taylor and most of the cast of *Cheers*. Next month the newlyweds purchase a $3.5 million colonial home in the L.A. community of Brentwood to house their extended family that includes her son and daughter from her marriage to Malcolm McDowell, and his two daughters.

His third, her second

"I'm deeply in love with a really good person who loves me back immensely. That is an amazing gift."

MARY STEENBURGEN

October 8 (1933)
Lupe Velez & Johnny Weissmuller

Him Tarzan, her... Lupe? Famous for rescuing damsels in distress, Johnny Weissmuller takes on a woman today who's known more for *causing* distress. Ex-Olympic gold medalist Weissmuller, 29, and Lupe Velez, a.k.a. the "Mexican Spitfire," 25, elope to Las Vegas for a quick, four a.m. ceremony for which **they "aroused a sleeping deputy clerk to obtain a license to wed**." She's just ended a tempestuous affair with Gary Cooper, whose future bride and Lupe have gotten into catfights at several Hollywood nightspots. In the bedroom, Velez takes a toll on her far larger but affable husband, inflicting hickeys, scratches and bites that keep the makeup department working overtime as he shoots his second Tarzan picture, *Tarzan and His Mate*. That film, which reunites him with screen love Maureen O'Sullivan, is acknowledged as the greatest of the forty-some Tarzan movies eventually made, and this portrayal cements his image as the immortal ape man.

"Fight? We all do. Johnny and I may fight, but no more than the rest of Hollywood. They call each other 'Darling' in public, and then go home and smack each other in private. When Johnny and I get sore, we get sore no matter where we are!" LUPE VELEZ

October 9 (1962)
Edith Piaf & Theo Sarapo

The public still adores their "little sparrow," even if critics carp that her voice has lost its timbre and strength. Thousands of fans line the streets in Paris's 16th arrondissement to catch a glimpse of frail chanteuse Edith Piaf, 47, and her new husband/protégé, Theo Sarapo, 26. After a civil service in the mayor's office the couple, both dressed in black, repairs to a nearby Greek Orthodox church lit by hundreds of candles. The handsome Greek groom, formerly a hairdresser, carries the diminutive Piaf through the throngs only partially controlled by six busloads of police. Inside reporters outnumber the guests, and outside screaming fans shower the newlyweds with rice. The next night the couple returns to their engagement at the famed Olympia music hall, where one reporter praises France's beloved torch singer with "**a voice of life itself**, refusing to die, refusing to be silenced, the voice of humanity itself."

Her second, his first, lasts one year until her death

October 10 (1975)
Elizabeth Taylor & Richard Burton

The epic battles, the drunkenness, the infidelities have played out on a global stage—so what's left for Elizabeth Taylor and Richard Burton to do but get remarried? Sixteen months after their divorce, they reconnected and embarked on a whirlwind tour from Switzerland to Italy to Israel to South Africa. Today they continue on to Botswana and remarry on the banks of the Chobe River. A district commissioner from the Tswana tribe performs **a 20-minute ceremony witnessed by two locals and two hippopotamuses**. Liz, 43, wears a long flowing green dress ribbed with feathers and beads, Dick, 49, a red silk turtleneck, white trousers, red socks and white shoes. The couple exchanges rings and afterwards celebrates with a champagne toast. "Sturm has remarried Drang," says *The Boston Globe*, "and all is right with the world."

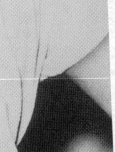

Never let it be said that the Taylor/Burtons traveled light: their luggage outside NYC's Regency Hotel

"I have never been so happy in my life. E[lizabeth] cured me with loving even lavish attention. This is far better marriage than the first despite its silly (and dangerous) beginning."

RICHARD BURTON, WRITING IN HIS DIARY ON HIS WEDDING DAY

Here Comes the Bride— Again!

"Always the bride, never the bridesmaid."

OSCAR LEVANT, ON THE OCCASION OF TAYLOR'S FITH WEDDING

Elizabeth Taylor's eight strolls down the aisle

Conrad "Nicky" Hilton, Jr. **(1950)**

Michael Wilding **(1952)**

Michael Todd **(1957)**

Eddie Fisher **(1959)**

Richard Burton **(1964 & 1975)**

John Warner **(1976)**

Larry Fortensky **(1991)**

Taylor and fourth hubby Eddie Fisher

The first time: Elizabeth Taylor and Conrad Hilton, Jr.

October 11 (1975)
Hillary Rodham & Bill Clinton

This morning the bridegroom breaks the news
to his mother: **his headstrong fiancée will be
keeping her maiden name**. She breaks into tears,
but regains her composure by the afternoon as family and friends gather for the
wedding of fast-rising Bill Clinton, 29, and Hillary Rodham, 27, at their modest
brick home in Fayetteville, Arkansas. She wears a floor-length, cream-colored
Jessica McClintock dress with a high neck, long sleeves and touches of lace,
which she and her mother bought last night at a Dillard's department store. He
wears a politician's standard-issue dark blue suit and silk tie. After exchanging
traditional vows and heirloom rings, the couple and 200 guests celebrate at a
reception at the sprawling home of a state senator replete with champagne from
a bubbling fountain. Bill & Hill cut into a seven-tiered wedding cake decorated
with yellow roses. After dancing the night away at a nearby motor inn, he's
awoken by a four a.m. phone call and must hurry down to the local jail to bail out
a brother-in-law hauled in for drunken driving.

"I thought, 'What can I say to him that he hasn't heard before? Gee, I loved 'E.T.?' That would be ridiculous. So when we finally met I said nothing. When the meeting was over, he got up and said, 'Thanks for not saying anything about "E.T."

KATE CAPSHAW

October 12 (1991)
Kate Capshaw & Steven Spielberg

No killer sharks, no intrepid adventurers, no aliens.
Just **a traditional black tie wedding** on the banks of a
peaceful pond in the Hamptons as mega-director Steven
Spielberg, 45, marries Kate Capshaw, 37, who'd previously starred in the
second Indiana Jones movie. Earlier today the star-studded crowd played
a Kennedy-esque touch football game on his posh Long Island estate.
Tonight guests include Richard Dreyfuss, Sally Field, Dustin Hoffman,
Barbra Streisand and Robin Williams, who performs his stand-up shtick
at the reception. Warner Bros. chairman Steve Ross, Spielberg's longtime
mentor and father figure, speaks after the service. Professionally it's been
a rare dry spell for the wunderkind filmmaker, whose only movie this year
is the underwhelming *Hook*. But two years later he returns to smashing
records with the gargantuan *Jurassic Park*.

His second, her second

October 17 (1945)
Ava Gardner & Artie Shaw

Big band leader Artie Shaw, whose version of Cole Porter's "Begin the Beguine" skyrocketed him to fame, wanted the raven-haired temptress to sing with his band. **She refused that offer, but not his offer of marriage**. Today actress Ava Gardner, 22, weds Shaw, 35, at the Beverly Hills home of the judge who'd granted his divorce the week before. She wears a blue tailored suit, white gloves and holds an orchid corsage. Her best friend Frances Heflin (wife of actor Van Heflin), who'd introduced the couple, serves as maid of honor. They honeymoon at Lake Tahoe, but fights quickly ensue. Overbearing Artie tries to school his young wife about music, art, politics and other worldly affairs. But after he hires an old Russian grandmaster to teach her chess, and she beats Artie in their first game, they never play again. He goes on to three more wives, she to one last husband, Frank Sinatra, and a successful cinematic career as one of the sexiest leading ladies of the day.

Her second of three, his fifth of eight, lasts a year and a week

"I fell in love with him, just like that. That's the way it always is with me, immediate or never."

AVA GARDNER

October 18 (1986)
Kathryn Lee Epstein & Frank Gifford

Mama's a born-again Christian, and a teetotaler. When she arrived last night for dinner before her son's wedding, **the bride she'd never met up and ordered a martini**—a drink the bride later admitted she'd never ordered before. Was it nerves? Staking out her territory? Regardless, mother smiles and all's well. Today's service on a gorgeous Indian summer afternoon goes off without a hitch. Veteran sportsman and sportscaster Frank Gifford, 56, marries TV personality Kathie Lee, 33, before 75 friends (naturally including the co-host she calls Reege) and family at the beachfront Long Island home of his attorney. Her brother David, a minister, performs the short ceremony for which the bride and groom wrote their own vows, and her sister Michie provides the vocals. Afterwards, with paparazzi in pursuit, the couple races off in the groom's red Jaguar for a brief honeymoon at Gurney's Inn in Montauk, since both have on-air gigs the following Monday.

His third, her second

October 19 (2012)

Jessica Biel & Justin Timberlake

Mission—accomplished! Favored targets of paparazzi throughout their five-year courtship, today these newlyweds pull off the unexpected: a wedding with absolutely no prying photographers afoot. Secretly plotting the affair since his proposal to her on a Montana mountaintop last December, Justin Timberlake, 31, weds Jessica Biel, 30 at the luxurious Borgo Egnazia Resort in remote Puglia, Italy, which sports both mountainous and seaside views. She wears a strapless rose-pink petal gown by longtime designer pal Giambattista Valli, with voluminous layers of chiffon and a floor-length veil, **a custom creation that the bride calls "romance, romance, romance—kind of whimsical and dramatic."** The groom, who wears a custom Tom Ford satin-piped tux, croons a self-penned tune as Biel comes down the aisle before a select crowd of family and friends including Jimmy Fallon, Beverley Mitchell (her *7th Heaven* co-star), Andy Sambert and Timbaland. At the candlelit, nondenominational sunset service the newlyweds exchange hand-written vows, and later step out for their first dance to Donny Hathaway's "A Song for You."

"We wanted to create a time for our family and friends to say goodbye to their lives and really feel like they were on vacation."

JESSICA BIEL

October 20 (1968)

Jacqueline Kennedy & Aristotle Onassis

The world's not so keen about their impending union. His adult children also hate the idea of their father remarrying, while her toddlers Caroline and John John are too young to understand. Regardless, cultured and classy ex-First Lady Jacqueline Kennedy, 39, marries short, paunchy billionaire Greek shipping tycoon Aristotle Onassis, 62, at dusk on the isle of Skorpios, which he owns. Amidst flowering bougainvillea and jasmine, **the tiny, whitewashed chapel is filled with candles and burning incense**. Jackie wears a long-sleeved, two-piece dress beige dress by Valentino of chiffon and lace, he wears a dark blue double-breasted suit and a red tie. Even in his elevator shoes, he barely reaches her nose. After the 45-minute Roman Catholic service, the small wedding party emerges to a howling wind and drenching downpour. His moored yacht *Christina* hosts the reception, an all-night celebration, while Greek police keep a flotilla of boats carrying journalists and photographers at bay.

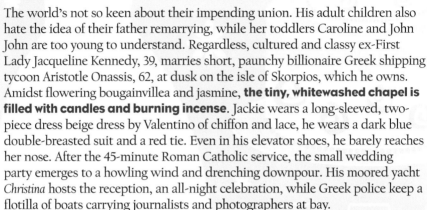

"Beautiful women cannot bear moderation. They need an inexhaustible supply of excess."

ARISTOTLE ONASSIS

October 21 (1965)

Christine Keeler & John Levermore

Two years ago her brief affair with a prominent British politician shocked the world and rocked the country's Conservative government. Pretty brunette call girl Christine Keeler, who'd also been sleeping with a Soviet spy, eventually drew a nine-month sentence for perjury and conspiracy to obstruct justice. Longing for a normal life far from the scandalous spotlight, she retreated to her mother's country home and met a rugged working bloke. Today Keeler, 23, marries John Levermore, 24, at a quiet registry office in Reading. She wears a simple two-piece green corduroy suit, a far cry from her flashy outfits during her swinging London days. "I desperately wanted to forget the past," says Keeler. **"I didn't want any more pointing fingers in the street."** A son is born next July, but the marriage quickly dissolves. Twenty-five years later a new generation rediscovers the tawdry tale in *Scandal*, with Joanne Whalley (Feb. 28) as Keeler and Ian McKellen as her politico paramour, John Profumo.

October 22 (1945)
Maria Eva Duarte & Juan Peron

Given her legendary fame, **one might assume that Evita Peron enjoyed a lavish, extravagant wedding**. One would be wrong. Because today she's but a little known, minor actress. She met strongman Juan Peron last year at a party after a fundraiser for earthquake victims, and soon they were living together, scandalous for two reasons: they were unmarried, and in Argentinean society, entertainers and politicians rarely mixed. Official documents falsely claim that the wedding occurs in her hometown of Junin, and lists her age as 23 to help hide her illegitimacy. The secret civil ceremony actually takes place this evening in their small apartment in Buenos Aires where the blonde bride, 26, wears an ivory suit and Peron, 50, wears a grey suit. Released from prison less than a week earlier amidst political upheaval, Peron soon begins a campaign for the presidency. He's elected less than a year later, boosted immensely by his magnetic, beloved First Lady who entrances a nation but dies tragically of cancer in 1952 at age 33.

Her first, his first of two, lasts seven years until her death

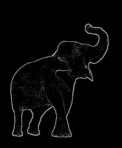

'I've never been in love before Katy, as now I rate love as being willing to change for someone... Of course marriage is for life, and that's what I wanted— but anything for the rest of life can be daunting."

RUSSELL BRAND

October 23 (2010)
Katy Perry & Russell Brand

Shy, retiring Russell Brand ties the knot today in a very subdued fashion—not! At a luxury resort in an Indian national park, Brand **rides atop an elephant in the tradition of maharajas**. The procession moves to the sounds of sitars and drums and sacred Vedic chanting. Brand, 35, wears a white kurta, loose informal trousers and a long baggy tunic, while bride Katy Perry ("I Kissed a Girl," though probably not tonight), two days before her 26th birthday, wears a plain red sari. A statement sent to MTV (they met at the 2009 MTV Video Music Awards) reads: "The very private and spiritual ceremony, attended by the couples' closest family and friends, was performed by a Christian minister and longtime friend of the Hudson [Katy's maiden name] Family. The backdrop was the inspirational and majestic countryside of Northern India." The ceremony caps a six-day celebration that included a Bollywood-themed bash last night where Perry, like a typical Indian bride, showed off the henna designs applied to her palms and hands.

His first, her first, lasts two years

October 24 (1969)
Ali MacGraw & Robert Evans

(speech bubble: I'm not sorry.)

He first laid eyes on her ten years ago when she was wearing a white mink on a sweltering summer day in New York. She was a part-time model, Wellesley co-ed and, in his words, "a star snot-nose." But years later their relationship blossomed on the west coast where her stock was soaring after a star-making acting turn in *Goodbye, Columbus*. Today Robert Evans, 39, head of production at Paramount, and Ali MacGraw, 31, hop into his Mercedes two-seater and head off for a marriage license. Then it's off to Palm Springs where a two-dollar judge marries them before three witnesses including his housekeeper and butler. Afterwards they uncork a bottle of Dom Pérignon on the courthouse lawn to celebrate. Then it's off to the east coast to begin shooting the weeper that catapults her to fame: *Love Story*, with its unforgettable line: "**Love means never having to say you're sorry.**" Evans, a quintessential Hollywood mover and shaker, later teams her with Steve McQueen in *The Getaway*. That she does: MacGraw falls in love with her costar and divorces Evans to marry him.

> His third of six, her second of three, lasts three years

October 25 (1973)
Marsha Mason & Neil Simon

Married for 20 years, playwright Neil Simon and his wife Joan raised two daughters, Ellen and Nancy, as his career soared with Broadway hits like *The Odd Couple* and *Plaza Suite*. After she died of cancer at age 40, he returned to work with a heavy heart. Attending the first reading of his latest play, *The Good Doctor*, he was struck by the performance and look of a young actress with dark reddish hair, a hint of freckles and a touch of makeup. This morning, three weeks later, under the delighted gaze of his approving daughters, Neil Simon, 46, and Marsha Mason, 31, marry in a civil ceremony in New York. An hour later the girls are back in school and the couple returns to rehearsals where producer Manny Azenberg pops the champagne, fills paper cups for the cast and offers a toast: "To the happy couple. **May the play run longer than the engagement.**" During their marriage he writes three films in which her roles net her Oscar nominations: *The Goodbye Girl*, *Chapter Two* and *Only When I Laugh*.

> His second of five, her second, lasts nine years

October 26 (2002)

Jessica Simpson & Nick Lachey

As their celebrity chronicles zoom off the charts, **what's left for the two adorable pop stars but to clinch the deal?** Heavy rains may not be the best omen as virginal Jessica Simpson, 22, arrives in a vintage Cadillac limo at the Riverbend Church in Austin, Texas. She wears a white strapless, beaded Vera Wang gown, with an 11-carat pavé diamond headband attached to her veil. Groom Nick Lachey, 28, sports a black Hugo Boss tux and white silk tie. Their mothers light a unity candle together during the ceremony, which ends with a 25-member gospel choir belting out "Oh Happy Day." At the reception in a ballroom decorated with 30,000 roses, the 350 guests enjoy Maine lobster bisque, spinach salad with candied pecans, chicken and crab cakes. Country singer Neil McCoy sings "Crazy Love" for their first dance, and Jessica and Nick later serenade each other with self-penned love songs. Their stupefying MTV reality show *Newlyweds: Nick and Jessica* debuts less than a year later.

> Her first, his first of two, lasts four tumultuous years

October 27 (1964)
Cherilyn Sarkisian
& Salvatore Phillip Bono

In the bathroom of his mundane Hollywood apartment, Sonny & Cher tie the knot. Sorta. Not really. Well... okay, here's the story. Ambitious musical jack-of-all-trades Sonny Bono, 29, has fallen in love with **his diamond-in-the-rough discovery**, the long-legged and longhaired Cher, 18. Today, they scrounge around an Indian souvenir shop near Sunset and Vine, finding a couple of cheap gold-plated rings. For an additional quarter apiece, they get their names etched on them. Then the crazy couple proceeds to his bathroom where, dressed in jeans and tee shirts, they exchange vows. Alone. Seriously. Later, in keeping with their groovy, baby, lifestyle, they float a fable that they married today in Tijuana, Mexico. Next year these unknowns become well knowns, as much for their outlandish outfits as their musical output, thanks to #1 smash "I Got You Babe." They maintain the fiction that they're married until they make it legal, shortly after the birth of their daughter Chastity (now son Chas) in 1969.

> His second of four, her first of two, lasts six years

October 28 (1986)
Marie Osmond & Brian Blosil

Perpetually perky singer Marie Osmond had been a bit blue since her divorce from Brigham Young University basketball star Steve Craig. So one of her eight brothers, Jay, invited her to a party where he especially wanted her to meet fast-rising BYU quarterback Steve Young, en route to a sparkling pro career. But Marie found herself drawn to another guest, a funny fellow who wanted to be a music producer. Today Marie, 27, marries that guy, Brian Blosil, 33, **at a traditional Mormon service at the towering Jordan River Temple** with only immediate family in attendance. She wears a full-length white dress with a high neck and long sleeves, decorated with sequins and pearls. Not much time for a honeymoon, though. Three nights later Marie, who just won a Country Music Award with Dan Seals for "Meet Me in Montana," performs at the celebrated honky tonk Gilly's in Pasadena, Texas, made famous in *Urban Cowboy*.

Her second of three, lasts 22 years

October 29 (1972)
Alana Collins & George Hamilton

The last of the red hot swingers ties the knot today in a very appropriate spot: Las Vegas. Perpetually tanned, oh so suave and handsome George Hamilton, 33, has been linked to a bevy of lovely ladies from Swedish bombshell Britt Ekland to LBJ's daughter Lynda Bird Johnson. Today he and model Alana Collins, 27, plus her cockapoo, Georgie, hop aboard the airplane of Colonel Tom Parker, Elvis's manager, and wing from Palm Springs to Sin City. In a suite at the International Hotel, with the Colonel as best man, the jet-setting couple marries. They celebrate with drinks, then **phone their respective mothers to share the news**. George and Tom head off to play roulette, and then it's back on the plane to spend their wedding night at his Palm Springs home. Within a few years Alana moves from matinee idol to musician Rod Stewart (April 6), who'd also had a fling with another of Hamilton's discards, Ekland.

His first and only, her first of two, lasts three years

"It was a far cry from any wedding I might have imagined for myself, though conjuring up ceremonies wasn't exactly how I spent my leisure time." GEORGE HAMILTON

October 30 (2004)
Shanna Moakler & Travis Barker

'Twas the night before Halloween, and all through the gothic house, **strange creatures were stirring as the drummer took a spouse**. Blink-182's heavily tattooed Travis Barker, 28, weds former Miss USA Shanna Moakler, 29, at a gala red-and-black affair at the Bacara Resort & Spa in Santa Barbara inspired by their favorite movie, Tim Burton's *The Nightmare Before Christmas*. She wears a long-sleeved, lacy Monique Lhuillier gown with a black sash tied around her waist, and carries a bouquet of crimson roses. He wears a black, gangster-ish suit with white pinstripes, and their year-old son, his hair styled in a Mohawk, wears a junior version of the same suit. Her five-year-old daughter is one of six flower girls in white sleeveless dresses with black sashes.

His second, her first, lasts two years

"Even though [the wedding] was different and wild, it was really upscale and romantic. It was like a fairy tale." SHANNA MOAKLER

October 31 (1970)
Dennis Hopper & Michelle Phillips

It's definitely **more trick than treat**. Fueled by the success of last year's counterculture hit *Easy Rider*, wild man Dennis Hopper hunkered down in his new digs in Taos, N.M. Hangers-on flooded his rural three-building retreat, partying hearty with booze and drugs aplenty. Amidst the madness, Hopper impulsively decides to turn a fling into a more permanent union. Today, in a living room lit with 150 candles, several hundred (probably mostly wasted) guests gather for the marriage of Hopper, 34, and Michelle Phillips, 26, the singer recently divorced from the Mamas and the Papas honcho John Phillips. In the ensuing days her erratic new hubby shoots off guns in the house and reportedly handcuffs her so she won't flee. She manages to escape, taking her two-year-old daughter Chynna, and eight days later files for divorce.

His second of five, her second of four, lasts eight days

November

Princess Elizabeth &
Prince Philip
November 20, 1947

November 1 (2003)
Elizabeth Berkley & Greg Lauren

When you're marrying someone named Lauren, **three guesses who dresses the entire wedding party.** Elizabeth Berkley (*Saved By the Bell*, *Showgirls*), 31, and Greg Lauren, 33, wed at the posh Esperanza Resort in Cabo San Lucas, Mexico. She wears a pale lime silk sheath dress, designed by the groom's uncle Ralph Lauren, with crisscrossing pearl straps down its low-cut back. The groom sports a white tuxedo jacket, black bow tie and black trousers. The attendants wear matching outfits in a kaleidoscope of tropical colors, creating a rainbow effect at the seaside service, a traditional Jewish ceremony beneath a chuppah decorated with orchids, hydrangea and roses. The couple met at a dance class several years ago, and their roots show as their reception dance routine, choreographed by their class's teacher, includes "Crazy For You" and "You're The One That I Want." The wedding caps three days of celebrations that included spa treatments, salsa dance lessons and a moonlight screening of *Casablanca* on the beach.

November 2 (1943)
Diana Dill & Kirk Douglas

The world's at war, so this patriotic lad put aside his acting aspirations and donned a naval uniform. Today Kirk Douglas, 25, wears it on the ferry from New Orleans to the naval chapel on Algiers Island where he marries model/actress Diana Dill, 20, who graced a *Life* magazine cover last May in a stylish checked outfit with matching parasol. The couple met several years ago in an acting class in New York. Young **officers in dress uniforms form an arch with their swords raised** as the newlyweds cross underneath and along a candlelit path to the reception at a nearby sculptor's studio. They enjoy a romantic month in an attic apartment overlooking St. Louis Cathedral and Jackson Square, until his ship is commissioned and Douglas sails off to war. En route to the Pacific months later, he's hospitalized at a naval facility in San Diego with amoebic dysentery when a letter from Diana brings news of their impending baby, Michael (Nov. 18), born the following September.

His first of two, her first of three, lasts seven years

November 3 (1972)

Carly Simon & James Taylor

Round midnight the folk rock star ambles onstage at Radio City Music Hall with his left hand jammed awkwardly in his pants pocket. He takes it out and **waves it about, a gold band on his ring finger**, and shares the good news. Earlier tonight Taylor, 24, wed girlfriend Carly Simon, 27, at her Manhattan apartment, a minimalist wedding with only their mothers and her songwriting partner Jacob Brackman attending. The intrigue surrounding the union of two rock royals fans mega-media attention. He's had serious drug problems, ended an affair with Joni Mitchell and enjoyed his only #1 single with pal Carole King's "You've Got a Friend." She's famously dallied with, among others, Warren Beatty (Mar. 12) and Mick Jagger (May 12), both of whom become prime suspected subjects of her forthcoming #1 "You're So Vain." Their subsequent *Rolling Stone* cover story mentions they've already named their hypothetical children Sarah and Ben, who materialize in real life in '74 and '77, respectively.

His first of three, her first of two, lasts 11 years

November 4 (1989)
Jenny Sullivan & Mark Sanford

They met on Memorial Day weekend in the Hamptons, an ambitious Southern businessman and a Wall Street investment banker. Jenny Sullivan, 27, liked that Mark Sanford, 29, a handsome, lanky, soft-spoken gentleman was so unlike her male co-workers, "suspender-snapping braggarts." They embarked on a two-year, long-distance courtship. But after his proposal, Jenny registers a tiny red flag today when **he insists they exclude a wedding vow promising fidelity**. Priest Leo O'Donovan, president of Georgetown University, her alma mater, performs the service at Christ Memorial Chapel on Jupiter Island, Florida. Her sister Kathleen serves as maid of honor, his brother William as best man. Soon they move into a house in Charleston, where their family and his political ambitions take root. Twenty years and four sons later, their union collapses quite publicly when he reveals, "I will be able to die knowing that I had met my soul mate"—not Jenny, but his Argentine mistress Maria Belen Chapur.

His first, her first, lasts 20 years

"It wasn't exactly love at first sight.
It was more like a friendship at first sight."

JENNY SANFORD

November 5 (1977)
Laura Welch & George Bush

They'd gone to the same middle school, but never really met. Three months ago friends arranged a blind date, and the next day the smitten twosome played miniature golf. Today George Bush, and Laura Welch, both 31, stroll down—**the church where she'd been baptized and sang in the choir**. With no time to have invitations printed, her mother hand wrote invites to 75 attendees. By the Texas standards of their well-heeled families, it's a downright small affair and short service. Pinning a gardenia in her hair, and carrying a bouquet of the same flower, Laura wears a simple, store-bought ivory silk skirt and blouse. After a reception luncheon tomorrow at the Midland Racquet Club, the Bushes honeymoon in sunny Cozumel, Mexico.

"Exactly 31 steps down the aisle and into the rest of my life."

LAURA BUSH

November 6 (1895)
Consuelo Vanderbilt &
Charles Spencer-Churchill

Take the insatiable public appetite for weddings like that of Prince Charles and Lady Di (July 29) or David Beckham and Posh Spice (July 4). Add in unimaginable wealth, dial back a century and you begin to get some sense of the hysteria that rages as Consuelo Vanderbilt, 18, great granddaughter of Cornelius Vanderbilt, marries the Duke of Marlborough, 24. **The arranged marriage of unbridled American riches and old-world British royalty**, imposed by her domineering mother Alva, attracts thousands eager for a glimpse of Gilded Age ostentation. The beautiful bride with the $20 million fortune wears a creamy white satin dress with graduated flounces of point lace and trails of orange blossom, and a long train embroidered with pearls and silver falling in double box pleats from the shoulder. Newspapers trip over themselves in delivering fawning praise of "the most conspicuous social function the metropolis has seen in recent years." In midtown Manhattan's St. Thomas' Episcopal Church, a 60-piece orchestra and 60-man choir provides appropriately grandiose musical accompaniment.

"The wedding was, without exception, the most magnificent ever celebrated in this country."

THE NEW YORK TIMES

Her first of two, his first of two, lasts 26 years

November 7 (1959)

Claudette Rogers & William "Smokey" Robinson

It's gonna take a miracle, ooh ooh... Actually **it takes two miracles to complete today's wedding** at Detroit's Warren Avenue Baptist Church. More than a year away from hitting the big time, two members of the Miracles—Smokey Robinson, 19, and Claudette Rogers, 17—tie the knot before a crowd that includes their fellow band members, soon-to-be Motown founder Berry Gordy and recording star Jackie Wilson who, Robinson recalls, "looked sharper than the bridegroom." A local paper proclaims, "Claudette Rogers to Sing Forever With Wm. Robinson." She wears a traditional, long-sleeved silk gown, cinched at the waist and flowing into a full taffeta skirt, with a white headpiece and sheer veil. After a one-night honeymoon at a nearby motel, it's back on the road for the Miracles, the lowest-billed act in a traveling show that features the Isley Brothers and the Drifters. Over a year later, the happily married Smokey pens a catchy mama-done-tole-me ditty, "Shop Around," which becomes Motown's first million-seller and ignites the label's stupendous success.

> His first of two, her first, lasts 27 years

"It wasn't just her mouth that smiled, it was her whole face. She was a cutie pie, a fox, flipping me out the first time I saw her."

SMOKEY ROBINSON

November 8 (1955)
Barbara Hutton & Gottfried von Cramm

First she was a princess (twice, actually), then a countess, then a movie star's wife (July 8). None of those worked out, so **today she becomes a baroness**. "Poor little rich girl" Barbara Hutton, 42, heiress to the Woolworth fortune (her maternal grandfather founded the five-and-dime chain), marries former German tennis star Baron Gottfried von Cramm, 46. At a civil ceremony performed by the mayor in Versailles's rambling stone town hall, the couple marries to only two witnesses: the groom's brother and the curator of the nearby famed chateau. She wears a smartly tailored black suit, he wears a navy suit. Back at their hotel, he chats up reporters while she changes into a low-cut black satin gown plus a double strand of pearls, diamond earrings and bracelet, and a simple gold wedding band. Despite a touch of bronchitis and a slight fever, Hutton seems more rested and happy than when she faced photographers after marriage to husband #5, Dominican playboy Porfirio Rubirosa, which lasted less than two months.

Her sixth of seven, his second, lasts four years

November 9 (1955)
Phyllis Gates & Rock Hudson

Millions of American girls mourn after hearing today's news: hunky heartthrob Rock Hudson has gone and gotten hitched. Fresh off filming *Giant* opposite James Dean and Elizabeth Taylor, 29-year-old Hudson and Phyllis Gates, also 29 and secretary to his flamboyant publicist Henry Willson, elope to Santa Barbara for a ceremony at the Trinity Lutheran Church. Then they jet off for a Bermuda honeymoon, and upon return he's off shooting *Written on the Wind* opposite Lauren Bacall. Born Roy Scherer, the rugged, dark-haired truck driver turned actor fast ascends Hollywood's ranks. Within two years he's the #1 box-office star, edging out macho John Wayne, and cements his leading man status by abandoning action roles for light battle-of-the-sexes comedies opposite stars like Doris Day. Too late Gates learns that the whispers are true: Rock's queer, and her boss orchestrated the nuptials to maintain his All-American hetero image.

His first, her first, lasts three years

November 10 (2007)

Julianna Margulies &
Keith Lieberthal

It'll still be **a couple years before she makes her name as the gutsy title character in *The Good Wife***, but today she becomes one. Emmy Award-winning (for E.R.) Julianna Margulies, 41, quietly marries lawyer Keith Lieberthal in rural Lenox, Massachusetts. Seven months pregnant, she wears a white Narciso Rodriguez gown with sheer elbow length gloves, he wears a black Armani tux with a red boutonnière. Her father Paul, a veteran adman who helped develop the Alka-Seltzer "plop plop, fizz fizz" campaign, walks her down the aisle. The honeymoon must wait as Margulies immediately continues shooting her co-starring role in Fox's *Canterbury's Law*. Unfortunately that drama lasts barely more than a month after it premieres next March, but by that time the newlyweds have welcomed son Kieran Lindsay.

> "He knows how to have a good time, how to enjoy life the right way. He is a deep thinker, but he knows, too, that life is short. He is a man who understands what a good meal and a decent bottle of wine can do." JULIANNA MARGULIES

November 11 (1975)

Toni Tennille &
Daryl "The Captain" Dragon

Love will keep us together, vow so many newlyweds. But only one couple manages to turn that promise into a multi-million seller. A few months after **"Love Will Keep Us Together"** (co-written by Neil Sedaka) topped the charts en route to being crowned the Grammy's Record of the Year, Toni Tennille, 35, and Daryl Dragon, 33, marry quietly at the Silver Queen Saloon Wedding Chapel in Virginia City, Nevada. Taking marital bliss to new heights, they succeed Sonny & Cher (Oct. 27) as America's favorite hitched musical duo, churning out treacly pop numbers like "The Way I Want to Touch You" and "Muskrat Love." Their subsequent, self-titled ABC variety hour doesn't quite click the way Sonny & Cher's did, though it does tickle America's fancy by featuring their English bulldogs, Elizabeth and Broderick. At last look, love has still kept them (the humans, that is) together.

November 12 (1969)
Julie Andrews & Blake Edwards

Julie Andrews' squeaky clean reputation has been burnished by starring roles in family favorites like *Mary Poppins* and *The Sound of Music*. But such popularity—she's been the #1 box-office star for two years running — naturally leads to sniping, as when director Blake Edwards was asked about her stardom. "I know exactly what that's about," he said. **"She has lilacs for pubic hairs."** Andrews roared upon hearing that line. Not only did she not hold it against him, it paved the way for their introduction and subsequent courtship. This afternoon, several nights after *An Evening with Julie Andrews and Harry Belafonte* aired on NBC, Andrews, 34, marries Edwards, 47, in the backyard garden of her hacienda-style home overlooking Beverly Hills. She wears a casual white and coral short-sleeved outfit, he opts for a more formal double-breasted suit.

His second, her second, lasts 41 years until his death

'Of course I know Julie Andrews. She's the last of the really great broads.' PAUL NEWMAN

'I wouldn't mind having that as my epitaph.' JULIE ANDREWS

November 13 (1993)
Michelle Pfeiffer & David E. Kelley

He's on a roll, having scored a hat trick for the first season of his offbeat drama *Picket Fences* with Emmy awards for Best Series, Best Actor and Best Actress. She's no slouch either, occupying a lofty perch as one of Hollywood's most popular and beautiful leading ladies with well-received turns in films like *The Fabulous Baker Boys* and *Dangerous Liaisons*. The two **met on a blind date engineered by friends**, and today David E. Kelley, 37, and Michelle Pfeiffer, 35, wed in a quiet non-denominational service in Santa Barbara before 40 guests. She wears an off-white, antique lace dress, and the ceremony concludes with the christening of her adopted eight-month-old daughter. Nine months later she gives birth to their son John Henry.

"Ultimately, I believe the only secret to a happy marriage is choosing the right person." MICHELLE PFEIFFER

November 14 (1996)
Debbie Rowe & Michael Jackson

The media is still picking through the bones after last summer's demise of the confounding, captivating two-year marriage of Michael Jackson and Lisa Marie Presley. Tonight **the Gloved One, 38, feeds a fresh tabloid frenzy** as he weds six-months' pregnant Debbie Rowe, 37, in his suite at the Sheraton on the Park hotel in Sydney, Australia during the HIStory world tour. They'd met in the early '80s at his dermatologist's office where she worked as a nurse and receptionist. Though the eager father had planned to keep his confidant/best pal strictly a surrogate, his mother insisted that they marry, and dutiful Michael complied. He gives Debbie, demurely dressed in black, a $100,000 diamond/platinum ring and a tentative kiss at the end of the brief ceremony. Next February she gives birth to Prince Michael, followed by daughter Paris the following year.

November 15 (1997)

Nerine Kidd & William Shatner

The captain takes a mate. "I pledge allegiance to you, Nerine, my queen," says William Shatner, 66, a.k.a. Captain James T. Kirk of the Starship Enterprise, as he slips an emerald-cut diamond on her finger. **"When it is dark and there is trouble, you need but wave that bauble and there will be light."** At the outdoor ceremony in Pasadena, *Star Trek* cohort Leonard Nimoy serves as first officer, er, best man. Shatner met former model Nerine Kidd, 37, when he was in Toronto directing an episode of the TV series *Kung Fu*. Years later Shatner tenderly recalled the moment: "I was struck instantly by her beauty and this marvelous sort of fuck-you attitude, this arrogance, that was so much a part of her. She had strawberry-blond hair and freckled pale Irish skin, the brightest blue eyes you've ever seen, and a spectacular figure." Unfortunately she also had an alcohol addiction, and after numerous alcohol-related incidents drowned in their pool one stormy year later.

"I had met the girl of my dreams. I fell in love with her and believed she was everything I'd spent my life looking for in a woman. WILLIAM SHATNER

His third of four, lasts one year until her death

November 16 (1987)
Lisa Bonet & Lenny Kravitz

Happy birthday—**will you marry me?** Just last week they turned heads when appearing at the L.A. premiere of *Barfly*. Today, Lenny Kravitz, 23, and Lisa Bonet, celebrating her 20th birthday, elope and marry secretly in Las Vegas. Both are children of interracial marriages with white fathers and black mothers. He's an unknown musician sporting the professional name Romeo Blue whose mother plays half of an interracial couple in *The Jeffersons*. Bonet is much higher profile, a household name as know-it-all teenage daughter Denise in *The Cosby Show*. But a nude scene in her controversial movie debut, *Angel Heart*, opposite *Barfly*'s Mickey Rourke, hastens her exit from the sitcom. With the help of fatherly Bill Cosby (Jan. 25), she shifts to the spin-off *A Different World*, but is fired after a year of chronic bad behavior. Meanwhile her hubby's musical career takes off and eclipses hers, and their marriage fizzles.

Her first, his first, lasts six years

November 17 (1981)
Laura Baldwin & Luke Spencer

Let's hope they've ordered a multi-tiered wedding cake, because there will be a lot of company—say, **30 million fans eager to witness the culmination of their star-crossed courtship**. Today the largest audience in daytime television history tunes in to the wedding of Romeo and Juliet sweethearts Luke Spencer (Anthony Geary) and Laura Baldwin (Genie Francis). The producers of *General Hospital* planned for 250 actual guests, but the exclusive private community that houses the site of the ceremony, a faux 17th century Norman/French chateau, limited the crowd to 140. No stranger to weddings, having married seven times to date, Elizabeth Taylor (Oct. 10) is such a fan of the show that she requests and receives a cameo role as a mysterious widow who curses the newlyweds.

Memorable Television Weddings

The Sixties

Samantha & Darrin *(Bewitched, Sept. '64)*

Laura & Rob *(The Dick Van Dyke Show, Oct. '63)*

Max & Agent 99 *(Get Smart, Nov. '68)*

Carol & Mike *(The Brady Bunch, Sept. '69)*

The Seventies

Mike & Gloria *(All in the Family, Nov. '72)*

Rhoda & Joe *(Rhoda, Oct. '74)*

Ted & Georgette *(The Mary Tyler Moore Show, Nov. '75)*

Margaret (Hot Lips) & Donald *(M*A*S*H, March '77)*

The Eighties

Richie & Lori Beth *(Happy Days, May '81)*

Mork & Mindy *(Mork & Mindy, Oct. '81)*

Latka & Simka *(Taxi, March '83)*

Ann & Stuart *(L.A. Law, Jan. '88)*

The Nineties

Kelly & Woody *(Cheers, May '92)*

Kelly & Zack *(Saved by the Bell, May '93)*

Emily & Ross *(Friends, May '98)*

Donna & David *(Beverly Hills 90210, May '98)*

The Aughts

Monica & Chandler *(Friends, May '01)*

Daphne & Niles *(Frasier, Sept. '02)*

Charlotte & Harry *(Sex and the City, Aug. '03)*

Pam & Jim *(The Office, Oct. '09)*

November 18 (2000)
Catherine Zeta-Jones
& Michael Douglas

New York's storied Plaza Hotel has hosted countless weddings over its 93 years, but **today's $1.5 million extravaganza registers as one of its most regal ever**. As a 40-member Welsh choir sings, the bride's mother enters with the couple's three-month-old son Dylan, dressed in a sailor suit. Then the 350 glittery guests—including Goldie Hawn, Jack Nicholson, Meg Ryan, and U.N. Secretary General Kofi Annan—watch the entrances of Catherine Zeta-Jones, 31, and Michael Douglas, 56. She wears an ivory-beaded Christian Lacroix satin sheath gown with a Chantilly lace train, and a diamond tiara in her hair. A sumptuous feast of New England clam chowder, terrine of foie gras, rack of Welsh lamb and lobster is followed by a 10-tier, six-foot vanilla and buttercream cake (that had to be disassembled to fit through the ballroom's doors, then reassembled). Live entertainers include Gladys Knight doing "You're the Best Thing That Ever Happened to Me" for the couple's first dance, followed by Jimmy Buffett, Art Garfunkel and Bonnie Tyler.

November 19 (2005)
Christina Aguilera & Jordan Bratman

What a pop goddess wants comes true today. Arriving in a white Rolls-Royce Phantom, Christina Aguilera, 24, marries musical manager Jordan Bratman, 28, in a sunset ceremony at a Napa, California vineyard before 130 guests. With her hair pulled back in a bun and decorated with jewels and white flowers, she wears a Spanish-style Christian Lacroix gown with an elaborate ruffled train. He opts for another Christian, a Christian Dior tux, entering to the strains of a 14-piece orchestra from the San Francisco Symphony. Under a gold and bronze chuppah wrapped with hydrangea, lilies and roses, he ends the traditional Jewish service by stomping on a glass. At the reception, after their first dance to "In a Sentimental Mood," Christina sings "Lady Marmalade" and later dedicates "At Last" to her new hubby. Guests dance through the night 'til 5 a.m. when waffles are served. In lieu of gifts, the couple asks that contributions be made to victims of Hurricanes Katrina and Rita.

"We have something called naked Sundays... You have to keep marriage alive, spice it up." CHRISTINA AGUILERA

Her first, his first, lasts five years

November 20 (1947)

Princess Elizabeth & Philip Mountbatten

As the royal bride gets dressed this morning at Buckingham Palace, her tiara breaks. Heavens! **Good thing the court jeweler is on hand to repair it.** And so the day that Britain has so eagerly awaited proceeds as scheduled. Princess Elizabeth, 21, marries her distant cousin, Philip Mountbatten (just named the Duke of Edinburgh), 26, before nearly 3,000 kings, nobles, statesmen and commoners in Westminster Abbey. Her elaborate Norman Hartnell dress, made only after the princess collected the ration cards necessary in postwar England, was reportedly inspired by a floral-themed Botticelli painting. Outside, hundreds of thousands of well-wishers cheer and millions more worldwide listen to radio broadcasts in 42 languages. As per her request, Elizabeth's bridal bouquet of white orchids and a sprig of myrtle is placed tomorrow on the grave of the unknown solider in Westminster Abbey.

"Elizabeth was wed in all the golden splendor and medieval magnificence that her father's austerity-pinched land could muster. Stunning in a dress of ivory satin embroidered with thousands of pearls, Elizabeth and her naval-uniformed bridegroom knelt on crimson pillows in the soft light of the altar." ASSOCIATED PRESS

November 21 (1987)

Demi Moore & Bruce Willis

Ever since the ABC sitcom *Moonlighting* elevated Bruce Willis to star status, he's been a major-league tabloid fixture for various on- and off-screen shenanigans. Today Willis, 32, and Brat Packer (*St. Elmo's Fire, About Last Night*) Demi Moore, 24, rock the media world by marrying in a private ceremony at the Little White Chapel in Las Vegas. Ally Sheedy serves as a bridesmaid and the inimitable Little Richard provides the music. The high and getting higher profiles of **Hollywood's hottest couple** soar as the movie he's currently filming, *Die Hard*, ignites the box office next summer—just around the time she delivers their first of three daughters. The follow-up *Die Hard II* does big business too, but pales before that year's #1 flick, *Ghost*, starring, yes, Moore, in a role that helps solidify her rarefied spot as Hollywood's highest paid actress. Her very pregnant, naked cover photo in *Vanity Fair* in 1991 further fans the celebrity fires.

His first of two, her first of three, lasts 13 years

November 22 (1965)

Sara Lowndes & Bob Dylan

With their high-profile visibility, isn't it only a matter of time before folk/protest singers Joan Baez (Mar. 26) and Bob Dylan tie the knot? That's what the public may think, but Dylan is nothing if not confounding. Privately he's been wooing a beautiful ex-Playboy bunny and model, Sara Lowndes, whom he met through the wife of his manager. Today, in the midst of touring, Dylan, 24, weds Lowndes, 26, in a secret ceremony on the lawn outside a judge's chambers in Mineola, New York. Not even telling his parents, Dylan misleads a reporter a week later by saying, "Getting married, having a bunch of kids? I have no hopes for it." Nora Ephron finally breaks the news next February in a *New York Post* story entitled, **"Hush! Bob Dylan Is Wed."** By then Lowndes has already given birth to their first son, Jesse. Songs she inspires include "Sad-Eyed Lady of the Lowlands," "Sara" and "If You See Her, Say Hello."

> **His first of two, her second, lasts 12 years**

November 23 (1996)

Malaak Compton & Chris Rock

He's been riding high with *Bring the Pain*, an HBO special that showcased his edgy comedic take on race relations in America. But today **he's bringing something else, the love**, as ex-*Saturday Night Live* star Chris Rock, 31, marries Malaak Compton, 27, in suburban Washington, D.C. He dedicates the ceremony to his late father, a blue-collar worker who didn't live to see his son's stunning career success. The couple met a couple years ago when he and several pals crashed the Essence Awards ceremony in New York where she was working as a publicist. To honor their unique gate-crashing encounter, they name their dog Essence.

November 24 (1954)
Pier Angeli & Vic Damone

Two fast rising young movie stars, one fierce love affair. But it ended badly when she jilted him, and today he sits, brooding, **on a motorcycle across the street from St. Timothy Catholic Church** in Santa Monica. Inside Pier Angeli, 22, and crooner Vic Damone, 26, marry in an elaborate service before a crowd of 400, serenaded by an angelic choir of 35 boys dressed in red, white and gold. She wears a white silk chiffon over crepe dress with a tight-fitting bodice, high lace collar, long embroidered sleeves and flowing skirt. Her Juliet cap anchoring her full-length tulle veil is embroidered with seed pearls. She wears no jewelry but carries a lace and beribboned bouquet of lilies of the valley. When the couple steps outside into the midday sun, photographers crowd about to get their shots as a motorbike revs up across the street and roars away, with the iconic and heartbroken James Dean aboard.

> Her first of two, his first of five, lasts four years

November 25 (1993)
Mary Matalin & James Carville

Oil and water, Democrat and Republican: **an improbable bipartisan courtship culminates in wedded bliss** in New Orleans' famed French Quarter. Political strategists (him Bill Clinton, her George H.W. Bush) James Carville, 49, and Mary Matalin, 40, marry to the strains of a string quartet at a civil ceremony at the Omni Royal Orleans hotel. She wears an ivory satin gown with an off-the-shoulder, draped portrait collar and bustle train trimmed with satin bows. Fortunately it detaches as the couple joins a dancing, swaying parade along the swinging streets, led by the Olympia Brass Band, to famed restaurant Arnaud's. The menu is a combo Thanksgiving/classic N'Awlins spread including turkey, gumbo, sweet potato and Andouille sausage soup and shrimp bisque. The 150 guests, mirroring the couple, represent both sides of the political spectrum: Paul Begala, Rush Limbaugh, Robert Mosbacher and George Stephanopoulos plus lawyer Alan Dershowitz, musician Al Hirt and actor Timothy Hutton.

> His first, her third

November 26 (1981)
Cicely Tyson & Miles Davis

On a chilly winter's evening in the Berkshires, **a midnight ceremony on Thanksgiving Day unites two high-profile celebrities**: Emmy award-winning actress Cicely Tyson, 47, and legendary Grammy award-winning jazzman Miles Davis, 55. Held at the home of actor/comedian Bill Cosby, who serves as best man and also gives away the bride, the ceremony is performed by Atlanta Mayor-elect Andrew Young, an ordained minister. The celebrated guests include friends on both sides including Dizzy Gillespie, Dick Gregory, Max Roach and Clarence Williams III. But the mercurial musical genius, an abuser and ex-addict, and the strong, successful actress are a bad fit.

His third, her first, lasts seven difficult years

"I respected her as a woman and felt like she was a good friend to me, but I also need that sex thing that I couldn't get from her. So I got it in other places." MILES DAVIS

November 27 (1960)
Lana Turner & Frederick May

Things didn't end so well with her last boyfriend, abusive mob lackey Johnny Stompanato. Her daughter Cheryl stabbed him to death two years ago in a sensationalistic crime that made headlines worldwide. Today, at the elegant pink stucco Miramar Hotel in Santa Monica, screen star Lana Turner, 40, marries retired sportsman and department store heir Frederick May, 43. She wears a simple honey-colored wool dress with alligator accessories and carries a small bouquet of yellow roses. Actress Virginia Grey serves as matron of honor, his best friend George Mann serves as best man. The only other guests are her mother, secretary and daughter Cheryl, whom the newlyweds drop off back at the school for wayward girls en route to a honeymoon in Carmel.

"My goal was to have one husband and seven children, but it turned out to be the other way around." LANA TURNER

November 28 (1962)
Yoko Ono & Anthony Cox

yes

From a rich family, **the diminutive Japanese native** emigrated as a teenager to the U.S. with her family in the early '50s. Drawn to the world of avant-garde art, she left college and began staging unconventional exhibits of performance art. An ardent fan, a young American filmmaker, pursued her zealously. Today Yoko Ono, 29, and Tony Cox, 25, marry, though her divorce from a Japanese composer isn't final. So next March the marriage is annulled, and the couple remarries in June. Two months later, in Tokyo, she gives birth to daughter Kyoko. But conflicts quickly arise between the driven Yoko and her equally ambitious husband, who puts his career on hold to promote hers and to raise their daughter. An art symposium in London triggers their relocation, and as the marriage falters she throws herself headlong into her art. At a gallery show in 1966 she charms an unshaven, stoned visitor, John Lennon, with her minimalist "yes" exhibit.

Her second of three, lasts six years

November 29 (1962)
Diane Cilento & Sean Connery

It's a secret assignment carried out in the finest cloak-and-dagger tradition, because he's a fast-ascending heartthrob to millions of ladies worldwide—so **news of his departing bachelorhood must be soft-pedaled**. Sean Connery, 32, the dashing cinematic embodiment of super sleuth 007, surfaces in Gibraltar with his pregnant ladylove, Australian actress Diane Cilento, 29. After a quick ceremony at its registry office, with two taxi drivers roped in as witnesses, the couple enjoys a night at the famed Rock Hotel before heading off for a honeymoon along Spain's Costa del Sol, accompanied by her five-year-old daughter from a previous marriage. No, that's not at all the image the producers want for the strapping Scottish star of the first James Bond movie, *Dr. No*, which is torching the box office in Europe and soon to have a similar impact in America. Six weeks later, as production readies for the follow-up, *From Russia With Love*, handsome Sean becomes a proud papa to son Jason.

"His thick eyebrows met between his eyes— he looked dangerous, but fun." DIANE CILENTO

His first of two, her second of three, lasts 11 years

> *"Once in his life, every man is entitled to fall madly in love with a gorgeous redhead."*
>
> LUCILLE BALL

November 30 (1940)
Lucille Ball & Desi Arnaz

Just yesterday she told reporters she had no plans to marry any time soon. Then her longtime steady arrived at her Pierre Hotel suite between his shows at the Roxy, and popped the question. This morning a light snow falls as their limo speeds up the Merritt Parkway en route to Greenwich, Conn. A justice of the peace decides his drab courthouse chambers won't do, so he rings up the Byram River Beagle Club, a nearby hunting lodge. So there, with a ring purchased hastily at a local Woolworth's, Lucille Ball, 29, weds Desi Arnaz, 23. She wears a light gray woolen suit under a silver fox coat and matching hat, he wears a double-breasted blue serge suit. After breakfast before a glowing fireplace, **they kiss each other and the marriage certificate**. Years later, when the paper shows signs of age, Lucy's lipstick still glows red. Alerted by the news media, a packed house at the Roxy this afternoon fetes the new couple with pounds of rice, supplied by the management. Tonight Desi hosts a formal bash at the El Morocco.

Her first of two, his first of two, lasts 20 years

December

Natalie Wood & Robert Wagner
December 28, 1957

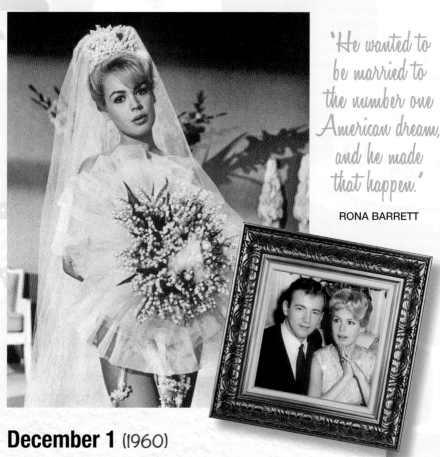

December 1 (1960)
Sandra Dee & Bobby Darin

As the story goes, they met last fall on a dock in Portofino, Italy, where they'd gone to shoot a movie, *Come September*, opposite leading players Rock Hudson (Nov. 9) and Gina Lollobrigida (Jan. 15). As she pulled in on a boat, he called out, "Hi, I'm Bobby Darin. You're gonna be my wife." She replied, "Not today." But **they fell hard for each other: the red hot, womanizing singer from the wrong side of the tracks and the shy but perky girl nicknamed "America's Sweetheart."** Tonight at 3 a.m. Darin, 24, and Sandra Dee, 18, marry in the Elizabeth, N.J. apartment of his producer pal Don Kirschner. A local magistrate performs the short ceremony attended by a handful of family and friends, but not her stage mother Mary, around whom rumors swirl about a fling with Darin during the movie's filming. Then, with a Yorkshire terrier tucked under her arm, they fly to Florida for his engagement at the Deauville Hotel and a rocky honeymoon.

His first of two, her first, lasts seven years

December 2 (1984)
Connie Chung & Maury Povich

Their relationship has gone the distance, and it continues to be long distance. Yet today **a made-in-TV marriage of two prominent personalities** occurs in a most private setting: the bride's apartment in the 19th century apartment building The Dakota aside Central Park, site of John Lennon's assassination four years before. Having dated for nearly seven years, NBC News anchor Connie Chung, 38, marries Metromedia anchor Maury Povich, 45. They met in their native Washington, D.C., and reconnected while briefly co-anchoring a news show in Los Angeles. Now the New York-based anchor's up at three a.m. every day to host *NBC News at Sunrise*, while he's an evening anchor at a station in D.C. Their back-and-forth relationship continues 'til he lands a new syndicated show, *A Current Affair*, based in New York.

"The telephone company and the airlines will be tying this marriage together... But you can bet we'll make up for it over the weekend." CONNIE CHUNG

December 3 (1965)
Shirlee Mae Adams & Henry Fonda

Gossip columnists have been whispering, including one who reported spotting a wedding ring on the young lady's finger during a dinner with her boyfriend at a posh NYC restaurant last fall. They've been dating since meeting at a screening of his film, *The Longest Day*. Today stalwart Henry Fonda, 60, makes it official, marrying 33-year-old ex-stewardess and model Shirlee Mae Adams in a judge's chambers in Mineola, New York. George Peppard and Elizabeth Ashley, who'll marry next spring, serve as best man and maid of honor, respectively. Returning to New York for Fonda's nightly appearance in the Broadway comedy *Generation*, the couple encounters a media horde encamped outside his midtown flat. At his new wife's suggestion, the publicity-shy groom invites them in. While the tabloids rage about **the May/December romance** (July 19) of Frank Sinatra (50) and Mia Farrow (21), this quarter-century-plus age disparity raises few eyebrows, and the marriage lasts until his death in 1982.

His fifth, her first, lasts 17 years until his death

December 4 (1999)
Prince Philippe & Princess Mathilde

As the days count down to a new century, is there **time for one more lavish royal wedding?** Why not, and in multiple languages too. Tens of thousands line the streets near Brussels' royal palace to celebrate the union between Belgian Crown Prince Philippe, 39, and speech therapist Mathilde d'Udekem, 26, whose secret two-year romance was revealed only a few months ago. After a civil service in French, Dutch and German, the couple marries at a medieval cathedral to the sounds of Bach in a Roman Catholic service conduced in Dutch and French. The smiling bride, who appears far more at ease than her serious groom, wears an eggshell gown of crepe and silk, with a five-yard, 100-year-old train of (what else?) Brussels lace emanating from her diamond tiara. One hundred and one cannon shots ring out as the couple rides back to the palace in a glass-topped Mercedes-Benz limo. If her husband assumes the throne as expected, Mathilde will become the first native-born queen in Belgium's history, succeeding women born in France, Austria, Germany, Sweden, Spain and Italy.

"The whole of Belgium fell for your charms."

THE MAYOR OF BRUSSELS TO PRINCESS MATHILDE

December 5 (2003)
Gwyneth Paltrow & Chris Martin

Two days ago, news broke that she was pregnant. Yesterday, at a taping of *The Ellen DeGeneres Show*, Gwyneth Paltrow received well wishes and baby gifts. Today Paltrow, 31, and Coldplay frontman Chris Martin, 26, pull off that most elusive feat: **a celebrity wedding with absolutely no paparazzi.** Or guests. After quietly taking out a wedding license this morning at the Santa Barbara County courthouse, the pair heads off and weds at the lush San Ysidro Ranch (where Vivien Leigh married Laurence Olivier) in the Montecito foothills of Southern California's wine country. After dark, wearing hooded sweatshirts, they stealthily (and successfully) slip out unnoticed en route to a honeymoon at the Esperanza Resort in Cabo San Lucas, Mexico. Five months later they welcome daughter Apple.

"I focus more on understanding than on being understood."

GWYNETH PALTROW, ON HER MARRIAGE

December 6 (2003)
Trista Rehn & Ryan Sutter

Hurry hurry, step right up: it's **romance-for-ratings time**. Given that they wooed before, only, say 20 million people every week, it's no great surprise that the couple from *The Bachelorette* should marry in a mega-hyped, reality-show wedding. Cameras roll as Trista Rehn, 31, strolls down the aisle at a Palm Springs resort to the strains of "Here Comes the Bride." She wears a strapless satin Badgley Mischka dress and diamond-encrusted shoes, carrying a bouquet of pink peonies swathed in silk and Swarovski crystals. Groom Ryan Sutter, 29, wears a black Kenneth Cole tux with vest and silver tie. ABC picks up the tab, estimated at nearly $4 million including the couple's $1 million fee, $500,000 for 30,000 roses imported from Ecuador, her $70,000 gown and a $15,000 wedding cake. Rather than a prenuptial agreement, the couple signs a contract that gives ABC control over all aspects of the "first class, high-end affair." The network inflates the made-for-TV event into a three-night miniseries airing next week. Defying the doubters, the marriage has endured.

"A publicity stunt that flouts the principles marriage is supposed to embody: a commitment of love and loyalty based on mutual respect and shared values."

COLUMNIST CYNTHIA TUCKER

December 7 (2003)
Mary J. Blige & Kendu Isaacs

No More Drama proclaimed the title of R&B/hip hop queen Mary J. Blige's multi-platinum album. Today there's **no hoopla, no celebrities, not even a band**. As a guest plays "Here Comes the Bride" on a piano, Blige, 32, walks down the aisle of her Bergen County, N.J. home to marry plus-size producer Kendu Isaacs, 33, before 50 guests. The two met when he was producing an album for Queen Latifah. Her mother and sister whip up a homemade dinner of oxtail, barbecued chicken, crab, red rice and salad, topped off with a cake from their favorite Yonkers, N.Y., bakery. Besides the nuptials, the happy couple also celebrates the Grammy nominations announced two days ago. Next February Blige wins her third Grammy for "Whenever I Say Your Name," her pop collaboration with Sting.

Her first, his second

December 8 (1963)
Barbara Walters & Lee Guber

Two weeks ago the world turned upside down when JFK was assassinated in Dallas. A few days later the former fiancé of a rising television writer who'd been pressed into on-air service to help cover the president's funeral showed up at her apartment. She answered the door with a towel wrapped around her hair, dripping wet from a shower. "Life is too short," he said. **"Let's get married right now."** Even though they hadn't spoken since she broke off their engagement three months ago, the moment had arrived. Today Barbara Walters, 34, and Lee Guber, 43, marry at the East Side apartment of one of her high school friends. Only a handful of guests witness the short ceremony uniting the *Today* show staff writer and an entrepreneurial showman who met on a blind date last year at the Friars Club. Last night Walters declined a last-minute proposal from one of her closest friends: closeted attorney and ex-Senator Joe McCarthy henchman Roy Cohn.

Her second of three, his second, lasts 13 years

December 9 (2005)

Luciana Barroso
& Matt Damon

Privacy si, paparazzi no. After a series of tabloid-friendly, high-profile affairs and breakups with fellow screen stars like Minnie Driver, Claire Danes and Winona Ryder, the groom-to-be opts for **a very private wedding** —just like his best pal Ben Affleck did six months ago (June 29). Matt Damon, 35, and three-months pregnant Luciana Barrosa, 29, exchange vows at a quiet ceremony at New York City Hall officiated by a justice of the peace. Her seven-year-old daughter Alexia from a previous marriage is the only family member to attend. The two met in Miami Beach where the beautiful Argentinean brunette was bartending. Afterwards the busy actor heads off to nearby Yonkers to continue filming *The Good Shepherd*, and tomorrow the family jets off to London for a quasi-honeymoon and continued shooting of the movie.

December 10 (2005)
Tricia Yearwood & Garth Brooks

Topping the engagement would have been difficult, so he didn't even try. Eight months ago, at the unveiling of his statue at Buck Owens' Crystal Palace in Bakersfield, California, Garth Brooks **crouched down on one knee, took off his trademark cowboy hat and proposed** to Tricia Yearwood. She wiped away a tear as 7,000 fans went wild. Today Brooks, 43, and Yearwood, 41, marry in a private ceremony at his Oklahoma ranch. The small service includes his three daughters Taylor, August and Allie, who also exchange rings with their new stepmother. "It's the perfect Christmas gift to each other – we could not be happier," says Brooks, who met his future bride when each was a struggling Nashville newcomer. His career took off first, and he helped put her career on the fast track by connecting her with a producer, hiring her as his opening act on tour before her debut #1 song, "She's in Love With the Boy."

His second, her third

'I'm beginning this next stage of my life with my best friend beside me. My new goal is to be known as Mr. Trisha Yearwood. GARTH BROOKS

December 11 (1924)
Georgia O'Keeffe & Alfred Stieglitz

No gala affair, no bouquet, no reception, no honeymoon for this odd yet so prominent couple: bushy-haired Alfred Stieglitz, with his bristling white mustache, and slender, dark-haired Georgia O'Keeffe. Stieglitz, 60, one of the world's most eminent photographers, and O'Keeffe, 37, a promising painter, marry at a friend's house in Cliffside Park, N.J. **The bride wears black**. Then they catch the ferry back to Manhattan and the apartment they've been

sharing for several years while he was still married to his first wife. O'Keeffe refuses to change her name, one that he has made prominent by displaying and selling her work at his renowned Fifth Avenue gallery. She becomes his somewhat recalcitrant muse. He photographs her obsessively, producing more than 350 prints, while she shifts styles to concentrate on the southwest, where she lives most of the rest of her life, painting the large-format flowers that make her famous.

His second, her first and only, lasts 22 years until his death

THE ✦ TIMES

"We got married because we love each other and we decided to make a life together. We are heterosexual and monogamous and take our commitment to each other very seriously."

FROM GERE & CRAWFORD'S NEWSPAPER AD

December 12 (1991)
Cindy Crawford & Richard Gere

Early tonight the owner of Las Vegas's famed Little Church of the West receives a telephone call from a Disney exec: an unnamed Hollywood couple will be arriving shortly for their hush-hush wedding. Several hours later in stroll supermodel Cindy Crawford, 25, and movie star Richard Gere, 42, accompanied by several friends including his agent Ed Limato and photographer Herb Ritts. Cindy wears a dark pantsuit and white turtleneck, Richard a leather jacket and jeans. With no special requests or handwritten vows, the private service is over in a flash—but the media hubbub has just begun. Next week she appears on *The Arsenio Hall Show*, answering the host's question about whether her husband is an officer or a gentleman in the bedroom, thusly: **"Well, you'll always wonder now, won't you?"** Three years later the couple takes out a full-page ad in London's *The Times* to quash nasty little rumors, but six months later they announce their separation via press release.

His first of two, her first of two, lasts four years

December 13 (2003)
Nicoletta Mantovani & Luciano Pavarotti

Music's in the air as 600 guests gather at the opera house in Modena, Italy. **As a gospel choir sings "Here Comes the Sun**," here comes the bride: 34-year old Nicoletta Mantovani, resplendent in a pale pink Armani gown and carrying a bouquet of pink roses. The happy groom's none other than storied tenor Luciano Pavarotti, 68, who completes the storybook saga that's become a staple of gossip columns: young student turned secretary turned love interest turns wife. Their year-old daughter wears a miniature version of her mother's dress. Other musical performances including Andrea Bocelli singing "Ave Maria." The shimming guest list includes Sting and his wife Trudie (Aug. 22), Bono (Aug. 21), designers Donatella Versace, Domenico Dolce and Stefano Gabbana, plus actress Gina Lollobrigida and soccer star Alessandro Del Piero.

His second, her first, lasts four years until his death

"As a general rule, I would warn against anyone marrying a person with more than a ten-year age difference. It almost never works."

JAMES BROWN

December 14 (2001)
Tomi Rae Hynie & James Brown

This is a man's world, according to one of the signature tunes of electrifying soul singer James Brown—but it's nothing, he aptly points out, without a woman or a girl. Today the hardest workin' man in show business again follows his own advice by hitching up with wife #4 at a private ceremony in front of 150 guests at his home in Beech Island, S.C. During the reception James, 68, and shapely redhead Tomi Rae Hynie, 32, sing **a duet: "Baby (You've Got What it Takes)."** Last summer the background singer gave birth to their first child together, James Brown II, his ninth child. But problems quickly develop, far beyond their age difference or the color of their skins (she's white). Brown's long history of abuse reemerges, with domestic violence charges, separations and reconciliations keeping the tempestuous couple in the news. After he dies five years later, word surfaces that she was married to another man at the time she wed Brown, so their marriage wasn't legal.

December 15 (1985)

Brigitte Nielsen & Sylvester Stallone

Last year while he was in the throes of a divorce, **she thoughtfully sent him a fan letter—accompanied by a revealing photo**. Before long she moved into his Pacific Palisades home. Today statuesque blonde Danish model Brigitte Nielsen, 22, marries macho mega-star Sylvester Stallone, 39, at the Malibu estate of his *Rocky* co-producer, Irwin Winkler. She wears a self-designed white silk dress trimmed with white fox fur and laden with pearls and heart-shaped crystals, and a tassled headpiece. She stands two inches taller than her husband who dubs her his "tower of power." This year alone *Rocky IV*, in which he cast her as the wife of his Russian opponent, and *Rambo* and have grossed more than $200 million. The money undoubtedly comes in handy for their shopping spree tomorrow along Beverly Hills' plush Rodeo Drive. Then it's off to co-starring roles in *Cobra*, but the marriage is rocky.

His second of three, her second of five, lasts 18 months

December 16 (1984)
Bette Midler & Martin von Haselberg

Flashy and brassy onstage, Bette Midler takes a decidedly opposite approach in her personal life. Tonight at 2 a.m., she strolls down the aisle aside Martin von Haselberg at the Candlelight Wedding Chapel in Las Vegas. Then again, **the minister does moonlight as an Elvis impersonator—hey, this *is* Vegas**—but Bette doesn't find this out until the end of the ceremony when he hands her his single. Days after her 39th birthday, Bette caps an intense six-week courtship with von Haselberg, a fellow with an unusual job combination: commodities broker/performance artist (a.k.a. Harry Kipper of the Kipper Kids). They'd been introduced by her pal Toni Basil several years earlier, but didn't reconnect until several months ago when he called her out of the blue. One date led to another, and another, a late-night proposal in L.A. and this midnight ride to Las Vegas.

December 17 (1969)
Miss Vicky & Tiny Tim

Ten thousand tulips imported from Holland fill a stage dressed in turn-of-the-century fittings. Swinging a hand-carved walking stick, gangly groom Herbert Khaury, 37, gambols down the aisle aside his bride, Vicky Budinger, 17. With her hair bobbed, she wears an off-white, Victorian-era gown of peau de soie lace. Welcome to **the made-for-television nuptials of Tiny Tim and Miss Vicky,** watched by a studio audience of 250 and an estimated 21 million home viewers—the biggest audience to date for *The Tonight Show Starring Johnny Carson*. The beak-nosed, scraggly longhaired singer with that inimitable falsetto met his intended at a book signing in a Philadelphia department store last summer. His remake of a 1929 hit, "Tip-Toe Thru the Tulips With Me," helped launch his unlikely stardom, and tonight the original singer, Nick Lucas, is on hand to sing it to the new couple.

His first of three, lasts seven years

December 18 (1983)

Patti Hansen & Keith Richards

A notorious womanizing bad boy and on-and-off drug addict, he cleans up nicely today and is right presentable in full evening dress and blue suede shoes. Outside the Hotel Finisterra in Cabo San Lucas, Mexico, Keith Richards, turning 40 today, marries model Patti Hansen, 27. **The Lutheran ceremony, conducted in Spanish, includes a novel twist**: Keith, who usually shuns organized religion, adds the Jewish custom of stomping on a glass wrapped in cloth. Mick Jagger, appearing without longtime gal pal Jerry Hall, serves as best man, and Keith's parents come too: the first time they've been together in 20 years. At the reception at a nearby trailer camp, Keith flings himself at her feet and serenades his new wife with Hoagy Carmichael's "The Nearness of You."

"I know I couldn't have beaten heroin without Patti. She's been of inestimable value. I ain't letting that bitch go!" KEITH RICHARDS

December 19 (1953)
Maggie Johnson
& Clint Eastwood

They **met on a blind date in Berkeley**, set up by a friend: a tall, attractive gal from a good family and a soon-to-be-released soldier. After his discharge he headed to L.A., juggling odd jobs as a building manager and gas station attendant, with a vague interest in becoming an actor. She moved home to the San Bernardino mountains and took a job as a manufacturer's rep. Today Clint Eastwood, 23, and Maggie Johnson marry in a South Pasadena home before a Congregational minister, then head off for a honeymoon in Carmel. His acting lessons don't have much effect, but Clint does have the attributes now in demand after Marlon Brando's star turn in *On the Waterfront*: he's young, handsome, cool and brooding. It's enough to get him signed by Universal for $75 a week, where he's soon bedding available starlets and getting bit parts in films like *Francis in the Navy*. Six lean years later CBS's western *Rawhide* makes him into a star.

His first of two, lasts 25 years

December 20 (1998)
Kimora Lee & Russell Simmons

A missed flight stranded the groom temporarily in Puerto Rico, but **the hip-hop impresario makes it to the church on time**. In the picturesque town of Gustavia on the Caribbean isle of St. Barts, Russell Simmons, 41, and supermodel Kimora Lee, 23, tie the knot before 150 guests including A-listers Jon Bon Jovi, Martha Stewart (July 1) and bridesmaids (in purple chiffon) Tyra Banks and Veronica Webb. Lee wears a white, body-hugging Susan Lazar creation of matte jersey and Jimmy Choo shoes, while Simmons wears a casual outfit from the Phat Farm collection. Simmons' brother Joey "Reverend Run" Simmons of Run-DMC, a Pentecostal minister, performs the service. Afterwards the party moves onto a yacht for a stupendous bash topped off with a five-tier wedding cake. World famous as the face of Chanel, the stunning half black, half Japanese model met Simmons during Fashion Week six years ago.

His and her first, lasts eight years

December 21 (1991)
Jane Fonda & Ted Turner

From the outset **they seem like a rather odd couple**: the glamorous, independent-minded Oscar winner (*Coming Home, Klute*) and the brash billionaire media mogul. Today Jane Fonda, celebrating her 54th birthday, and Ted Turner, 53, marry at his vast Florida ranch. Down a red clay road lined by arching oak trees, a guard on horseback keeps uninvited news media away though Ted's CNN reports, "It is a fact – that long-rumored wedding." While photographers and reporters outside the gates play with the caretaker's dog, two news helicopters buzz overhead. About 30 guests gather as Fonda's 18-year-old son Troy, from her marriage to Tom Hayden, walks her down the aisle. She wears a Victorian-styled ivory linen gown accented with eyelets, with a cameo brooch pinned onto its high lace collar. En route to their honeymoon at his Montana ranch, Ted and Jane stop in Cincinnati to visit his ailing mother, who dies shortly thereafter.

Her third, his second, lasts ten years

December 22 (2000)
Madonna & Guy Ritchie

There's something about a man in a Mackintosh plaid tartan kilt (who, as is the custom, wears nothing underneath) marrying **a woman known for her own unique sense of fashion**. Today she dons a strapless ivory silk gown with a fitted corset bodice and long train, and an antique embroidered veil. Her mega-bling includes an Edwardian diamond tiara (once worn by Princess Grace), a 37-carat diamond cross necklace, and pearl-and-diamond bracelets. At the 19th century Skibo Castle in the Scottish Highlands, Madonna Louise Ciccone, 42, marries kilt-wearing filmmaker Guy Ritchie, 32. (Her first choice was Althorp House, where Princess Diana is buried, but her brother Earl Spencer nixed it due to security concerns.) A high-tech security team with heat-seeking equipment and infrared cameras successfully keeps paparazzi away from the chichi event that attracts 50 select guests including maid of honor (and wedding gown designer) Stella McCartney, Gwyneth Paltrow (Dec. 5), Donatella Versace escorted by Rupert Everett, Sting and wife Trudie (at whose estate the newlyweds first met), Jean Paul Gaultier, Debi Mazar, and two stars of the groom's *Lock, Stock and Two Smoking Barrels*, Jasons Statham and Flemyng.

Her second, his first, lasts eight years

"I don't want to look back on my wedding pictures in ten years and say, 'What was I thinking?'" MADONNA

December 23 (1997)
Soon-Yi Previn & Woody Allen

The incest and pedophilia jokes have grown a bit stale – and the couple, aged 62 and 27, respectively, remains together. Tonight two unassuming travelers leave the 16th century Hotel Gritti Palace in Venice as blustery winter winds blow. He wears an overcoat, tweed cap and muffler, she wears a long camel-colored coat. At a secret twilight ceremony in the elegant Palazzo Cavalli overlooking the Grand Canal, **the city's mayor marries the notable, some might say notorious couple**: Woody Allen and Soon-Yi Previn. Only his sister Letty, her husband and one of their children witness the short civil ceremony. Afterwards the wedding party pops into Harry's Bar, a grand restaurant made famous by Ernest Hemingway in the '20s, where they dine on pasta with truffles, scampi, and crêpes a la crème. Combining business with pleasure, the couple flies to Paris on Christmas Day for the publicity junket for Woody's latest, *Deconstructing Harry*.

"He needs a psychiatrist more than an attorney."

LAWYER RAOUL FELDER, UPON BEING TOLD THAT WOODY ALLEN DID NOT ASK SOON-YI TO SIGN A PRENUPTIAL AGREEMENT

December 24 (1990)
Nicole Kidman & Tom Cruise

Days of thunder, nights of... well, we'll just have to wonder, won't we. When she auditioned for the aforementioned movie, **sparks instantly flew between the willowy, ginger-haired Australian and one of the biggest, handsomest movie stars on earth**. Only problem: he was married to Mimi Rogers. After their divorce, he rented a $2 million house with spectacular views of the Rockies in Telluride, home of the famed film festival and a favorite wintering spot of the stars. In a super secret Scientology ceremony on Christmas Eve, Tom Cruise, 28, weds Nicole Kidman, 23, who wears a '30s brocaded gown. Dustin Hoffman, currently filming *Billy Bathgate* with the bride, serves as best man while her sister Antonia is maid of honor. Hoffman and his wife Lisa give them his-and-hers tenpin bowling balls, to match the newlyweds' new sporting passion. Tom makes Nicole the leading lady in his next movie, *Far and Away*, a spectacular flop.

His second of three, her first of two, lasts 11 years

December 25 (1999)
Jessica Sklar & Jerry Seinfeld

Notoriously, neurotically commitment-phobic on television, Jerry Seinfeld takes the plunge in real life. The 45-year-old comedian marries publicist Jessica Sklar, 28, in a hush-hush evening wedding presided over by a rabbi in a Greenwich Village penthouse loft. She wears a simple white, spaghetti-strap, empire-waist gown designed by her boss, Tommy Hilfiger, while the groom wears a dark Hilfiger tuxedo and bow tie. None of his *Seinfeld* co-stars are among the handful of guests. The newlyweds elude the press by using a decoy limousine, and spend their honeymoon in a swank suite at the Carlyle Hotel. Previously, Jerry and Jessica had **engendered mega-media speculation ever since being spotted together** at a posh health club. That came shortly after her Italian honeymoon with new hubby, Broadway producer Eric Nederlander, who gets the news of his ex's remarriage while partying in Aspen.

December 26 (2001)
Joanne Kathleen Rowling & Neil Murray

Harry Potter fever is rising. The first film based on the smash book series has just arrived in theaters to sterling reviews and adoring masses. As the world simultaneously celebrates its success and the Christmas season, **the acclaimed creator of the world's most famous wizard quietly ties the knot**. At a mansion in remote Aberfeldy, Scotland, J.K. Rowling, 36, marries dark-haired anesthesiologist Neil Murray, 30, whose boyish good looks and round glasses suggest an adult Harry Potter. Her daughter Jessica, from her first marriage, and sisters of the bride and groom serve as bridesmaids. The handful of guests includes her father and stepmother, and his parents. The couple met earlier this year at a party given by a mutual friend, and Rowling was especially impressed that he wasn't overwhelmed by her mega-success. Earlier plans to marry during a cruise to the Galapagos Islands were scotched after the press got wind and swarmed the site. Now honeymoon plans stay on hold as she gets to finishing her eagerly awaited next novel, *Harry Potter and the Order of the Phoenix*.

"There were a lot of candles and flowers and Van Morrison music, but you don't have to bedazzle women with wonderful gifts. It can be a simple thing like a quiet meal somewhere." **PIERCE BROSNAN**

December 27 (1980)
Cassandra Harris & Pierce Brosnan

He's a handsome but struggling Irish actor, she's **a beautiful, elegant Australian model dabbling in acting**. Her career got a major boost after Sammy Davis, Jr. spotted her walking past the London Palladium and they posed for a photo that ran in the local papers. Today Pierce Brosnan, 29, and Cassandra Harris, 28, tie the knot at the Chelsea registry office on Kings Road. Earnings from a role in a James Bond movie helps finance their relocation two years later to Los Angeles, but it's not his part as the smooth sleuth—that's still 15 years off. No, it was Harris's short but well-received turn in *For Your Eyes Only* that bankrolled their move, which paid off when Brosnan landed the title role in NBC's tongue-in-cheek spy drama *Remington Steele*. Sadly, his soaring career coincides with her diagnosis of ovarian cancer. Four years after she passes away, he makes his debut in the role Cassie had so wanted him to play: agent 007 in *GoldenEye*.

His first of two, her second, lasts 11 years until her death

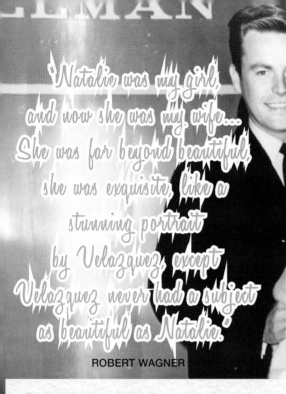

"Natalie was my girl, and now she was my wife... She was far beyond beautiful, she was exquisite, like a stunning portrait by Velazquez, except Velazquez never had a subject as beautiful as Natalie."

ROBERT WAGNER

December 28 (1957)
Natalie Wood & Robert Wagner

Three weeks ago the gorgeous Hollywood couple, fan magazine favorites, were celebrating the one-year anniversary of their courtship with dinner at famed L.A. eatery Romanoff's. There Natalie Wood **discovered a pearl-and-diamond ring in her crystal champagne glass** of Dom Pérignon, engraved with the words, "Marry me." In time-honored tinseltown tradition, Wood's first call was to gossip columnist Louella Parsons, who breathlessly recounted their movie-scripted engagement. But to avoid studio meddling Wood, 19, and Robert Wagner, 27, repair to Arizona and marry today at a Methodist church in Scottsdale. Her ankle-length white lace dress and matching head coverlet come courtesy of costume designer Howard Shoup. It's a well-publicized affair, since a reporter and photographer accompanied them on the train ride from L.A. The fairy-tale romance endures ups and downs, ending with her tragic and still mystifying drowning off Catalina Island in 1981.

Her first of three, his first of four

Wedding Bells are Ringing... Again

Booking a return engagement, these fickle Hollywood couples took second strolls down the aisle.

ROBERT WAGNER AND NATALIE WOOD

How They Met: At the studio when she was $1,000-a-week child star and he was a promising 18-year-old heartthrob. Nearly a decade later they went out for a date on her 18th birthday and married the following year.

Why They Split: As rumors swelled of her supposed affair with Warren Beatty, her co-star in *Splendor in the Grass*, Wood filed for divorce.

Reunited: After each had married and divorced others (her, Richard Gregson; him, Marion Marshall), they reconnected at a Hollywood party. Old sparks flew and they remarried in 1972.

Goodbye: She drowned in 1981 under still mysterious circumstances in the waters off Catalina Island after falling off the boat *Splendour* where their remarriage had taken place.

— — — — **Married 1957 Divorced 1962 Remarried 1972** — — — —

ELIZABETH TAYLOR & RICHARD BURTON

How They Met: Nearly a decade after meeting at a Hollywood pool party, they reconnected on the set of *Cleopatra*. They married in 1964 after each divorced their respective spouses (him, Sybil Burton; her, Eddie Fisher).

Why They Split: Dubbed the "Battling Burtons," they made several more films together amidst torrid tabloid headlines of infidelity.

Reunited: Apart only a year, they each dated others but were inevitably drawn back together.

Goodbye: Two years later the split was final. Each went on to two more marriages.

— — — **Married 1964 Divorced 1974 Remarried 1975 Divorced 1977** — —

LANA TURNER & STEPHEN CRANE

How They Met: At a Hollywood restaurant where each was dining with friends. Months later they eloped to Las Vegas.

Why They Split: After she became pregnant he broke the news that the one-year waiting period from his first marriage wasn't over, meaning their vows weren't legal.

Reunited: Despite his deception, he begged her to remarry for the sake of their forthcoming baby. When she hesitated, he reportedly attempted suicide twice before she gave in.

Goodbye: The thrill was gone. But each re-reached the altar: her five more times, him three. Their daughter Cheryl made headlines in 1958 when she stabbed her mother's mobster boyfriend Johnny Stompanato to death.

— — — **Married 1942 Divorced 1943 Remarried 1943 Divorced 1944** — —

December 29 (2006)
Nikki Cox & Jay Mohr

They met **not only in Las Vegas but on *Las Vegas*** when he guest starred on an episode of her Sin City drama on NBC. Today Jay Mohr, 36, and Nikki Cox, 28, and tie the knot in a rose- and candle-filled garden at the elegant, lushly landscaped Bel-Air Hotel in the Hollywood Hills. She wears an ivory strapless Monique Lhuillier gown and a diamond-encrusted tiara, later changing into a pink dress by the same designer for the reception. After exchanging vows and wedding bands, they present Mohr's four-year-old (and best man) Jackson, from his marriage to Nicole Chamberlain, with his own ring. Two years later, things are going so swimmingly for the couple that he petitions to have his name changed to Jay Cox Mohr.

December 30 (1988)
Louise Hoogstratten & Peter Bogdanovich

In ancient times, it was common practice for a man to marry his brother's widow after he died. But in modern times, the world shudders to learn of a jarringly unpleasant familial match. Filmmaker Peter Bogdanovich, 49, had been obsessed with *Playboy* Playmate of the Year and budding starlet Dorothy Stratten, who was shockingly and gruesomely murdered by her jealous, soon to be ex-husband in 1980. Eight years later he quietly weds her half-sister Louise, 20, in Vancouver, a fact the couple conveniently neglects to mention to her mother whom they visit after the private ceremony. When reporters inform mama, she wails, **"If he is in love with one daughter, how can he be in love with the other daughter?** I've cried before, and I cry now because I've lost another daughter." The media mercilessly pillories Bogdanovich, whose once-promising directorial career (*The Last Picture Show, Paper Moon*) fades.

> His second, her first, lasts 11 years

December 31 (1997)

Jada Pinkett & Will Smith
Helen Mirren & Taylor Hackford

Two talented and highly successful actors whose names rarely appear in the same sentence, let alone on the same marquee, **choose the same day to marry an ocean apart**. In a secluded castle in rural Maryland that hints of medieval Europe, Will Smith, 29, marries Jada Pinkett, 26. She wears a high-necked, long-sleeved ecru gown of silk and velvet by Badgley Mischka. The groom opts for a harmonizing suit and ascot. Across the Atlantic, in a true medieval setting, Helen Mirren, 52, marries director Taylor Hackford on his 53rd birthday. At the parish church of tiny Ardersier, Scotland, she wears a lavishly embroidered cream damask jacket and bronze-colored skirt. Afterwards the reception at a nearby 16th century castle includes much revelry and traditional Scottish music. Guests troop outside at midnight to welcome the new year by banging on pots. A local resident who plants a proper kiss on the bride enthuses, "You don't see things like that in a Highlands village very often."

PHOTO CREDITS

20th Century Fox: 132
3 song photography/Shutterstock.com: 136
ABC Television: 147, 218 bottom, 222/cover
Alan Light: 156 left, 244 top
Alfred Stieglitz: 240 bottom
amyandstuart.com: 63/cover, 77 top, 104, 105
Andrea Raffin: 236 bottom
Anton Oparin/Shutterstock.com: 143 top, 238/cover
Associated Press: 83, 129, 233
Attit Patel: 81
BMCL/Shutterstock.com: 99 bottom
CarlaVanWagoner/Shutterstock.com: 173/cover
Christa Hickey: 3 left
cinemafestival/Shutterstock.com: 247 bottom/cover, 248 top
Clinton Family Historical Collection: 199 top/cover
Corbis: 23, 151
Dana Nalbandian/Shutterstock.com: 146 bottom
Daniel Ogren: 250
David Fowler/Shutterstock.com: 155
David Shankbone: 111 bottom, 157 top, 249
dbking: 149
Eckhard Pecher: 56 right
Ed Roman Guitars: 209 top
Elke Wetzig: 148
Featureflash/Shutterstock.com: 5, 6 both/cover, 16 bottom, 17/cover, 18, 25 top, 26 top, 38 both/cover, 41 top, 45, 47 top, 51, 52, 54 bottom, 58, 67/cover, 69, 70, 71, 72, 82 bottom, 85, 86, 95 top, 97, 98, 99 top, 102, 111 top, 114 both, 115 both, 124 top, 125, 126, 127, 131/cover, 134, 140 both, 143 bottom, 144, 164, 165, 172 bottom, 180 couple/cover, 185, 189, 190 bottom, 194, 195/cover, 199 bottom, 201 top, 208 top/cover, 210 top, 220, 222 top, 226, 229 top, 237/cover top, 242/cover, 248 bottom/cover, 254 both/cover
Food Network: 47 bottom
Fotoschab/dreamstime.com: textured paper
Fraser MacPherson: 121
gdcgraphics: 3 right
George Bush Presidential Library and Museum: 214/cover
Helga Esteb/Shutterstock.com: 3 top, 50 top, 75, 80, 103/cover, 132 top, 135, 141 bottom/cover, 159, 162 top, 181, 218 top/cover, 224 top/cover
JCREATION/Shutterstock.com 162 bottom
Joe Seer/Shutterstock.com: 20, 53 top, 78, 88 top, 113, 119, 152, 170, 177 bottom/cover, 221, 227, 240 top/cover
Joel Baldwin: 44
Justin Hoch: 84
kojoku/Shutterstock.com: 56 left
Kris: 37
Larisa Bozhikova/dreamstime.com: square frame

Leah Mark: 25 bottom
lem/Shutterstock.com: 31
lev radin/Shutterstock.com: 112
Library and Archives Canada: 225/cover
Library of Congress/New York World-Telegram & Sun: 4, 10, 11, 15, 20 bottom/cover, 21 cover, 32, 39, 41 bottom, 46/cover, 53 bottom, 54 top, 57 bottom, 65 top, 76 bottom, 79, 90 bottom, 93, 108, 120 top, 124 bottom, 133, 138, 139, 142 top, 154, 158, 160, 167 bottom, 168, 169 bottom, 175, 183 bottom, 184, 187 bottom, 188 all, 190 top, 196 both, 197 both/cover, 198 left, 201 bottom, 211, 219, 228, 229 bottom, 230, 234 both/cover, 235, 247 top, 251, 252 all
LiliGraphie/Shutterstock.com: 76 stamps
Martin Putz: 91
Martyna Borkowski: 57 top
MGM: 118, 177 top, 191
Miro Vrlik Photography/Shutterstock.com: 95 bottom, 167 top
Morris Edwards/National Archives of Canada: 55
Nicolas Genin: 239/cover
Olga Galeeva/dreamstime.com: wedding background
Paramount Pictures: 94 bottom
Paul Cush: 68
PETA: 35
Peter Denton: 208 bottom
PRNewsFoto/Sandbox Entertainment: 1, 2/cover
Prolineserver: 107, 120 bottom
Rafael Herremans: 236 top
Raffaele Fiorillo: 224 bottom
Raywoo/dreamstime.com: film strip
Rena Schild/Shutterstock.com: 27, 157 bottom, 161
Rolenstone /dreamstime.com: oval frame
Ronald Reagan Library: 43, 156 right, 243
rook76/Shutterstock.com: 82 top
Roger Costa Morera/dreamstime.com: cake
Rozaliya/dreamstime.com: gems
s_bukley/Shutterstock.com: 7, 8, 16 top, 34, 74, 77 bottom, 90 top, 94 top, 146 top, 169 top, 178 top, 206, 209 bottom/cover, 212, 245/cover, 246, 253
Solters, O'Rourke & Sabinson: 141 top
stocklight/Shutterstock.com: 122
Tiago Chediak: 40
TLC: 116
Toni Frissell/U.S. Library of Congress: 171/cover, 179 both
Vadim Kozlovsky/dreamstime.com: flower frame
Valery Bareta/Shutterstock.com: 29
vipflash/Shutterstock.com: 187 top/cover
Webster & Associates: 36
WFIL-TV: 80 top

INDEX

About the Author

Veteran freelance writer Harvey Solomon has written several books about pop culture, and hundreds of articles about media and entertainment for magazines and newspapers from *Adweek* to *The Los Angeles Times* to *Variety*. His corporate writing includes speeches and video scripts, and his creative credits include *Law & Order*.